ADOLESCENT BOYS
IN HIGH SCHOOL:
A Psychological Study
of Coping and Adaptation

ADOLESCENT BOYS IN HIGH SCHOOL:
A Psychological Study of Coping and Adaptation

Edited by
JAMES G. KELLY
Institute for Social Research
The University of Michigan

LAWRENCE ERLBAUM ASSOCIATES, PUBLISHERS
1979   Hillsdale, New Jersey

DISTRIBUTED BY THE HALSTED PRESS DIVISION OF
JOHN WILEY & SONS
New York   Toronto   London   Sydney

Lawrence Erlbaum Associates, Inc., Publishers
62 Maria Drive
Hillsdale, New Jersey 07642

Distributed Solely by Halsted Press Division
John Wiley & Sons, Inc., New York

Library of Congress Cataloging in Publication Data

Main entry under title:
Adolescent boys in High school.

1. High school students' socio-economic status—
Addresses, essays, lectures. 2. Social interaction—
Addresses, essays, lectures. I. Kelly, James G.
LC203.A33 373.1′8′1   78-21652
ISBN 0-470-26591-4

Printed in the United States of America

To
Erich Lindemann
Who Charted the Way
and
Inspired Many
To Do Community Research
About Persons and Settings.

His Ideas, His Care, and
His Curiosity Have
Made a Difference.

Contributors

GEORGE BELL
Principal, Wayne Memorial High School, Wayne, Michigan

NORMAN BOYEA
Social Science Faculty Member, Wayne Memorial High School,
Wayne, Michigan

TERRENCE E. DEAL
Associate Professor, Harvard Graduate School of Education,
Cambridge, Massachusetts

DANIEL W. EDWARDS
Assistant Professor of Psychology in Psychiatry, The University of
California, Davis/ and Chief, Program Evaluation Section,
Division of Mental Health, Sacramento Medical Center,
Sacramento, California

GEORGE E. GILMORE, JR.
Independent Practice, Austin, Texas

PAUL V. GUMP
Professor of Psychology, The University of Kansas,
Lawrence, Kansas

JACK R. HARMS
Principal, Lee M. Thurston High School
South Redford, Michigan

JAN W. JACOBS
Assistant Superintendent for Curriculum and Instruction,
South Redford School District, South Redford, Michigan

WILLIAM H. JONES
Independent Practice and Director of Aftercare and Day
Treatment Services, Desert Community Mental Health Center,
Palm Springs, California

JAMES G. KELLY
Dean, School of Community Service and Public Affairs, Professor
of Psychology, University of Oregon, Eugene, Oregon*

JACK KNOX
Counselor, Lee M. Thurston High School, South Redford,
Michigan

MARILYN MARSH
Caseworker, Catholic Social Services, Ann Arbor, Michigan

EVIE McCLINTOCK
Research Psychologist, Family Care Center, Santa Barbara,
California

BARBARA M. NEWMAN
Associate Professor of Psychology, Russell Sage College, Troy,
New York

PHILIP R. NEWMAN
Niskayuna, New York

RICHARD R. RICE
Research Associate, Institute for Social Research, The University
of Michigan, Ann Arbor, Michigan

DWIGHT ROPER
Senior Associate, Contemporary Research, Inc.,
Stanford University, Stanford, California

DAVID M. TODD
Associate Professor of Psychology, Department of Psychology,
The University of Massachusetts, Amherst, Massachusetts

*Fulbright-Hays Scholar, University of Osnabrück, Federal Republic of Germany,
1978–1979 Academic Year.

Contents

Preface

Community psychology emphasizes social interventions that are designed to facilitate growth and to prevent the development of emotional disorders. Developing community-based programs to reduce the expression of maladaptive behavior and to encourage positive coping can be aided by knowledge of the interdependence of persons and social settings. The research reported in this volume is based on investigations of how tenth-grade boys cope and adapt to the high school environment in, specifically, two high schools in suburban Detroit in 1970. In addition to information about the ways that students relate to the high school environment, this volume presents examples of how multiple research methods can be used to investigate the expression of complex person and environment relationships.

The volume is divided into four parts. Part I includes four chapters in which background information about the research is provided. Chapter 1 discusses the theoretical backdrop and indicates, from the ecological point of view, factors that influenced the choice of topics and variables. This chapter also includes a brief overview of the entire volume and a commentary on how the chapters relate to each other. Chapter 2 presents a historical perspective on the role and the development of the high school in the United States. Chapter 3 summarizes major trends in the research literature that pertain to the way in which students, faculty, and the school environment all contribute to the socialization of students. Chapter 4 presents demographic and research data about the communities, the two high schools, and the students who were the subject population for this research.

Part II consists of five chapters that describe the results of the various methods that were used to identify the personal characteristics of the boys in the study. The primary variable was the boys' preferences for exploratory behavior that engaged the social structure of the high school. Characteristics of exploratory behavior were measured by self-report questionnaires and are related to other behaviors observed and reported in Chapters 5 through 9. Chapter 5, for example, presents psychometric and correlational data for the exploratory variable. Chapter 6 presents a summary of self-report data regarding the views and perceptions of the youth. Chapters 7, 8, and 9 elaborate upon the empirical validity of the exploratory variable based on three other methods of observation: structured interviews, small group observations, and problem-solving exercises.

Part III presents research on the relationship between the personal qualities of the students and important features of the social structure of the high school environment. Chapter 10 examines peer-group helping behavior in two contrasting subgroups in one of the high schools, while Chapter 11 reports a method that was used to describe the psychological properties of the social environment of the two high schools.

Part IV completes the volume with three chapters. Chapter 12 consists of commentary by representatives of the two participating high schools, giving their appraisal of the research findings and their relationship to the study. Chapter 13 provides commentary on the various studies by Paul Gump of the University of Kansas, who has himself investigated social settings and the social life of schools. Chapter 14 presents an interpretative summary of the research reported in this volume, including commentary about the measures of exploratory behavior and the ecological point of view that stimulated and guided the research.

This volume has been prepared to illustrate the application of an ecological point of view for research on person-environment relationships. It is hoped that the community psychologist, social psychologist, and school psychologist interested in doing research with adolescents and the high school environment will find the presentation of research methods informative and encouraging. For those readers involved in teaching and administering in secondary education, the volume is an example of how research can illustrate the ongoing personal and social characteristics of students and the high school environment.

This research program, with its several approaches to inquiry, has benefited from the efficiency and extra effort of many persons. Executive secretaries of the Opinions of Youth Project at the Institute of Social Research, University of Michigan—Merikay Bryan, Colby Wartenberger, and Terry Rogers—made difficult tasks easier and enjoyable. Michael J. Donovan developed the initial baseline measures of exploratory preferences at The Ohio State University. Reinhard Fatke, Tom Gordon, Phil McGee, Richard Roistacher, Harriet Stillman, and Jim Swan made substantial contributions to the research program. Rosemary Boss and Susan Evans of the School of Community Service and Public Affairs, University of Oregon, helped with editing and final typing. Kathryn McInnis Gay prepared the author and subject indexes. Phil Runkel of the Center for Educational Policy and Management of the University of Oregon improved the presentation of material. Dan Adelson suggested additional material to benefit the manuscript, including Chapter 2, prepared especially for this volume by Terry Deal and Dwight Roper. Charles Spielberger's interest in the research and conspicuous editorial help encouraged and prompted the completion of the work.

The research also had the advantage of the active interest of the following high school faculty and administrative staff, who helped their high schools, the study, and the students benefit from one another: Jack Knox, Norm Boyea, George Bell, Jack Harms, and Jan Jacobs. The staff, faculty, and especially the young adults of Thurston and Wayne High Schools are the real authors. The staff of the Opinions of Youth project at the Institute of Social Research have worked to measure and communicate their perceptions, feelings, and aspirations of their school and their lives in progress.

To the many colleagues who have expressed a persistent, supportive inquiry for the research to be published, and to the colleagues whose commitment and diligence is expressed in these pages, my deep and long lasting appreciation.

JAMES G. KELLY
Eugene, Oregon*

*The original work reported here was conducted while Dean Kelly and the contributors were affiliated with the Institute for Social Research, The University of Michigan.

ADOLESCENT BOYS
IN HIGH SCHOOL:
A Psychological Study
of Coping and Adaptation

SETTING THE SCENE

1 The High School: Students and Social Contexts— An Ecological Perspective

James G. Kelly[1]
Institute for Social Research
The University of Michigan

Ecology is an ambiguous and spongy word in the behavioral sciences, with multiple and even conflicting meanings. The word can refer to such varied phenomena as citizens working to promote the quality of community life, research on the structure of social settings, community mental health workers studying the prevalence and incidence of various mental disorders, or doing naturalistic research. Ecology may also simply refer to a personal value for studying how social contexts affect our lives.

The work reported in this book is concerned with analysis of the personal preferences and attitudes of adolescent boys and how adolescent boys adapt to the high school setting. There are three unique features of this work that distinguish it from other research. One is that the psychological qualities of two high school environments have been assessed in order to evaluate the effects of the social structure upon individual students. Second, the characteristics of the high school environment and the characteristics of students over three years of the high school period are compared. Third, the research employs a variety of methods to achieve these goals. In planning and carrying out this work, constructs from biological ecology have served as metaphors and analogies for viewing how individuals relate to social environments and, more specifically, how individuals and the environment are interdependent social units (Kelly, 1966, 1968, 1975, 1977; Mills & Kelly, 1972; Trickett, Kelly, & Todd, 1972).

The use of ecological in this volume refers to a conception of the high school as a social institution, which includes places and events, and as a culture that

---

[1] Present address: School of Community Service and Public Affairs, University of Oregon, Eugene.

both constrains and helps the socialization of students. In the same way, students are viewed in relationships to the school of which they are a part each day. Both the school environment and the students, then, are interrelated in a process of mutual social development.

Making conceptual leaps from biological to social systems is risky, incomplete, and even implausible. It is the opinion of the authors, however, that a systematic view of how individuals are affected by their social contexts can be enriched by analogies from biological ecology. This volume describes research that illustrates how a particular social environment, the high school, can be viewed as an interdependent social system.

Two criteria have been employed to select both person and contextual variables:

1. Individual difference variables were selected to illustrate a specific social context.
2. Social context variables were selected to illustrate how the context affects different persons.

These two criteria, how persons and social variables are interdependent, have guided this research.

The criteria for the selection of dependent variables in psychological research generally derive from a particular theory rather than from the immediate social context, and the specific variables that are studied are often located inside the body. Only recently have psychological premises included behaviors that are expressed in natural settings uncontrolled by the investigator (Willems & Raush, 1969). The psychological point of view assumes the validity of the theoretical idea and then attempts to verify the theory by assembling empirical facts. Validity is defined in terms of external criteria that are not derived from a social context. Sociological inquiry is equally incomplete, assuming that social organization affects most persons in the same way, i.e., that the consequence of participation in a social setting is the same for everyone.

In contrast to traditional psychological and sociological theories, an ecological perspective affirms that it is important to determine the impact of social settings on individuals and, reciprocally, how persons respond to varied environments. For the work described in this volume, the principle of interdependence is superordinate to the premises of psychological or sociological causation. To specify the conditions in which persons and social settings are mutually related, varied research methods have been employed. Varied methods expand the range of observations that are possible for evaluating relationships between persons and settings.

The high school environment was studied, because the authors believed that an educational setting — particularly one serving adolescents — was particularly appropriate for investigating personal and social adaptation. We assumed that during the high school period students and faculty express a wide variety of responses to school that reveal the diverse ways in which social settings and persons are related. Another important focus for the study was an attempt to specify the varieties of social development during adolescence. Empirical data are available through repeated interviews with students and faculty regarding their views of the school environment, their perceptions of themselves, of each other, and of their school-oriented social interactions. Thus, much-talked-about but little-known "varieties" of adolescent experience are one major focus for the study.

In accordance with our research goals, we selected a group of boys in junior high school and followed them through their high school careers. They were selected on the basis of the first criterion — according to their preferences for exploring (engaging) the school environment. In the spring of 1969, 1,144 eighth-grade boys in junior high schools being served by the study schools were administered a self-report measure of exploration preferences. In the spring of 1970, they were selected according to their high, moderate, or low preferences.

The specific aim of the study was to examine how boys with different needs to explore the school environment adapted to two contrasting schools. We have also assessed the two schools and evaluated how the social interactions and personal satisfactions of students and faculty changed over time. Observed differences in the ways the cultures of the schools developed and the ways boys with different levels of social exploration responded to their school environment provide evidence of how socialization processes functioned in the two high schools.

Longitudinal study is applicable not only to the study of persons but also to the study of social settings. Among other changes, schools may alter their ways of teaching, planning, and controlling students; and such changes affect the kinds of students and faculty who thrive or succumb in any given period of time. How a social environment changes and how persons adapt to the changes are essential topics for a view of the person and the environment. The chapters in this volume report research with multiple methods and a longitudinal perspective. The authors have endeavored not only to describe the adolescent and the high school environment but also to provide a general conceptual framework for conducting person—environment research.

BACKGROUND

This research was stimulated by a deep interest to create knowledge that could be useful for the design of social and community interventions. It is my belief that the design of social and community interventions will be aided by understanding how persons adapt to varied environments.

Initial research on students' adaptation to a school environment began in the spring of 1965. Preliminary studies carried out in two high schools in Columbus,

Ohio, led to the development of several measures of coping preferences in adolescents and to an appreciation of the complexity of varied types of social settings (Kelly, 1966, 1968, 1969). In the fall of 1966, a more formal study was charted with the collaboration of several high schools in the Detroit metropolitan area. After a year of background work and planning, the administrative staff and principals of Wayne Memorial High School in Wayne, Michigan, and Lee M. Thurston High School in South Redford, Michigan, agreed to participate in the *Opinions of Youth Study*, a longitudinal study of coping preferences of adolescent boys.

In the spring of 1968, with the award of a research grant from the National Institute of Mental Health (MH—15606), the work with high school students and their social context began. In the fall of 1968, a sample of eighth-grade junior high school boys was selected on the basis of the boys' preferences for exploring the social environment of the high school. Plans were made to follow these boys throughout their high school careers. Studies of the boys while they were finishing the eighth grade are described by Kelly et al. (1971). The work presented in this volume describes in detail the data that were obtained during the 1970—71 school year when the boys were in the 10th grade.

THE CHOICE OF TOPICS: EXPLORATION AND ADAPTATION

Exploratory preference, a measure of individual differences, was selected as a major concept for study, because this concept could be related to how individuals behave in different environments. The intent was to learn about characteristics of students in terms of their level of exploratory preferences in the two high school environments. Of particular interest is to specify how boys with different levels of exploratory preference interact with their high school and how high school environments encourage the expression of different exploratory preferences.

In addition to the broad general objectives of the research, two additional goals were set: (1) to analyze the developmental characteristics of adolescent boys; and (2) to use the research findings whenever possible to recommend improvements in the curriculum and in the social organization of the high school. In addition to describing the correlates of exploratory behavior, the chapters in this volume present characterizations of boys at their grade level and suggestions for the practical use of the research findings.

Adaptation was a second major concept in this research. Whereas exploration focuses upon the students' preferences for *moving* the environment, adaptation refers to social processes of how the student and the organization *react* to the social environment. Adaptation was also selected to clarify how different individuals are affected by their membership in a particular social setting. The work presented in the following chapters focuses on individual differences in

levels of exploration and on differences in how the two high school environments responded to the boys.

AN OVERVIEW OF THE METHODS AND APPROACHES
TO THE STUDENTS AND HIGH SCHOOLS

The research reported in this volume was conducted in two Midwestern high
schools in the early 1970s, but it is important to understand the broader context
for this work. Terry Deal and Dwight Roper, in Chapter 2, have summarized the
major themes underlying the role of the high school in the United States, focusing
upon five functions: sorting persons for future roles in society, training for
specific cognitive skills, certification of educational accomplishments, the high
school's custodial role in society, and the role of the high school in socialization
for adult roles. Although the research described in this book focuses primarily
upon the last function, Deal and Roper have set the scene by providing an
historical and sociological commentary on the high school.

The third chapter, by Evie McClintock, reviews the literature on the socialization of adolescents in the high school. This chapter provides a frame for reference in which the teacher, parents, and peers may be viewed as important resources for the socialization of students. It also offers illustrations from the
literature of prevailing specific gaps in our knowledge and illustrates how the
social system of the high school can be studied via multiple levels of analysis —
cultural, organizational, interpersonal, and personal — and how each one of these
levels is important to understand the effects of the social order upon individuals.

Chapter 4, by Richard Rice and Marilyn Marsh, reports descriptive data about
the Wayne and South Redford communities, as well as data showing similarities
and differences among the social characteristics of the faculties and the boys
who attended the two schools. In the high school communities, a pivotal issue
for the research is the relationship between patterns of adaptation reflected in
the high school and patterns of adaptation that emerged from the culture of the
larger community. The data presented by Rice and Marsh illustrate consistencies between the analyses of 1960 and 1970 Federal Census data for the school
communities as well as consistencies between the census information and the
data derived from self-reports of faculty and 10th-grade boys attending the
schools.

In Chapter 5, Daniel Edwards summarizes extensive research on the properties of the questionnaire measure of exploration preferences and the status of
the exploration concept as an explanatory term. This chapter also reports an
empirical analysis of self-reports to assess how the boys perceived their school,
in which Edwards used categories derived from the boys' actual responses to the
school to examine individual differences. When the study began, the selection of
students for the longitudinal study was based upon a priori assumptions with

regard to the salient features of exploratory preferences as a coping style. In the strict sense, we introduced a foreign body into the social organization of the high schools to help define characteristics for effective or ineffective coping. The measuring instrument for exploration preferences was imposed on the boys, and we have subsequently followed the effects of our "divining rod."

In Chapter 6, Daniel Edwards reports from the same source of data that generated the analysis reported in Chapter 5. In this chapter, however, the self-perceptions of the boys and their perceptions of their peers and the life of the school environment are described. These data provide a clear and comprehensive statement of the social norms of boys in the 10th grade attending the two high schools. The overwhelming features of the data, as Edwards emphasizes, are the variability and the diverse level of responses. Implications of this fact alone suggest a humble appreciation of the complexity in designing educational programs to meet the needs of boys at different levels of personal and social development. The developmental variety of the 10th-grade boys attending these two schools is vivid.

The very low salience of the classroom as a powerful social setting was also quite strong. The classroom as the setting of choice contributed to the negative evaluation of the high school environment in both schools. Seventy percent of the 10th-grade boys say the worst thing about high school is the classroom!

Other data reported by Edwards encouraged us to examine in greater detail the informal social structure of the high school. The startling conclusion we derived from the findings reported in Chapter 6 was that if schools had additional places to learn beyond the classroom, schools could be attractive places to learn. Except for classes, the rest of school life is potentially very satisfying. We need to know more about the informal school environment, for it is these social settings that produce the sources of emotional support for making school not only tolerable but even enjoyable.

In Chapter 6, Edwards has given us ample reason to focus on the informal sources of socialization in the high school. It appears that Wayne Memorial High School helps to increase this informal social process by having more *structured* social settings available for informal social interaction within the school building; whereas at Thurston, the boys seek such settings outside of school. Data reported in this chapter, along with other findings about school differences, make it possible to conceive of contrasting environments that encourage varied adaptations. This topic is developed further in Chapters 10 and 11 by David Todd and Philip Newman.

Chapter 7 presents an example of our efforts to go beyond the use of a self-report questionnaire in elaborating the personal concerns of the 10th-grade boy. George Gilmore used a structured interview with small groups of students. He selected 6 high, moderate, and low explorer boys — a total of 18 boys at each of the two schools — and analyzed these boys' responses to the interviewer's inquiries about their feelings of competence, their perceptions of self-identity, and their satisfactions with the expression of these competences in the high school. Gilmore also reports some provocative findings regarding differences in responses to questions of identity development at the two schools. The work of Gilmore highlights again the uncertainty and diffusion of the identities of the 10th-grade boys and has helped us take a more realistic view of the level of development at these two suburban high schools. Gilmore and Barbara Newman, in Chapter 8, in addition to presenting their reports of research, include a case example of the responses of a high-explorer boy at one school and a moderate-explorer boy at a second school. These case presentations illustrate the additive information about identity and small group behavior that is revealed by the two different research studies.

Chapter 8 presents the work of Barbara Newman, who used a different approach to assess the characteristics of 10th-grade boys. Her work involved half of the sample of boys from Gilmore's study — three each of high-, moderate-, and low-explorer boys from each school (nine boys in each school sample) — meeting together in a series of eight semiformal group discussions. Observing both verbal and nonverbal behavior, Barbara Newman found that the high-explorer boys at Wayne interacted more with each other and with the leader than did the boys with other levels of exploration preferences. The reverse was true, however, at Thurston High School, where the low-exploration boys were the most active in small group discussion.

Barbara Newman's work provided us with specific hypotheses for defining the socialization process at Thurston and Wayne High Schools. We concluded that the boys at Wayne were less experienced in small group discussion but more able to involve themselves in a school-related task than the boys at Thurston. We also speculated that the boys at Thurston, as a result of the Thurston culture, learned to cool their affect and to respond to novel intrusions with unfamiliar adults by not revealing themselves.

In Chapter 9, William H. Jones investigates the use of an experimental method in a seminatural school situation to test out the validity of the exploration construct. Pairs of boys varying in level of exploratory preferences were asked to prepare solutions to realistic school problems. This particular research reports some modest relationships between the exploration variable and solutions of everyday events such as: trying to be admitted to a class when an application permit was lost; helping a friend who has been evicted from school as an unwilling partner in a fight; etc. This chapter provides an example of adapting the experimental method to the natural conditions of the high school environment.

The chapters by Edwards, Gilmore, B. Newman, and Jones provide complementary data regarding the types of findings related to differences in levels of exploration preferences at the two schools. Although the findings are modest, we were encouraged by the new directions that emerged from this research. The coping style of choice, exploratory preferences, does seem to be related to both individual and social variables.

Chapters 10 and 11 present examples of studies that focused more directly on the social structure of the schools. Chapter 10, by David Todd, illustrates a research approach that is prototypic for conducting person–environment research. From both theoretical and methodological standpoints, the work presented in Chapter 10 was rooted in an ecological perspective. Trickett, Kelly, and Todd (1972) previously discussed the value in social research to define the nutrient, social support features of a social environment. Help-giving behavior was selected in the earlier article as a variable to understand both interpersonal and social processes. In Chapter 10, Todd reports an empirical test of these ideas. The theoretical discussion of helping behavior, derived from an ecological perspective, suggests that how young persons learn to help and how they define relationships with peers and adults will vary from place to place. Working at Thurston High School, Todd employed a series of successive procedures including informal interviews, sample surveys, and log reports of helping acts in an intensive study of the help-giving process in two subcultures.

One subculture of boys identified in Todd's study serves as an example of active participants in school life ("citizens"), whereas a second group of boys illustrates a marginal social group ("tribe"). Todd found that help-giving behavior among these two groups not only varied according to the subgroup but also according to the methods employed and the types of interpersonal relationships that were characteristic of each subgroup. Until Todd's research, the social structure of Thuston High School was ambiguous and confusing to the research staff, and it was difficult to assess what the possible effects of being a member of the environment would be. We did not know whether the uncertain or "foggy" quality of the social environment was due to the nature of the school or to our inability to ascertain the genuine world of Thurston. As a result of Todd's work, we now understand better that the peer structure of Thurston can in fact be represented as a series of loosely tied groups of small numbers of students rather than as a pyramidal hierarchy of well-defined status levels.

The work of Philip Newman in Chapter 11 was designed to assess the quality and quantity of social interaction as reported and perceived by a representative sample of faculty and students. This chapter reports the development of a survey research instrument (the Environmental Assessment Questionnaire) to identify differences in the perceived environments of the two high schools. Both students and faculty at Wayne Memorial High School report more social interaction and more satisfaction with their social interaction than do the faculty and students at Thurston High School. It was also found that there were more social settings for interaction at Wayne than at Thurston.

On the basis of Philip Newman's research, we are now in a position to examine more critically the relationship between social interaction among students and social participation in the life events of the school. Newman's work has provided us with an empirical guide for examining in more detail whether or not the socialization for adult roles *is* in fact more pervasive at Wayne than at Thurston, and whether the socialization processes favor social participation at Wayne in contrast to favoring personal autonomy at Thurston. We can now work from the hypothesis that boys at Wayne have an opportunity to be socialized as active participants in a well-structured and responsive environment, whereas boys at Thurston are socialized to become more solitary members of a loosely connected social environment.

In summary, the chapters in this volume illustrate the research style at one point in time in a longitudinal study of students and the schools they attend. Different research methods, including questionnaires (Edwards), structured interviews (Gilmore), observational studies (B. Newman), and experimental methods (Jones), have been complemented by alternative sampling procedures and organizational research methods (Todd and P. Newman). We wanted to design studies that could provide an integrated view of the high school environment.

The specific studies that are reported in this volume have focused upon different aspects of the integration of data. There is also an effort at the integration of data collected by several investigators at the same time — such as the work of Edwards, Gilmore, and B. Newman — and the integration of data obtained from the same persons at different times — as in the work of Edwards.

There is the integration of data obtained from large samples of faculty and student respondents (P. Newman) and of data generated by matched and unmatched pairs of students from different schools offering solutions to a problem (Jones). Thus, it was possible to compare data collected about persons and about environments, as well as to compare data collected from the two schools.

We have invested in research to unfold facts that illustrate the significance of person—and—environment relationships. We have tried not only to emphasize the characteristics of the 10th-grade boy but also to present the point of view that research can be designed sequentially and can be derived from the events of the locale.

Chapter 12 presents commentary by the administrative staff and faculty who coordinated the research. These comments are included to provide accountability of what it was like to collaborate in this research process. In Chapter 13, Paul Gump of the University of Kansas provides an evaluation of the research. Paul Gump, in his early collaboration with Professor Roger Barker and through his own research, has been a major contributor to ecological research in school settings. In Chapter 14, the first author provides commentary on the study and presents closing interpretative comments regarding the research and its status after the initial high school year.

Relevance of This Research to Community Psychology

Community psychology requires concepts and methods for assessing how the individual and the environment are related (Kelly, 1970, 1971). A community intervention designed to stimulate beneficial change requires an assessment of both persons and settings. Such assessments cannot be made without concepts and methods that articulate the relationship between persons and settings.

The issue of the relationship between person and environment, which has long faced scientists who study social systems and cultures, is also becoming increasingly critical for the community psychologist, whose work involves creating therapeutic solutions within diverse social systems. The community psychologist works from a world view that personal, organizational, and community change is created at all levels of a social organization. As the community psychologist works with varied cultures and designs therapeutic services, he/she must be able to visualize and then carry out community programs that demonstrate that persons can improve their abilities to cope with their immediate social conditions. What the community psychologist works toward is a conception of a dynamic relationship between person and social setting similar to the psychodynamic view of the individual that has been so much a part of the perspective of the clinical psychologist.

The authors hope that the volume provides an overview of the methods of a study of coping preferences and social contexts in two Midwestern high schools.

REFERENCES

Kelly, J. G. Ecological constraints on mental health services. *American Psychologist,* 1966, *21,* 535–539.

Kelly, J. G. Towards an ecological conception of preventive interventions. In J. W. Carter, Jr. (Ed.), *Research contributions from psychology to community mental health.* New York: Behavioral Publications, Inc., 1968.

Kelly, J. G. Naturalistic observations in contrasting social environments. In E. P. Willems & H. G. Raush (Eds.), *Naturalistic viewpoints in psychological research.* New York: Holt, Rinehart and Winston, 1969.

Kelly, J. G. Antidotes for arrogance: Training for community psychology. *American Psychologist,* 1970, *25,* 524–531.

Kelly, J. G. Qualities for the community psychologist. *American Psychologist,* 1971, *26,* 897–903.

Kelly, J. G. The ecological analogy and community work. Paper presented at the Symposium on Public Policy and Ecological Change, International Society for the Study of Behavioral Development Biennial Conference, University of Surrey, Guildford, England, July 1975.

Kelly, J. G. Community psychology: Ecological approach. In B. B. Wolman (Ed.), *International encyclopedia of psychiatry, psychology, psychoanalysis, and neurology.* New York: Van Nostrand, Reinhold, 1977.

Kelly, J. G., Edwards, D. W., Fatke, R., Gordon, T. A., McClintock, S. K., McGee, D. P., Newman, B. M., Rice, R. R., & Todd, D. M. The coping process in varied high school environments. In M. S. Feldman (Ed.), *Buffalo studies in psychotherapy and behavioral change, No. 2, Theory and research in community mental health.* Buffalo: State University of New York at Buffalo, 1971.

Mills, R. D., & Kelly, J. G. Cultural and social adaptations to change: A case example and critique. In S. Golann & C. Eisdorfer (Eds.), *Handbook of community mental health.* New York: Appleton–Century–Crofts, 1972.

Trickett, E. J., Kelly, J. G., & Todd, D. M. The social environment of the high school: Guidelines for individual change and organizational redevelopment. In S. Golann & C. Eisdorfer (Eds.), *Handbook of community mental health.* New York: Appleton–Century–Crofts, 1972.

Willems, E. P., & Raush, H. G. (Eds.). *Naturalistic viewpoints in psychological research.* New York: Holt, Rinehart and Winston, 1969.

2 A Dilemma of Diversity: The American High School

Terrence E. Deal
Harvard Graduate School of Education, Harvard University

Dwight Roper
Contemporary Research, Inc., Stanford University

INTRODUCTION: ADOLESCENT SOCIALIZATION IN CONTEXT

Secondary schools play a diverse social role. High schools develop the cognitive capabilities of students and are judged according to how well students perform reading, computational, and conceptual skills. High schools are also given considerable responsibility for developing attitudes, expectations, and skills that will prepare students for adult social and occupational roles. But the role of the American high school is not limited to either cognitive instruction or socialization. In addition, high schools sort students into social strata that determine or restrict social or occupational opportunities. High schools perform evaluation functions by providing certificates of educational accomplishment. Finally, high schools perform a custodial function by assuming control over students within the jurisdiction of the school. The adolescent entering high school should therefore expect to be more than academically prepared. Considerable time is spent by schools — acting *in loco parentis* — socializing students in a variety of ways (Spady, 1974).

Although secondary schools are expected to attend to each of the educational functions just mentioned, some functions are assigned more importance than others. In different historical periods, one or more of these functions may be emphasized over others. European antecedents of the American high school, for example, emphasized social selection and vocational training (Krug, 1969). American normal schools of the 19th century focused mainly on the development of specific vocational skills for the students and techniques of classroom management and practice teaching (Pangburn, 1932). Educational reformers of the early 20th century emphasized the development of social skills for the

15

students and strengthened the role of the schools as a form of social control (Krug, 1964). Sputnik produced a new emphasis on cognitive development of students and the selection functions of high schools. The late 1960s as a period of unrest probably placed new importance on the socialization or personal development of students.

Even within the same historical period, high schools in different geographical regions face varied societal expectations for the educational functions that should be emphasized. Some communities expect schools to stress academics, whereas others focus on vocational training or social development. Some high schools are, by demand, oriented toward "keeping the kids off the street and out of trouble." Others are asked to take seriously their role in sorting students into the "appropriate" societal niches.

Organization and operation of high schools are greatly influenced by what emphasis is given to the five educational factors. High schools established as "sorting" institutions will differ structurally from those whose mission it is to help students grow personally. Vocational schools will likewise differ from high schools emphasizing the academic growth of students. For any historical period, the programs of secondary education can be viewed as a reflection of the prevailing priorities assigned to the five basic educational functions.

But high schools cannot be categorized simply as vocational, academic, socially developmental, evaluative, or custodial. An interplay among the five functions can be observed operating at any one time. In addition, there is a complex interaction between the functions and the basic structure of secondary schools. This creates a constant need for balance between the structure and the mission of the high school. The variety of expected roles of secondary education and the variety of roles taken make it necessary for the high school to accommodate a diversity of educational aims. A historical perspective on the five functions of the American high school helps to elucidate the contemporary scene.

The primary purpose of this chapter is to provide a historical and contemporary context for studies conducted by the author of this volume and his associates. Their research focuses on the relationship between the environmental structure of the high school and socialization of adolescents. Emphasis is placed on how the socialization function is affected by the structure of the high school. In this chapter, a historical backdrop and contemporary analysis of this relationship between the five educational functions and the structure of high schools is provided to give continuity with the past. Our discussion raises a set of current issues, some of which are addressed by the research reported in this volume, others of which are not. Together, the history and broad context should give the reader a basis for evaluating research reported in later chapters and enable him/her to relate the topic of adolescent socialization to an expanded set of institutional issues.

This chapter explores the evolution of the American high school, focusing on the nature of its mission in educating young people and the impact of this mission upon the social structure of the high school. The examination notes some European antecedents of American secondary education but severs the American high school from some of its mythical European roots.

This discussion also examines the historical interaction among the five functions of the high school, particularly the interaction between academic preparation and vocationalism (socialization).[1]

High schools have over time inherited and even sought additional responsibilities. Legal mandates for attendance, the demands of pluralistic communities, and adaptation to changes in adolescent life styles have made the responsibilities of the high school diverse and demanding. High schools are certainly no longer given a clear set of educational priorities or social expectations. They often attempt to pursue all five functions with equal vigor, providing quite different experiences for widely dissimilar groups of students.

Discussion in this chapter proceeds from this to the modern period and argues that schools in the last two decades have confronted diversity in several ways. Diversity was accommodated in the 1950s through changes in the structure of the comprehensive high school. Diversity in the 1960s was provided for by the creation of new institutions or "alternative schools." In the 1970s the challenge of diversity remains, and it is more intensified; and the American high school is faced with some tough decisions about how it will respond to the challenge. Our discussion identifies three options: (1) restructing diversity of student interest; (b) adapting the high school social organization; and (c) coordinating existing community agencies to provide a community-wide approach to secondary education.

The work of Kelly and associates reported in this book expands the second alternative by providing empirical data concerning the relationship between high school organization and adolescent socialization. From the point of view of the present chapter, the high school's role in the socialization of adolescents must be placed in some historical perspective. Structuring the high school environment to promote socialization must be weighed against other options as the high school confronts the diverse expectations of students and parents.

SOME ANCESTORS OF AND MISCONCEPTIONS ABOUT THE ORIGINS OF THE AMERICAN HIGH SCHOOL

There was no need for John Baker to recount the votes after roll call. His official job as clerk was to make sure the tabulation was accurate. But a vote of 249 in favor and 143 opposed was obviously decisive. The motion had passed. On that

---

[1]Throughout the discussion, we treat vocationalism as a subject of socialization. Vocational training prepares the students for the adult world of work. There is, however, another aspect of socialization that prepares students for adult life. Under this rubric are such activities as personal development, social training, and citizenship training. Together, vocational training and these other activities constitute the socialization function.

March evening in 1860, citizens of Beverly, Massachusetts, had just voted to close their high schools.

When educational historian Michael Katz (1968) first told this story, many educators and laymen alike were surprised. In the age of failing bond issues and diminishing public faith in schooling, high schools might close — but surely not in the golden era when reformers were responding to a swelling popular demand for more formal education. Such a review shows that the commonly accepted genealogy of American high schools has rested to some degree on stereotype and misconception.

A common stereotype of the beginning of American public, secondary education stems from misconceptions about its historical roots. Americans look at the function of their secondary school system and draw immediate parallels with earlier structures in Europe and on this side of the Atlantic. There are, of course, some similarities. Elements of all the functions — instruction, socialization, custody—control, evaluation, and certification — are found in these earlier beginnings. In addition, at least a small percentage of adolescents in Western civilization have participated in various ways with institutions of secondary education since Roman times. But the presence of these similarities between 19th-century American secondary institutions and older beginnings leads to easy, erroneous, and often nonexistent connections.

Of the multitude of alternative mechanisms that European and American societies provided for adolescents from the 1st through the 20th centuries, this examination is limited to the three forms of grammar schools, academies, and normal schools. A discussion of the many major alternatives that existed from the first to the middle of the 16th centuries for the adolescents of Western civilization is omitted from discussion. The monastic orders of the Church, the manorial system of the agrarian Middle Ages, and later, apprenticeship opportunities were but a few of those alternatives. Indeed, until well into the 20th century, only a tiny percentage of adolescents at any time were participants in secondary education. The vast majority of adolescents were involved in other institutional provisions of their particular societies.

One of the noticeable paradoxes of history is that there was a greater variety of institutional outlets during the longer periods of time when the adolescent population was fewer in number and more homogeneous in nearly all local communities. Current society has provided only the high school for the very diverse adolescent population. It is important to keep that paradox in mind when examining examples of early secondary education.

Grammar School

One of the earliest forms of secondary schooling (and appearing 1,500 years later in colonial America) was the Latin grammar school of Donatus. From its early Roman beginnings, the Latin grammar school continued and was the most prevalent form of organized secondary education in England. On this side of the Atlantic (as early as 1640), Massachusetts enacted a series of laws proposing — among other educational mandates — a Latin grammar school for every 100 families in the colony. Later, in Revolutionary years, Thomas Jefferson emphasized the Latin grammar school as an important link with the "hundreds schools" and William and Mary College. Together, these three kinds of institutions provided (in Jefferson's mind) universal education for the most capable intellects in Virginia.

With the Protestant Reformation in Europe came a practical educational emphasis that gave secondary grammar schools a different twist. Johann Sturm (1507–1589) altered and consolidated the grammar schools of Strassburg into what eventually became the prototype of the German *Gymnasium* (Power, 1970). But even with the emphasis on vernacular instruction and on practical sciences, the Gymnasium remained concerned with preparing a limited number of young men for the higher professions or the university. Two hundred years later, Johan Julius Hecker opened the *Realschule* in Berlin, which trained young men in mundane occupations (Power, 1970). This was the first example of a secondary school with a mission limited to vocational training.

The Realschule emphasis crossed the Atlantic, and Benjamin Franklin proposed, 2 years after Hecker, a vocational orientation for secondary education at the Philadelphia Academy (Woody, 1931). But it is significant to note that in order to have his proposal for vocational secondary education accepted, Franklin also had to include a classical Latin grammar division. Americans were willing to have a school emphasize the vocational function but not to the exclusion of academic preparation.

Although there were overlaps between European and American education, educators often relate such European secondary equivalents as the Gymnasium and French *lycée* to the later development of the American high school. But contrary to that assumption, European secondary institutions provided a kind of education for purposes apart from the apparent or implied goals of public high schools in America. The European schools had a strong economic class and vocational stamp. In addition to this bias, European secondary schools were different in financial support and *structure*. National ministries of education provided standardized policy and fiscal control. This form of centralized national administration for secondary education was directly opposed to the state and local financial support and control of American high schools.

To some extent, the attempt to emphasize the European roots of American secondary schooling is a holdover from 19th-century reform attempts in public elementary schooling. Early schoolmen such as Horace Mann, Henry P. Barnard, and John Philbrick sought, found, and used the precedent of Prussian elementary education to justify their own efforts to consolidate and standardize formal schooling for Massachusetts in particular and the United States in general. There was a similarity of *product* from the universal secular literacy and patriotism that characterized both Prussian and American elementary systems. In addition, both developing systems soon assumed, with the exception of parochial competition, the centralized district *structure* and virtual monopoly of all elementary educational services. The same kinds of connections simply never existed between European and American secondary education.

Although there were several significant differences between the control and purpose of American and European secondary educational systems, there was an early similarity in the emphasis assigned to the five educational functions. The Latin grammar school, the Gymnasium, and the Realschule were all concerned primarily with cognitive training. They placed minor emphasis on evaluation and credentialing. Socialization was incidental, and the thought that secondary students needed custodial care would have sounded like so much nonsense to the colonial society.

Adolescents in colonial institutions, of course, had a much different relationship with their secondary schools than do adolescents today. To some degree, the secondary schools of both Europe and colonial America were a parallel alternative to the apprenticeship system. Both the apprenticeship system and colonial secondary schools held a common assumption about young people that appears very benign and reassuring when compared to the harsher assumptions of our own time.

The American colonial society believed in and practiced a full employment program. Twentieth-century observers viewing that phenomenon often interpret universal apprenticeship from the present-day perspective, which is concerned with a fear of idleness. But colonial people went beyond the concept that effort was good and leisure was bad. The colonists believed that every adolescent should have a place in society and moreover that it was society's responsibility to provide that place. The current admonition to adolescents – "you have to compete for your place in the sun" – would have rung like cruel, barbarian gibberish to colonial ears. American colonials would have interpreted the phrase, "They think the world owes them a place," as an appropriate expectation for adolescents to hold. The formal designation of school as the only social institution to fulfill this expectation would have, once again, sounded like nonsense.

Academies

Benjamin Franklin's Philadelphia Academy was not the only attempt in early America to create a different kind of secondary school. During the 19th century, several privately financed American "academies" provided instruction that varied from university preparation to finishing schools for the offspring of affluent parents. The careless observer of education often arrives at the conclusion that public high schools were merely an attempt to imitate for the less fortunate what was already in existence for the well-to-do. Some factors argue against the complete acceptance of that conclusion.

In the first place, so-called public high schools often charged tuition to supplement local and state funding. Frequently, high school students bought their own texts and paid additional fees for materials and activities. In addition, the "classics" were always suspected guests on the public high school curriculum. From the beginning, "public" schools required classical studies and languages to offer justification for their inclusion in course work (Krug, 1969). These "classics" were the backbone of private academy studies, but they were often intruders with no visible means of support for the public high school graduate.

Normal Schools

One early and unique example of the emphasis on certification at the secondary level was the development of normal schools. The rapid expansion of public elementary organization, standardization, and consolidation resulted in an increased need for certified teachers in the last part of the 19th century. There were three common means of preparation for this credential in most states: (1) completion of college; (2) completion of high school; or (3) completion of normal school.

Normal schools often limited their curriculum to techniques of classroom management and practice teaching. Because of the abbreviated curriculum, average normal school completion time was 1 year. This brevity placed normal schools in direct competition with high schools for elementary school graduates who wished to become teachers. School districts often mitigated this competition in showing preference to high school graduates for elementary teacher appointments. A direct result of that policy shows in high school attendance records. From 1880 to the first decade of the 20th century, there were significantly more young women students than men in high school (Krug, 1969). This was the same period when the average national education level was only 5 years of schooling (Tyack, 1974).

In the South during the same period, colleges often competed with high schools for students (Krug, 1969). Southern colleges lured high school students from public education through admissions policies that did not require a secondary school diploma before entering the academic portals of higher education. All these elements influenced a unique development in American public, secondary education that was different from European schools, private academies, or normal schools.

THE AMERICAN HIGH SCHOOL TO 1950

The commonly accepted roots of American secondary education may be misleading. But in spite of those false leads, there are some direct and indisputable antecedents to the present American high school. Boston had one as early as 1821. By 1860, there were several hundred public high schools in the United States. Most of these institutions were concentrated in New England and the Midwest, but there were also scattered representations in the other regions of the nation. Even at that early time, some of the public high schools provided preparation for college. Another argument is that the current secondary school system has descended during the last 100 years from the combination of the unique demands and desires of society and structured schooling.

As noted in the introduction, the five functions of instruction — cognitive development, socialization, custody—control, evaluation—certification, and selection — have appeared in the changing context of high schools. In connection with the appearance of those five functions, the development of secondary education to the 1970s has emphasized three main themes. These themes form a simple operating equation : *function + constraints = demands.* This presentation reduces the examination of functions to the two tangible curriculum items: vocational training and college preparation. The discussion of constraints on secondary education provides a brief exploration of compulsory schooling, expanding social and institutional expectations, and decreasing resources. The resultant demands on high schools yield the problem of diversity as the sum residue. The equation in its simplest form is:

Vocationalism and/or College Preparation	+	Mandatory School and and Increased Social, Institutional Expectations and Decreasing Resources	=	Diversity

The equation, of course, is an oversimplification that shrouds or excludes some other important factors. Social and institutional expectations, for instance, include a cluster of subfactors concerned with growth in student numbers and percentages. In 1900, only 5! of the total American population attended high school. During the last 75 years, population has jumped from 80 million to over 220 million. At the same time, the percentage of adolescents attending high school reached nearly 100 percent. Such growth is an important part of diversity. In addition to numerical growth, diversity was affected by the characteristics of students included in the secondary population. At least in urban high schools, immigration and the extension of publicly financed, secondary education to groups formerly excluded from such opportunities were important factors. The influx of these various ethnic and economic groups was one of the main contributions to the increase in social and institutional expectations for secondary education.

Despite these exclusions, the relationships between the factors in the equation have resulted in diversity. Having the equation as a framework, the discussion now turns to the development of the American high school to 1950.

Goals or Functions

Two main currents form the stream for development of public secondary schooling in America to 1950. The first current is what has often been loosely identified as vocationalism. At times, this current has been swollen by input from the social training emphasis of the 1920s or other social or personal development institutions. The second influence is the idea of high school as a steppingstone between elementary school and higher education. In these two currents, one finds two of the five functions noted in the original framework. The other functions are somewhat obscured by incorporation into the main two. Both vocational and college preparation have certainly incorporated certification—evaluation and selection. In addition, both vocational and college preparation imply a socialization to roles of work or academic achievement. Some commentators have also argued that college preparation and even college attendance was a lesser degree of custory—control in a society that had more people than occupational places prepared for them.

Materialistic vocationalism.   As noted before, European secondary education sometimes served as a training and screening institution for specific vocations. European secondary schools often trained students, especially boys, in specific skills such as watchmaking and clockwork, electronics assembly, printing, or toolmaking. The influence of vocationalism in American high schools differed markedly in two ways from European vocational training. First, American high schools began and maintained vocational training in general rather than specific terms. "Industrial arts" and "vocational agriculture" finally emerged as the two broad categories devoted solely to preparation for employment. Other areas of the curriculum such as typing, bookkeeping, and "business" mathematics provided a brief, unfocused exposure to the general, clerical domain of the bureaucratic/technocratic world. The curriculum and organization of secondary schooling served as a preview to the job culture requirements of punctuality, standardization, and obedience to unmerited hierarchy.

Second, the specific aspects of the developing American high school curriculum were often secular and materialistic as well as vocational. There was and is a strong emphasis on the job culture as the natural and fitting end of education. As noted before, early America practiced through apprenticeship the humane belief that society should provide a place for every individual. But there was also a corresponding emphasis on "seek your fortune" rather than the present admonition of "jet a job!" Early American folk considered working for someone else as second-rate to self-sufficiency. Independence was not compatible with salaried employment. The appropriate reward for service or production was a negotiated price or fee, not a set wage. With the consolidation of industry and proprietorship and the abolition of slavery came a dramatic shift of American attitudes (Higham, 1969). Since the middle of the 19th century, Americans have generally condoned working for hire as an adequate goal in life (Wiebe, 1967). This job orientation of working for others is reflected in the vocational curriculum of secondary education.

There is also a corresponding lack of emphasis and support on the American high school for any nonutilitarian value. At one time, the exclusion of Latin from the secondary curriculum could evoke considerable debate (Krug, 1969). But over the period of development, it became apparent that the institution of American secondary education was increasingly prone to demand justification for nonutilitarian curriculum — while rarely inspecting the alleged necessity for "practical" courses.

College preparation.   Present-day American high schools are obviously either steppingstones or barriers between elementary school and college. Because of this current status, there is a corresponding assumption that American high schools began for that purpose. Contrary to that assumption, high schools were originally often an educational end in themselves. High schools served as the "college of the common man" and originally provided an additional "secondary education" for that portion of the population that had neither expectations nor intentions of going to college. As recently as the 1920s, only a very few public high schools served as the main feeder institutions for universities and colleges. Public high schools in general did not assume the role of major college and university supplier until after World War II.

Constraints

Two recurring issues have exerted a continuing influence on American high schools. The first of these concerns is the relationship of a society and an institution to its adolescent clientele as reflected in various forms of compulsory attendance legislation. The second problem is the increasing social expectations and responsibilities that high schools must bear in addition to an expanding curriculum. These issues have placed high emphasis on the functional elements of custody—control and socialization.

Society, institutions, and mandatory participation.   Until recently, education enjoyed popular acceptance as the main expression of social mobility. Getting an education was the pathway to success, financial rewards, and social status. The effect of that faith was a voluntary increase in the number of adolescents who attended secondary institutions.

The requirements began to escalate. The same success, financial rewards, and social status demanded increasingly longer periods of "qualifying" education. Ivan Illich recently noted that the gestation period for entrance to adult society is steadily lengthening (Illich, 1971). This period has been and is now increasing 2 years in every decade. Such escalation of general employment and society requirements reduces even further the likelihood that secondary education can continue to function even partially as an end in itself. High schools are apparently doomed to be the steppingstone from elementary schools to postsecondary institutions.

The first paragraph of this subsection noted that attendance in secondary schools was originally voluntary. Mandatory schooling laws began with Massachusetts in 1852 and were not nationwide until 1918. The laws were directed primarily at insuring attendance in elementary and basic literacy training. High schools stumbled into the jurisdiction of compulsory attendance laws mainly because some of the age group that attended high school was partially below the upper legal limit for required schooling. The combined efforts of professional education lobbies and labor unions eventually extended specific legal control to high school attendance. To some extent, this legislation was a protection to the shrinking job market from the competition of lower prices, adolescent labor.

Increasing social expectations and responsibilities.   At one time, the mission of the secondary school was largely to transmit practical knowledge, instill some utilitarian attitudes, and provide a smattering of culture. From the assassination of William McKinley to the success of Sputnik, public education curriculum and activities extended in geometric proportions. As noted before, this growth in curriculum and activities corresponded to the increase in percentages and numbers attending public high schools. With this growth came a commonly accepted faith in "consolidation," "sophistication," "complexity," and "expertise" that allowed public education to usurp an increasing proportion of the prerogatives of the family, church, and other training and social institutions.

Before the institutional takeover, the family provided sex education, driver training, and most of the vocational guidance. As modern complexity increased the list of required skills and attitudes, loud educational spokesmen and lobbyists such as Cubberley (1934), Terman (1922), and Sears (1950) sought and obtained legal sanction to annex even more of family and church domain as "educational responsibilities." Families, churches, and other natural, social arrangements rarely had such a combination of spokesmen and laws to protect their interests from organized education. The result was that the public schoolmen stole more gold than they could carry. The last 25 years have disclosed the spectacle of public education driven to its knees and general, clamorous decline under the burden of responsibility that families bore with quiet dignity for all preceding generations.

Results = Diversity

American secondary institutions must face all the characteristics discussed earlier in addition to the diversity of social backgrounds, physical differences, and academic abilities. At the same time, parents, communities, and teacher groups often provide conflicting demands in a short span of time. Pluralistic or fragmented societies produce offspring and demands that are more different than alike. On the other hand, consolidation tendencies such as desegregation and comprehensive high schools push heterogeneous populations under one roof with more force than good faith.

As noted before, adolescence has not always been the same as it is now. The report *Youth: Transition to Adulthood* (1974) asserts that even puberty is coming earlier now than a few decades ago. The average tells very little about the variations that occur during the "high school" years. Averages are silent on the diversity of backgrounds, personal needs, values, attitudes, and skills displayed in the adolescent population of a pluralistic or fragmented society. Young people enter and leave adolescence at different ages. There is just as much variation in the different ways young people face the changes they experience during their time. Adolescence is a time of ambivalence and inconsistency. It can also be a period of rigid conformity and self-imposed collective uniformity.

The central argument is that the conflict between socialization and academic preparation, together with the extension of mandatory attendance laws and the expansion of social and institutional expectations, have resulted in a net increase in the overall diversity with which American high schools must contend. The development of secondary education until 1950 can be viewed as an accumulation (planned or unplanned) of responsibilities and clientele. This legacy has made one question critical: How can high schools organizationally provide for diversity? Three options seem evident:

1. The range of responsibilities or clientele can be reduced.
2. Schools can be restructured to accommodate diversity of clientele.
3. Schools can coordinate various community agencies in providing the full range of educational functions.

The history of secondary education since 1950 can be interpreted as an attempt to experiment with these options. We focus on restructuring and coordinating. The various ways in which secondary schools institutionally reduce diversity are not discussed.

THE 1950s AND EARLY 1960s — PROVIDING DIVERSITY WITHIN THE TRADITIONAL STRUCTURE

In the 1950s, the American high school was confronted with one significant event and two prominent individuals. The Russian satellite "Sputnik" contributed directly to an increased emphasis on the scientific and mathematical side of instruction and focused attention on the educational problems of the gifted. Much of this attention was directed to the selection function of secondary education: How can we identify and provide experiences for those students who will eventually get us to the moon ahead of the Russians?

Several individuals influenced the response of the American high school to the societal demands engendered by Sputnik, but two seem worthy of special mention. James B. Conant laid the foundation for this new emphasis but also argued that secondary schooling should continue to occur within the comprehensive high school rather than in specialized institutions (Conant, 1967) The price of specialization was not to be exacted from the high school's contribution to the socialization of young people for a pluralistic, democratic society.

J. Lloyd Trump (1961) provided a new model for a more highly differentiated version of the comprehensive high school for many secondary school practitioners. His plan provided for large-group, small-group, and individualized modes of instruction as an alternative to the traditional, self-contained classroom. By means of "flexible scheduling," students could enroll in or be assigned to various configurations of these three modes, depending on their particular instructional needs and desires. The plan attempted to make better use of instructional resources. It called for a new physical plant and new patterns of social organization. Administrators, teachers, and students assumed new roles. The structure of teaching particularly was affected. Teaching roles were differentiated even to the point where different teaching roles had different salaries.

In essence, the 1950s and early 1960s can be viewed as a period that emphasized providing diversity at the local school level. Sputnik imposed new academic demands on the high school in addition to the instructional and other functions it had always been asked to assume. But there was an implicit, often explicit, requirement that these new emphases be added so as not to encroach upon the other educational functions: socialization, custody—control, certification—evaluation, and selection.

In one sense, internal tracking or the assignment of students to college preparation or vocational streams made the coexistence of diverse instructional demands possible. Without jeopardizing the selection or certification functions of the high school, students could mingle in social studies classes or in extracurricular activities to fulfill the socialization task or democratic ideal. But, interestingly, as students in flexibly scheduled high schools had more spare time to wander about the community, communities often exerted pressures on the schools to fulfill their responsibilities in the area of custody—control.

In theory and practice, the impact of the 1950s on the social organization of the high school was not exceedingly great. The agenda following the launching of Sputnik was to provuce talent that would one day get us to the moon first. But equalitarian values and the socialization function of education prevented the creation of specialized institutions to reach this goal.

THE LATE 1960s — RESPONDING TO
DIVERSITY BY CREATING NEW INSTITUTIONS

One way to characterize the late 1960s is as a humanistic reaction to the technocratic emphasis of the 1950s. For high schools, the main issues associated with the emerging "counterculture" were student alienation and disaffection and a related demand for alternatives to the existing educational program of the high school. In part, these issues may be related to the aborted implementation of many of Trump's ideas to reorganize the high school. Flexible scheduling, differentiated staffing, and small-group or individualized instruction in many instances never reached full implementation (Charters, 1974). As a result, it was difficult for secondary schools to accommodate diversity by restructuring when the new structures had never been implemented. But the predominant issues of the late 1960s may also be related to the agenda of instructional specialization, excellence, and the selection emphasis of the 1950s and early 1960s. It was these issues that the "counterculture" singled out for attack.

The first pressure to be felt by high schools in the late 1960s and even early 1970s was student alienation and disaffection. Sometimes subterranean, student alienation was manifested in lethargy, classcutting, and frequent absenteeism. Openly, students expressed the alienation in aberrant patterns of dress, demonstrations, demands for greater student voice in decision making, and demands for a new emphasis on experience and preparation for other than academic or traditional vocational careers.

Viewed from the functional scheme outlined earlier, one thrust of the late 1960s was away from certification—evaluation, selection, custody—control, and a narrow conception of instruction and toward an expanded version of instruction and, particularly, socialization. This thrust emphasized the importance of high school in preparing one for life — especially a counterculture life style. The issues raised by this counterforce polarized communities, high school students, teachers, and administrators and confronted high schools with more diversity than they had faced in earlier periods. So great was this diversity that most high schools, with the exception of those that created "schools—within—schools," could not respond. Consequently, in the late 1960s, new institutions — or alternative schools — attempted to accommodate the diversity produced by the counterculture and resultant student disaffection.

Within these alternative schools, socialization was a paramount function; and character development, or personal growth, received emphasis over formal instruction (McCauley, 1971). Schools de-emphasized custody—control, certification—evaluation, and selection. In many alternative schools, the scope of instruction expanded to incorporate a greater breadth of activities (such as homemaking and organic gardening); students received a greater voice in making decisions about instructional activities and schoolwide governance, and the number of adults other than teachers included in the educational process increased (Deal, 1975).

Although alternative schools inside and outside the public area provided initially for the diversity of students and the educational functions produced in the late 1960s and early 1970s, many of these institutions were temporary. During this initial period, many alternative schools failed, either by collapsing or reverting to the practices they had once sought to replace. Such schools did not realize that in responding to some educational functions, they were neglecting others that society also values.

To some extent, alternative school patterns were co-opted by the traditional high schools, many of which organized schools—within—schools to provide for the diminished numbers of students seeking an "alternative" learning environment. The net impact of the 1970s was a modified version of the comprehensive high school, differentiated further than in the 1950s to accommodate — through schools or programs-within-the-school — the residual diversity of the "counterculture" revolt.

THE 1970s — AN ACCUMULATION OF DIVERSE EXPECTATIONS

The 1970s have brought a new emphasis to the fore — career education. But this emphasis is actually a vocational wolf in career-education clothing. Partially instructional (developing occupational skills) and partially socialization (providing students adult role models to equip them with the social skills and outlooks necessary to the work place) preparing students for occupational careers beyond high school has been rebilled as an important educational function. The emphasis on the vocational side of socialization is here once again.

This emphasis, however, has not replaced the instructional—vocational duality of the 1950s and before. Nor has it replaced the socialization or personal development strand of the late 1960s and early 1970s. In short, the demands placed on the American high school have accumulated. To be sure, there continues to be an emphasis on cognitive growth and college preparation. But there is an equally vigorous emphasis placed on career development. And if the California Commission for the Reform of Intermediate and Secondary Education (RISE) and a related renewed interest in alternative schools can be accepted as valid indicators, there continues to be a major importance on socialization or on preparation for life outside the world of work. Just as vigorous are the societal values attached to the function of high schools as certifiers, selectors, and institutions that control and "care for" young people.

In its development, the American high school may be witnessing a period that is unparalleled historically. It is a time when each of the five educational functions has attained major value. The priorities that have characterized various periods of the past may be nonexistent; consequently, high schools are held accountable for a remarkably diverse, if not impossible, contradictory set of functions. At the same time, high schools have assumed these functions with a remarkable, diverse clientele in pluralistic communities with decreased fiscal support. And they have continued to be buffeted with the factors outlined earlier in the equation characterising the development of the high school to 1950. The plaguing question is how secondary education will handle this diversity in clientele, environments, and expectations.

Options Available to Secondary Schools in Coping with Diversity

There are three basic strategies available to high schools in coping with diversity. First, high schools may attempt to reduce diversity itself. Of course, there are elements of diversity outside the control of high schools. They cannot make communities less pluralistic, reduce the range of societal expectations for schools, or change the basic nature of the adolescent. They can through legislation, however, reduce the mandatory attendance age, thereby reducing a range of clientele and the emphasis placed on custody—control. They can also decrease the educational responsibilities of the high school. For example, high schools could focus on the cognitive growth of students in language and quantitative areas, leaving the responsibility for socialization to the family and other resources within a particular community.

Second, high schools can reduce diversity by adapting structurally. Specialty high schools focusing on either college preparatory, vocational, or broader socialization functions can organize diversity. In fact, schools—within—schools are examples of existing attempts to organize diversity at the school level. Following the schools—within—schools idea, it is conceivable that a high school could develop several schools within the comprehensive structure, each with a different educational character. Within these could be established a different equilibrium among the five basic functions. For example, one school-within-a-school could emphasize vocational training and socialization to the world of work. Another could emphasize the experience side of instruction and socialization to a broader spectrum of life while de-emphasizing custody—control, evaluation, and selection. Certain schoolwide activities and a vigorous extracurricular program could integrate these distinct programs into a single high school program.

Third, high schools can cope with diversity by changing the role of the high school in the community. Presently, communities place on the high school diverse expectations. As noted above, high schools can legally divest themselves of certain responsibilities, or they can alter the organizational structure to accommodate these diverse expectations. The third alternative is to take an active role in cultivating other community agencies to share the educational responsibilities now assigned formally to the high school. The colonists of early America set an interesting precedent for this option. The third alternative could involve exploring systematically interdependencies with other agencies in the community or actively coordinating other agencies in providing certain educational experiences for students. For example, to provide adult role models and experiences that foster the passage into adulthood, high schools might create student internships with adult organizations in the community. The high school could coordinate and monitor these interns' experiences, but the actual responsibility for the socialization function would rest with the adult "mentors." Similarly, these internships could take a vocational emphasis; and businesses, craftsmen, and semiprofessionals within the community could formally have the responsibility for developing the salable skills of students. As another example, high schools could create among physicians, social agencies, and community action groups consortia to focus resources on a particular instructional area. Sex or drug education would be prime examples.

In responding to a historically unparalleled diversity in education, modern high schools have three options to increase their ability to cope. Any one of the options may enable high schools to survive effectively, even though the costs of reorganization and the establishment of new patterns will undoubtedly run high.

Various combinations of these three alternatives are certainly possible. This latter possibility appears particularly attractive. In a particular community where the high school is expected to be all things to all people, these changes could be made. First, state laws could lower the mandatory attendance age. Second, schools could create new educational missions aligned closely with the community. The primary responsibility of these roles would be to develop the educational potential of the community. This responsibility would involve developing consortia, identifying "mentors," and supervising internships within the community. At the same time, several programs within the high school could emphasize different educational functions. Some programs could focus on cognitive outcomes, others on broader socialization goals.

Pursuit of this latter alternative will need additional knowledge about the relationship between the high school environments and the intellectual and socialization outcomes of schooling. In the cognitive area, there has been work to show the impact of high school structures and climates on academic achievement and aspirations. But our knowledge of the relationship between the characteristics of schools and adolescent socialization is an area that needs considerable development. The work of Kelly and associates described in this book moves us in that direction.

CONCLUSION

The purpose of this chapter has been to provide a historical and contemporary backdrop for the topic of person—environment fit in secondary schools presented in this book. The historical analysis identified some misconceptions of secondary school origins and emphasized the historical continuity of many of the current issues in secondary education. The underlying significance is that adolescents in public high schools have often faced and attempted to cope with institutional efforts in development, expansion, and responding to diversity.

At the same time, this interpretation of the historical development of the high school focused on the contribution of reformers and centralizers to increasing the educational responsibilities of the high school and extending the responsibility into functions once reserved for other agencies and institutions in the society.

The historical assumption of broad responsibilities has coupled with other developments to carry into the contemporary scene a heavy burden for high schools to assume. They are asked to perform each of the five basic functions at a high level, even though many of these are contradictory. At the same time, they are given fewer resources with which to accomplish this expanded task. The modern high school is therefore faced with critical decisions about the diversity with which it must cope. It can either reduce the scope of its functions, change its role to one of coordinator rather than provider of educational experiences, or modify its structural form to foster a broad range of educational functions, including responsibility for the personal development of adolescents. This latter alternative will require more knowledge about the impact of high schools, both on socialization and intellectual development. The uppermost notion is that high schools have several functions to perform and that they have additional options other than providing for each function directly. Each one or a combination of those options should receive full consideration. The final measurable product of such consideration is, in the words of Kelly, the number of adolescents in high schools who succumb or thrive.

REFERENCES*

Callahan, R. E. *Education and the cult of efficiency*. Chicago: University of Chicago, 1962.

Callahan, R. E. The superintendent of schools: An historical analysis. Final report of project S212. Washington, D.C.: Cooperative Research Branch, United States Office of Education, Department of Health, Education and Welfare, 1966.

Charters, W. W., Jr. On neglect of the independent variable in progressive evaluation. Eugene, Oregon: Center for Educational Production and Management, University of Oregon, 1974.

Conant, J. B. *The comprehensive high school: A second report to interested citizens*. New York: McGraw–Hill Book Co., 1967.

Cremin, L. *The transformation of the school, progressivism in American education, 1876–1957*. New York: Vintage Books, 1964.

Cremin, L., & Borrowman, M. *Public schools in our democracy*. New York: The Macmillan Company, 1956.

Cubberley, E. P. *Public education in the United States: A study and interpretation of American educational history*. Boston: Houghton–Mifflin Co., 1919, 1934.

Deal, T. E. *An organizational explanation of the failure of alternative schools*. Stanford, Calif.: Standford University School of Education, 1975.

Ellsbree, W. *The American teacher*. New York: American Book Company, 1939.

Higham, J. *From boundlessness to consolidation. The transformation of American culture, 1848–1860*. Ann Arbor, Mich.: William L. Clements Library, 1969.

Illich, I. The institutionalization of truth. In L. Robinoff (Ed.), *Tradition and revolution*. Toronto: Macmillan of Canada, 1971.

*This bibliography includes references not cited in the chapter. The references provide additional historical background.

Katz, M. *The irony of early school reform.* Cambridge, Mass.: Harvard University Press, 1968.

Krug, E. A. *The shaping of the American high school* (Vols. 1 & 2). Madison: The University of Wisconsin Press, 1964, 1969.

McCauley, B. Evaluation and authority in radical alternative schools and public schools. Unpublished doctoral dissertation, Stanford University, 1971.

Pangburn, J. *Evolution of the American teachers' college.* New York: Columbia University Bureau of Publications, 1932.

Power, E. *Main currents in the history of education.* New York: McGraw–Hill Book Co., 1962, 1970.

Sears, J. B. *The nature of administrative process with special reference to public school administration.* New York: McGraw–Hill Book Co., 1950.

Spady, W. G. The authority system of the school and school unrest: A theoretical exploration. In C. W. Gordon (Ed.), *Uses of the sociology of education.* Chicago: National Society for The Study of Education, 1974.

Terman, L. M. *Intelligence tests and school reorganization.* Yonkers-on-Hudson, New York: World Book Co., 1922.

Trump, J. L. *Focus on change.* Chicago: Rand McNally, 1961.

Tyack, D. B. *The one best system.* Cambridge, Mass.: The Harvard University Press, 1974.

United States President's Science Advisory Committee Panel on Youth. *Youth: Transition to adulthood.* Chicago: University of Chicago Press, 1974.

Wiebe, R. *The search for order, 1877–1920.* New York: Hill and Lang, 1967.

Woody, T. *Educational views of Benjamin Franklin.* New York: McGraw–Hill Book Co., 1931.

3 Adolescent Socialization and the High School: A Selective Review of Literature

Evie McClintock[1]

Institute for Social Research
The University of Michigan

INTRODUCTION

The study of socialization is an important topic for a study of the high school and for the field of community psychology. The topic of socialization is of particular concern to the community psychologist who is attempting to understand the ways in which communities influence the young adult who will eventually perform adult social roles. The preparation for adulthood involves the transmission of skills and values carried out informally by the family, tribe, or clan. With industrialization and urbanization, the number of young people to be socialized has increased, and the complexity of knowledge and skills to be imparted has multiplied to such a degree that it is very difficult for the family and other informal, community agencies to transmit this knowledge effectively. Over the years, many of these tasks have been gradually given up to schools.

In order for the high school to cope with society's demands, students' needs, and its own organizational tasks, it has evolved into a complex formal organization, often with an elaborate bureaucratic structure. It is capable of coping with large numbers of students, transmits large amounts of complex information in a regulated and sequential manner, and prepares children and adolescents to take up adult responsibilities in a constantly changing world (Bidwell, 1965; Coleman, 1965).

There seems to be a firm belief in the United States today that schooling is essential for future occupational success and upward social mobility, both of which are highly valued. Given the roles that the school is expected to play in

---

[1]Present address: Family Care Center, P.O. Box 74, Santa Barbara, California.

the community and for the development of the young, it is not surprising that the school has attracted the interest of researchers from various disciplines. Most observers acknowledge that what is learned in school probably involves much more than what is included in the curriculum. Yet there is considerable lack of information about the nature and quality of the "noneducational" outcomes of schooling and marked skepticism among researchers and educational reformers about the actual contributions of the high school to what can be referred to as "social learning." Patricia Sexton (1967), for example, voices the opinion of a substantial group of investigators when she states:

> The contribution of the school to total learning is a matter of speculation rather than certain knowledge. With the competition of other media and other relationships, it may be that little of significance is learned in school [p. 1].

The purpose of this selective review is to ask some questions about the role of the school as a socialization resource in the community and to report empirical and speculative responses currently available in the literature. Before presenting the discussion, a general frame of reference is offered, and concepts that are used in this chapter are defined.

A FRAME OF REFERENCE AND DEFINITION OF TERMS

The high school is a social setting characterized by a spatial and geographical location. The daily life within the high school consists of regular and patterned interactions among its participants. These interactions are the medium through which socialization is accomplished. The nature and outcomes of these inter-

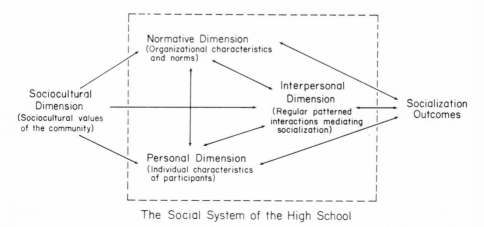

The Social System of the High School

FIG. 3.1   Framework for the study of socialization in the high school.

personal relationships are related to at least three components of the social system of the school: (a) the sociocultural context of the community surrounding the school; (b) the organizational structure and norms of the high school staff; and (c) the personal characteristics of faculty and students. At any point in time, the sociocultural context affects the organizational structure and the characteristics of the students and faculty of the high school. The organizational structure has an impact on the personal characteristics of the participants that, in turn, affect the norms and goals of the organization as well. Figure 3.1 represents graphically these interrelated dimensions and their influence on the interpersonal interactions that take place in school. This general framework is an elaboration of one utilized by Getzels (1969) in reviewing research related to the "Social Psychology of Education." Similar frameworks have been employed by Bachman, Kahn, Mednick, Davidson, and Johnston (1967), Bachman (1970), and Edwards (1971).

The topic of socialization refers to changes brought about in an individual's beliefs, feelings, and behavior as a result of their interactions with other members in a social group. Some of these changes occur incidentally, but in most cases the socialization process involves planned influence efforts carried out by persons (*agents*) and addressed toward certain *targets*. From the standpoint of the targets, the interactions with agents, and the perceptions of and reactions to the influence efforts define the *socialization experience*. The changes effected in the beliefs, skills, and motivation are the *outcomes of socialization*.

THE ORGANIZATION OF THIS REVIEW

The information available on the relationships of the high school and the adolescent is often confusing. Following the general framework described above, we ask a number of questions about what takes place in the high school. First, we consider whether the high school is a unique setting in the community in terms of the experiences it provides to adolescents. Second, we focus on each of the dimensions of the high school environment and describe their reported impact on the high school experience. Third, we focus upon the specific, interpersonal interactions that take place in the high school setting and evaluate their influence on the adolescent by contrasting them with adolescent behavior outside the high school. Finally, we discuss some of the most and some of the least widely researched outcomes of high school socialization.

IS THE HIGH SCHOOL A SETTING FOR
UNIQUE SOCIALIZATION EXPERIENCES?

Several sociologists like Parsons (1959), Dreeben (1968, 1971), Clark (1964), and Goslin (1965) have addressed this question. Dreeben (1968) summarizes their views best by noting that:

Schools provide experience that allow children to pass through that phase of the life cycle bounded by immersion in the family of orientation at one end and participation in adult public life at the other [p. 110].

According to Dreeben, these experiences derive mainly from the *unique* social structure of the high school that differentiates it as a socialization setting from the family, the primary school, or the informal peer group. For example, the size and boundaries of the high school setting are greater, and thus the number of possible interpersonal relationships is increased. The duration of the social relationships is shorter, providing the students with extensive experience of impersonal, short, and transient relationships.

The relative number of adults compared to nonadults is small. Although nearly all those adults share common roles as teachers, the personal characteristics of the adult population are varied, and students learn to differentiate between the positions and the people who fill them. Additionally, students learn to accept being in a role position and being responded to according to universalistic, rather than particularistic, criteria. They are exposed to different types of authority and expertise and learn to evolve differentiated relationships with authority figures. Finally, in the high school students are exposed to a large and highly varied group of peers who provide multiple standards of comparison and a variety of referents. Dreeben argues that the patterning, quality, and quantity of these interpersonal relationships differentiate the high school from the family and from peer groupings. These experiences prepare students to fulfill their adult roles by teaching them norms that will facilitate future organizational adjustment.

Another aspect that differentiates the high school from other agencies of youth socialization is the methods for *allocation of status.* Parsons (1959) notes that in primary schools, students are confronted for the first time with competition and allocation of status on the basis of standards of achievement and not of ascription such as sex, age, etc. In fact, students are evaluated on the basis of their performance and have to compete for "academic status." The competition that begins in primary school is intensified in the high school, where success or failure in academic tasks has a multiple impact on students' feelings about the school and about themselves and their futures. Students who do well in high school tend to like school, to have positive self-concepts, and to stay in school longer.

On the other hand, failure in academic tasks is an experience that has unique consequences for the future and the development of the adolescent. It leads to dropping out and tends to be correlated to negative self-evaluation and lowered achievement aspirations (Bachman, Green, & Wirtanen, 1971). It has also been suggested that delinquency might be a consequence of academic failure (Gold & Mann, 1970). Some adolescents whose self-esteem is threatened by academic failure may use delinquency as a defense. Havighurst and Newgarten (1962) have stressed the negative consequences of experiencing failures and the need for provision of alternate routes to adult competence.

The availability of *varied opportunities* for success is an aspect of the high school that differentiates it from other settings influencing the young. Diversity of opportunities for success, potential for acquisition of different skills, and provision of alternate opportunities for crystallizing identity are listed among the major functions of the high school as a socialization resource (Trickett, Kelly, & Todd, 1972). From the students' standpoint, a varied opportunity structure implies that they have the chance to participate and get involved in a wide variety of activities. They establish transient, organizational involvements and have an opportunity to play different roles, become leaders and followers. Although able to provide varied opportunities for success, schools have not developed appropriate mechanisms to cope with student failure. It is possible that failure to succeed in any of the school-related activities has a stronger impact on negative outcomes than success has on positive ones.

Furthermore, not all high schools provide the same opportunities for experiences to their students. Barker and Gump (1964), Wicker (1968), and Willems (1967) have extensively documented the impact of the size of the high school on student experiences. Larger schools offer more varied instruction and more out-of-class activities, and students in such schools participate in a larger number of activities. However, students in small schools participate in more varied settings; get more experience in leadership and responsible participation; find their participation more gratifying in terms of developing competence, meeting challenges, and working closely with peers and friends; and finally, experience more sense of responsibility for school affairs. These findings stress that it is not the absolute number of activities available in the high school that is important per se but rather the opportunities for active and responsible participation that make a difference in terms of student experiences. They also indicate that participation and position held in the informal structure of the school is a central facet of adolescent experience.

Coleman (1961) has provided a detailed analysis of the meaning and norms of status allocation in the peer culture. He reports that the peer structure in the high schools he studied promoted values independent of those espoused by the formal structure of the school. Peer status was allocated on the basis of nonacademic and anti-intellectual criteria that mostly involved athletic prowess, involvement in school activities, and social leadership. Status in the peer group had various consequences for the adolescents, as it particularly affected their self-esteem and educational aspirations.

Another unique characteristic of the students' experience in the high school is related to the special type of *power* that society allocates to the school over the academic and nonacademic aspects of the lives of adolescents (Brookover & Erickson, 1969; Nelson & Besag, 1970). The high school, *in loco parentis*, imposes rules and regulations and demands organizational compliance. Vis-'a-vis its students, the high school has been characterized as a "total institution" in Goffman's (1961) sense, i.e., it has total power over its members' lives. As a consequence, Friedenberg (1970) observes that adolescents experience a protracted state of infantilization. They learn to assume that the state has the right to compel them to spend 6 or 7 hours a day, 5 days a week, in a specific place. They also learn to conform to the authority and the regulations of the school that controls not only their educational development but other often nonacademic aspects of their lives. Such authority, instead of enhancing feelings of autonomy, simply substitutes one form of control for another, legitimizing dubious sources of power.

Jenks and his co-workers (1972) raise similar points in their discussion of the impact of schooling on adult occupational and educational attainment. They note that one of the powers assigned the school is the certification of students' ability and motivation. Student experiences in the high school consist mostly of learning to obey instructions, performing under supervision to detect and meet the requirements of various situations. Those unable to conform to these expectations are ejected as troublemakers or are persuaded to drop out. Those evidencing the aforementioned skills are certified and referred to prospective employers as reliable and responsible potential members.

Summary and Critical Comment

The high school undoubtedly provides adolescents with experiences, types of relationships, and involvements that are not encountered in other settings. Unfortunately, the majority of the discussions that pertain to these points are speculative and with only sporadic empirical documentation. Thus, our present empirical knowledge of the nature of the socialization experience in the high school needs to be expanded. Any of the assertions presented in the previous section could provide the "seeds" for systematic research into what is learned in school above and beyond the "three Rs."

How Do Sociocultural Values Affect High School Socialization?

What takes place in a high school is to a large extent affected by the culture and the values of the group whose needs the school meets as an institution. Among other things, these values define who should be educated and who should educate; and through these selection rules, they determine the personal characteristics of the participants in the school system. Furthermore, they define the duration of the relationships that occur in school and, more importantly, the nature and goals of schooling (Clark, 1964; Goslin, 1967). These latter constraints are particularly significant in establishing the length and quality of high school socialization.

Inkeles (1966) notes that every group establishes a number of "functional requisites," i.e., qualities necessary for its members if the group is to survive. The functional demands of a culture affect the influence processes that take place in a high school, because they determine what skills and information should be transmitted to new members (Parsons, 1959). As agents of the majority culture, schools teach young members about the role structure and role requirements that guide interpersonal behavior; they assign them to societal positions on the basis of their ability and societal needs; they mediate the continuation of social patterns by transmitting shared communication modes, shared orientations and goals, as well as acceptable means to achieve these goals (Mead, 1969).

Beyond the long-range goals of the culture that affect school functioning, there are also important, short-range goals that influence the social structure of the school and, through it, student experiences. Some of the central, short-range objectives of the high school involve controlling and "keeping out of trouble" the student population as well as certifying their ability and motivation to parents and future employers. These functions predicate the power structure of the school and affect the rules for allocating status, for refusing further participation into the school system and the overall nature of opportunities that high schools provide to different categories of students (Goslin, 1967; Slater, 1963).

How Do the Organizational Demands of the School Affect Its Socializing Role?

The shaping processes that take place in the school depend not only on socio-cultural factors but also on the tasks that it has to accomplish in order to function effectively and to survive as an organization. Organizational theory suggests that social systems, in order to establish and sustain stable and regulated patterns of interaction: (a) avoid undesirable behavior and motivate desirable behavior; (b) sustain innovative and expressive behavior to ensure actualization of available resources for individual growth and organizational development; (c) adapt their functions to individual and societal needs so as to optimize capacity for stressless functioning and acquisition of resources (Bennis, 1968). These organizational demands in turn determine the socializing relationship of the school and the students. First, they define a need for order and behavioral homogeneity within the setting that defines the power structure in the high school. Then they stress the necessity to internalize values and dispositions in the students in order to avoid constant surveillance. To accomplish this, the high school develops a system of rewards status and punishment, and communicates this to the students. Furthermore, in order to actualize individual and organizational potential, the high school has to motivate students toward innovative behavior, provide varied opportunities for participation, and motivate students to utilize the available resources. Finally, to survive as an organization, the school has to meet the sociocultural demands we discussed earlier and also bring these demands in line with the needs of its adolescent members. The need to align sociocultural, organizational, and individual needs illustrates the constant interaction and interdependency of these aspects of the social system, which both individually and jointly affect the interpersonal interactions that comprise the core of the adolescent school experience.

How Do the Individual Characteristics of Students Affect Their Socialization Experience?

The sociocultural context of the school and its normative structure provide the general background within which individual behavior and interactions occur. Sociocultural and organizational demands guide the processes that determine who will be educated and who will educate. This selection affects the individual characteristics of the students participating in the system and, to a large extent, affects the eventual outcomes of the socialization process. Individual differences in student socioeconomic background, ambition, intelligence, motivation, and aptitude render students differentially able to utilize the resources of the school and differentially susceptible to school influences (Backman & Secord, 1968; Coleman et al., 1966; Turner, 1964).

Several investigations have used the concept of person–environment interactions to explain individual student variations in the experience and outcomes of schooling. In essence, this concept proposes that socialization is affected not so much by an individual's abilities and motivation in any absolute sense, but by the extent to which they are congruent with the expectations and demands of the school setting (Getzels, 1969; Pervin, 1968). Although the factors that contribute to optimal person–environment fit have not yet been defined or measured successfully, several studies have documented interesting relationships between global measures of fit and short-term or long-term socialization outcomes. Perceived congruence between student and school has been negatively related to dropping out (Pervin, 1968), and positively related to academic success, positive relationships with teachers, low school deviance, and involvement in school life (McClintock, 1972). As it stands, person–environment fit is more an intuitively appealing idea than an empirically validated one.

Nevertheless, person–environment fit raises some questions about the much discussed influence of differences in student background and the outcomes of schooling. There is consistent empirical evidence indicating that familial background, including family socioeconomic level, parental aspirations, etc., affects student socialization. More specifically, it has been demonstrated that white, middle-class students do better in school and attain higher eventual social status than lower-class or minority students attending equally "good" schools. These facts are taken as proof of the limited contribution of the high school to adult success, which is viewed as mostly dependent on family factors. However, what such explanatory models do not take into consideration is the topic of student–

school congruence and the possibility that white middle-class students do better, because the schools have been geared to meet their needs and values and are not congruent to those of lower-class or minority students. This basic lack of fit may in turn render students unable to internalize the values of the school system, utilize the resources, and actualize their own potential.

Our discussion indicates that individual differences within the student population are partly determined by selection criteria set by the social and organizational context of the school. These individual differences, in turn, affect student interactions with teachers and peers that are the essential part of their socialization experience in school. The subsequent sections focus on these interactions and on their impact on student skills, abilities, and motivation.

What Is the Nature of Students' Interactions With Influence Agents in the High School?

In order to understand the impact of these school relationships, we need not only to describe their nature and outcomes but also to compare them to relationships that students have outside the school. Such comparisons focus on the impact of teachers and school peers relative to that of parents, who are the major sources of extraschool socialization. It would have been interesting to compare school relationships to relationships in other community settings; however, in our society, such relationships seem to be limited, and information on them is scarce.

WHAT IS THE SOCIALIZING ROLE OF THE TEACHER?

In extensive review articles, Stern (1963), Boocock (1966), and Getzels (1969) have listed and evaluated many studies dealing with teacher behavior, classroom interaction, and classroom climates. Yet relatively little of this research provides conclusive evidence on the nature of teacher–student interactions inside and outside the classroom and their consequences for student behavior. An adequate understanding of the role and impact of the teacher will require a description of teacher–student relationships, of the norms moderating them, and of systematic comparisons to relationships with peers and parents.

Teacher–Student Relationships in the Classroom

The teacher's role in the classroom is dependent on normative expectations that define its main functions: First, the teacher has to establish rules of deportment and control undesirable behavior; second, the teacher must transmit information and motivate students to learn; and third, the teacher is responsible for evaluating students and for integrating several conflicting expectations (Bidwell, 1965; Gordon, 1955).

Studies of administrators,' teachers,' and students' expectations of the teacher show that the ability to control and dominate the classroom is considered a major indicator of teacher effectiveness (Brookover & Gottlieb, 1964; Bryan, 1970). However, the particular techniques used by teachers to enforce discipline seem to affect the behavior and motivation of their students. Several studies have indicated that supportive, integrative leadership styles in the classroom were more successful than dominative styles in evoking friendly, cooperative behavior in students. Additionally, more permissive, supportive teachers evoke more positive attitudes in their students (Stern, 1963). The dimension of "warmth" or "supportiveness" has also been found to relate to classroom performance (Getzels, 1969). Cogan (1958) demonstrated that students' reports of teacher warmth and supportiveness were related to student performance. Alexander, Epson, Means, and Means (1971) operationalized warmth and interest as teacher-initiated interactions with students and found an improvement of students' performance as a function of the number of teacher-initiated interactions with them.

Thus, to satisfy organizational expectations and student needs, the teacher has to be "firm" enough to control undesirable behavior and "warm" enough to motivate positive performance. As adolescents grow older, their views of power in organizations change. Authoritarian views of control are replaced by more democratic and participatory attitudes (Adelson & Beall, 1970). During the last years of high school, students who perceive control in the social structure of the school as a joint administration—teacher—student venture tend also to perceive their teachers in a more positive light and report closer relationships with them (McClintock, 1972). The implication is that at this level of schooling, teachers who make students feel they jointly control the classroom and what happens in it are more likely to evoke positive responses from the students.

Another task of the teacher in the classroom is to evaluate students and give them feedback on their performance. Teachers inform students about their ability and their personality, both directly through grades and reports and indirectly through their behavior in the classroom. Goslin and Glass (1967) note that the major source of information that students report having about their intelligence is their classroom performance and the teachers' evaluations. Rosenthal and Jacobson (1966) demonstrated how teachers' expectations can, in fact, affect students' measured intelligence. Brookover, Paterson, and Shailer (1962) found that the students' "academic" self-concept was correlated with their perceptions of expectations held by their teachers. Finally, Davidson and Lang (1960) report that the more positive the children's perception of their teacher's feelings, the higher their own self-image, the better their academic achievement, and the more desirable their behavior as rated by the teacher. It should be noted that the majority of these studies were conducted in elementary schools, where the relationships between teachers and students may be closer and the impact of teachers possibly stronger. However, there is evidence indicating that at the high school level, although teachers are not seen as referents or sources of influence, perceived teacher expectations have a considerable effect on high school students' self-perceptions of academic ability and a lesser effect on their educational aspirations (McClintock, 1972).

Teacher—Student Relationships Outside the Classroom

Teachers' formal interactions with students have been extensively studied, and still we know very little of a systematic nature about them. Teacher—student informal relationships outside the classroom have been investigated very rarely; and as a result, we know even less about them. Students tend to report positive feelings toward teachers who interact with them in informal settings and participate in extracurricular activities. Phil Newman, in an investigation carried out in two high schools reported in Chapter 11 of this volume, provides some evidence relevant to this question. He found that in the high school, where students reported interacting with teachers and other school adults across more settings, these same students tended to perceive school adults as being more interested in them, to perceive behavioral norms more clearly and the consequences of norm violation as harsher. It is obvious that the more frequent and intimate the interactions between students and teachers, the more effective the teacher can be in influencing the adolescents. Nevertheless, the situation is highly paradoxical. Although teachers are expected to act as models and referents to students, at the same time there are strong organizational constraints against teachers becoming friendly with students within or outside the classroom (Gordon, 1957; Goslin, 1967). The net effect of these pressures is that teachers end up playing a predominantly instructional role and have very limited influence on any of the nonacademic aspects of adolescent socialization.

Teacher Versus Parental and Peer Influence on the Adolescent

Teachers, as we have noted, as adult models in the school, are constrained by conflicting organizational demands. Consequently, their influence is much less than that of parents, who have more frequent and more intimate contacts with adolescents (McClintock, 1972). In the classroom, they often have to promote values and rules that are different from those espoused by the students' peers. At this point, we really do not know how successful teachers are in instilling values that run counter to those of the peer group. Studies comparing teacher and student attitudes toward appropriate classroom behavior identified as wide a variation of opinions among teachers and students as among the students themselves (Mutiner & Rosemier, 1967; Strom, 1963). However, when students are put under hypothetical cross-pressures from adults and peers, they are more likely to conform to peer expectations, even when these expectations involve violating adult norms (Bronfenbrenner, 1970).

It seems reasonable to speculate that teachers become more intimate with some of their students on whom they consequently have more influence than on the rest of the students. Teachers are more likely to encourage and advise students whom they consider bright and also students who share some of the same values and orientations that they do. Gurin and Katz (1966), for example, report that black college students retrospectively attributed their decision to attend college more often to teacher encouragement than to peer pressures. McClintock (1972) explored some of the correlates of reported positive relationships with teachers and found a syndrome of positive adjustment to school. Students who reported positive orientations toward their school also tended to report positive relationships with teachers and with their parents. These same students were more likely to aspire to college and to view both their parents and teachers as expecting them to do so.

What this latter research implies is that teacher influence tends to be in a direction that is congruent with familial influences and expectations. The real question in high school socialization is whether the teacher as an adult model can counteract family and peer influences and promote different norms. What we know from empirical or speculative work is indeed scarce, and it does not exclude the possibility that under certain conditions and for certain categories of students, some teachers can be very effective agents of socialization. The understanding of such unique relationships and the conditions surrounding them could prove extremely valuable both from a theoretical and a practical standpoint.

WHAT IS THE IMPACT OF THE PEER GROUP?

The majority of interpersonal interactions of adolescents inside and outside the school occur within their peer group. The rate, regularity, intensity, and closeness of these interactions contribute to the important role they play in adolescent life (Ausubel, 1954; Douvan & Adelson, 1966). However, there is no general agreement about the nature and extent of peer influence on the high school student. Several investigators have documented the existence of an independent "youth culture" whose values and goals are not identical with those of the adult society, of the school, or of the family and whose influence on the adolescent is pervasive, powerful, and diverse (Coleman, 1961; Gordon, 1957; Gottlieb & Ramsey, 1964; Waller, 1932). A minority of researchers, on the other hand, report that their investigations did not provide any support for the hypothesis of an adolescent subculture and that the nature and extent of peer influence is superficial and trivial (Elkin & Westley, 1955; Epperson, 1964; Turner, 1964).

Sherif and Sherif (1969), summarizing the conclusions of several studies about the natural groupings of adolescents and their impact upon member behavior, present a balanced view of the findings:

1. Associations among adolescents that recur regularly over time are patterned affairs. Although their organization is informal and is subject to change, these groups are sufficiently stable that their status and role structures can be reliably assessed.

2. Such groups do generate norms of their own that are binding for members in varying degrees. These norms may or may not promote conformity to values and goal striving approved by society. Whether they do cannot be predicted solely on the basis of the class and ethnic rank of the members, but is a complex product of the group's interaction in its particular environment and its relationships with other adolescents and adults.

3. Such groups are reference groups for individual members and do serve to provide standards for the individual in evaluating his own behavior and that of others [p. 454].

To briefly document the role of the peer group as model and referent, we review some studies that investigate the effects of the peer group on the self-concept and the educational and occupational choices of the adolescent.

The opinions of peers play an important role in the adolescent experience. Adolescent tastes, appearance, speech, and social deportment are shaped by the norms of the peer group. Furthermore, peer evaluations have been found to have several effects on the adolescent. Status or popularity in the peer structure, which can be considered an indicator of peer esteem, has been found to relate to the way adolescents view themselves (Coleman, 1961; Rosenberg, 1965) and also to their ambitions about the future (McDill & Coleman, 1963, 1965) and to the satisfaction and involvement they experience in present school life (Douvan & Gold, 1966).

Another group of studies has compared the fates and choices of adolescents to those of their best friends. Elliot, Voss, and Wendling (1966) for example, established in a longitudinal investigation that frequency and intimacy of contacts of high school students with dropouts were associated with eventual dropping out. Students' educational and occupational aspirations have been found to be associated to those of their best friends (Alexander & Campbell, 1964; Duncan, Haller, & Portes, 1968; Haller & Butterworth, 1960; McDill & Coleman, 1965). These studies indicate that high school students are more likely to aspire to go to college if their best friends do so and are more likely to attend college if their best friends do so.

Peer Versus Parental Influences

The ultimate issue in the study of the role of the peer group in adolescent socialization, however, is the input of peers when compared with that of the family. The findings in the literature appear to be in conflict on the issue, some authors supporting that the peer group is more influential than parents and others supporting the opposite. However, when studies are grouped on the basis of their methodology and the areas of adolescent life they investigate, it becomes apparent that the results are to a great extent dependent on choice of method and focus of variables.

Investigators who base their results on interviews with adolescent high school students report that for important matters in their lives, adolescents turn to their parents, whereas for everyday choices of matters related to their life in the peer group, they follow their peers' advice (Brookover & Erickson, 1969; Douvan & Adelson, 1966). Additionally, similar conclusions are reached by investigations that present their respondents with hypothetical dilemmas and ask them to report whether they would follow parental or peer advice. These researchers found that conformity to parental suggestions decreased with age (Utech & Hoving, 1969) but that the tendency toward parental conformity increased with the perceived difficulty of the choices (Brittain, 1962).

A large number of studies has been concerned with the relative effects of the family and the peer group on educational plans. One group of studies, employing family socioeconomic status (SES) as an indicator of parental influence and average socioeconomic status of the school as an indicator of peer influence, found that lower-class students attending middle-class schools are more likely to aspire to go to college than lower-class students attending lower-class schools. These findings are interpreted to indicate that middle-class peers promote higher educational standards and goals and hence affect the attitudes and plans of lower-class students. This relationship has been found to hold in urban centers more than rural communities, where parental SES is the main correlate of college plans (Boyle, 1966; Coleman et al., 1966; Meyer, 1970; Ramsoy, 1961; Wilson, 1959).

On the other hand, perceived expectations of parents have been found to more strongly affect adolescent educational aspirations than the expectations of peers or teachers (McClintock, 1972). Furthermore, studies that compare actual choices by the adolescents, their best friends, and the actual educational expectations of their mothers reach the same conclusions. Kandel and Lesser (1969) conducted one such study and demonstrated that educational plans of students are more congruent with maternal aspirations than with peer plans, regardless of social class. These authors conclude that adolescent future goals are strongly influenced by parents, whereas peer relationships and values related to school behavior are affected by the peer group.

In short, there seems to be some agreement among researchers that parents and peers are used as referents for different segments of the adolescent life and that they are perceived as having different types of competences.

Summary and Critical Comment

We reviewed numerous investigations assessing the impact of various socialization agents on the high school student. In general, results tend to indicate, not surprisingly, that the different "significant others" tend to have different areas of maximal influence and that their instigations are sometimes complementary and other times conflictual. Nevertheless, there exists no systematic attempt to describe the processes through which parents, teachers, and peers influence the adolescent. Consequently, the need arises for research that would conceptualize and compare the way through which adults and peers socialize the adolescent and that would map the areas and extent of their relative influence. Such efforts would integrate knowledge about the impact of the high school and would clarify its standing as a socialization agency in the community.

WHAT ARE THE OUTCOMES OF HIGH SCHOOL SOCIALIZATION?

A central question in the study of institutionalized socialization concerns the nature of its outcomes. What is it exactly that the school does to and for the adolescent? What are the results of the shaping processes that take place in these settings and that have implications for societal functioning, individual well-being, and organizational survival?

To answer these questions, we organize the discussion around three general topics that have been suggested by Orville Brim (1966) as the major results of socialization. Brim has proposed that socialization transmits information, skills, and motivation that permit the person to perform adequately in his or her adult roles. Information refers to knowledge about the social reality and the self. Skills involve competence to perform role-related tasks; motivation is the willingness to conform to role-related expectations with continuous societal surveillance, i.e., the internalization of norms and values of the society. Of course these categories, although conceptually distinct, tend to overlap empirically. It is often true that knowledge of values or acquisition of skills has motivational consequences and the other way around. However, these conceptual groupings are utilized mostly for the sake of clarity and organization.

What Do Adolescents Learn About the Social World in the High School?

Socialization involves teaching the young about the norms, values, and structure of the social world. This knowledge prepares youth to perform their social and political roles as adults. The high school is expected to make major contributions to this type of learning. However, there is very little empirical evidence suggesting that this is happening.

Let's take political values and orientations, for example. Hess and Torney (1967) and Torney (1970), after conducting major surveys among school children and adolescents, conclude that school experience is important for the formation of political attitudes. However, findings on the subject are mixed. Political affiliation of adolescents is mostly accounted for through political preferences of parents (Jennings & Langton, 1969). There are also studies indicating that the formal curriculum does not have an impact on political attitudes and values or knowledge of the political system (Ehman, 1970; Langton & Jennings, 1968). On the other hand, there is consistent evidence that as adolescents progress through high school, their political ideology and sense of community change (Adelson & Beall, 1970; Adelson & O'Neil, 1966). How much of this is due to the cognitive maturation of adolescents that permits them to view society as a more abstract system? How much is due to exposure to the mass media, and how much is due to exposure to parents and others outside the school? There are no answers in the current literature. Undoubtedly, the developmental and environmental factors interact to contribute to increased political maturity, but the separate impact of each and the contexts that optimize them have not been studied.

Unfortunately, we have very little information on the acquisition of any other type of value in the school. Jenks et al. (1972) have suggested that the school does not teach values; it merely certifies that individuals are able to conform to norms and therefore will be good risks for prospective employers. On the other hand, Dreeben (1968) has suggested that the high school does transmit norms necessary for future organizational adjustment: independence and accountability, achievement, universalism and specificity, role distance and equity. His suggestions, however, have not been empirically pursued; and therefore, we are left with simple speculation on the possible impacts of schooling and with hope that future research will clarify some of these issues.

What Is the Impact of the High School Experience on Self-Evaluations?

The ability to view the self as an object and to evaluate it positively has important personal and social implications, because it has been found to constitute an important element in mental health and adult competence. It is widely accepted that the self is a social product resulting from interactions with others in the environment that either provide direct evaluations or standards of comparison (Backman & Secord, 1968; Jones & Gerard, 1967). The school, through the interpersonal opportunities it provides its students, qualifies as a setting for acquisition of information about the self and the development of identity (Sherif & Sherif, 1969).

We have already mentioned several investigations reporting relationships between teacher and peer evaluations and the self-perceptions of adolescents. Brookover, Thomas, and Paterson (1964) found that interpersonal interactions with teachers are crucial in the development of a favorable self-concept of academic ability. Goslin and Glass (1967) found that teachers' evaluations are a major source of information about intelligence. Gordon and Wood (1963) report that accuracy of students' self-evaluations are a function of teacher and peer appraisal. Additionally, behaviors in the school such as successful academic performance, extracurricular participation, and informal status have all been found to correlate positively with self-appraisal (Bachman et al., 1971; Backman

& Secord, 1968; Coleman, 1961). Here, it should be noted that these studies simply establish trends and relationships but provide no information about the causal direction of such relationships. It is obvious that students with high self-esteem and ability will evoke positive evaluations from their environment, which in turn will further support their self-image.

The classroom seems to be a setting where important social comparison processes take place that shape the adolescent's self-concept. An illustration of the comparison functions of the classroom is presented by Pettigrew (1967) on interracial classrooms. Pettigrew notes that black students attending predominantly white schools tend to perform better academically and have higher educational aspirations than their counterparts in all-black schools. At the same time, they tend to have more negative self-concepts regarding their academic ability. This latter finding he attributes to the fact that in a predominantly white school, the others available for comparison set higher comparison standards; and thus, the resulting self-evaluation tends to be lower. Such illustrations, though interesting, are not sufficient. We definitely need more systematic studies of the interpersonal processes in classrooms and of their impact on self-concepts with adequate controls for individual differences on prior self-attitudes.

What Competences Are Learned in the High School?

The transmission of skills for adequate adult role performance is an essential part of any socialization effort (Brim, 1966; Parsons, 1959). Education is considered one of the major determinants of adult competence. Educational attainment has been found to correlate with adult occupational and social status. Zigler and Phillips (1962) also demonstrated that education is related to adult mental health and other indicators of adult competence.

The question is: What aspects of schooling contribute to the acquisition of competences conducive to successful adult role performances? Jenks et al. (1972) argue that the school does not "improve" but rather "certifies" the student's ability to perform in organizational settings and to conform to organizational expectations. If this is true, the question becomes: If school simply certifies the presence of competences, where are they learned? At home? Through the mass media? In the neighborhood? A look at adolescents' lives makes it obvious that the high school is the only large-scale organization in which they participate. Consequently, it is not unreasonable to speculate that the school does teach them some strategies for coping with organizational demands as well as competences for dealing with a large variety of peers and adults.

Several investigators have tried to assess such interpersonal competences acquired in schools of varying socioeconomic context, size, and other organizational characteristics (see Trickett et al., 1972). The argument underlying such research has been that if variation in competences can be related to variation in high school characteristics, then it can be said that the school indeed contributes to the learning of such skills. These studies, although they add to our understanding of what happens in the high school, have still to solve the problem of extracting the causal influence of school from the confounding influences of the family, the mass media, etc.

Thus, presently, our personal experiences, our subjective observations, and students' reports point out that the high school teaches its students interpersonal and organizational skills that are useful for future role performances. However, there has been no systematic listing or investigations of such competences or of the processes through which they are acquired. Kelly (1968, 1969, 1971) has initiated a longitudinal investigation with the objective of studying the effects of the social environment of two high schools on the socialization of competences of their students. This volume presents a summary of the early findings.

What Types of Social Motives Are Acquired in the High School?

One of the major contributions of the school to adolescent socialization is what Katz and Kahn (1966) refer to as 'generalized role readiness." This they define as "an ability to meet the demands of many organizational settings with the proper cooperation. These requirements may shift from situation to situation, but the individual must be able to pick up his cues and play his part [p. 132] " Several observers have noted that adequate role behavior depends on the willingness to perform in socially expected ways (Parsons, 1959) and that this willingness, or conformity, is a function of the susceptibility of the person to social rewards, expectations, and punishment. The school, through the systematized interactions of students with their peers and with school adults, instigates such susceptibility.

The majority of research of school outcomes has focused on the socialization of achievement motivation which is conceptually related to generalized role readiness. The socialization of achievement motivation is considered a major requisite for the induction of the young into an achievement and mobility-oriented society. The extensive research investigating the role of school, family, and neighborhood in creating an achievement orientation has been reviewed by Getzels (1969) and Boocock (1966). Findings indicate that the school, through its formal structure, its academic climate, and the expectations of the teachers, and through its informal structure and the composition and the values of the student population, may support or discourage achievement. However, the unique impact of the school on such outcomes is hard to assess, because the choice of school and even the nature of the peer group within the school is tremendously affected by parental background, values, and aspirations.

The most interesting information about the role of the school in the socialization of achievement motivation comes from studies that demonstrate the impact of different types of schools on minority group or lower socioeconomic status students. It has been found that minority group students in general do not exhibit lower achievement performance and aspirations than students from white middle-class families. However, a series of studies has demonstrated that minority students attending classes with predominantly white middle-class students have higher academic achievement scores and higher educational aspirations than comparable groups of students attending segregated classrooms (McPartland, 1969). The social comparison processes that mediate these effects have been documented by Epps (1969). In a study that varied experimentally the comparison groups, he found that black students perform better on cognitive tasks when they anticipate comparison with white peers.

Unfortunately, there has been little research carried out on any other aspects of social motivation enhanced through schooling. Willems (1967) studied the impact of school size on sense of obligation and found that in small schools, students report more sense of obligation than students in large schools. Todd (1971) investigated help giving mediated by high school socialization (see Chapter 10 of this monograph). Bachman et al. (1967) assessed a variety of motives, values, and attitudes that are dependent on socialization processes in the school. They report that students remaining in the high school indicated a higher level of trust in people than students who had dropped out. None of the other beliefs and attitudes investigated differed between the two groups.

CONCLUSION

The principal characteristic of the reviewed work is a lack of unifying theory that, as a result, has generated empirical evidence that is fragmented and methodologically uneven. Consequently, in view of the present state of the research evidence, the primary need is for an adequate theory of socialization that would provide the basis for a systematic and integrated study of adolescent socialization in the high school and other socializing agencies. Such a theory, as Inkeles (1966) has noted, should start by describing in detail the qualities and attributes required of adults in the society and then should postulate through what processes such qualities are acquired, what socialization settings contribute to their acquisition, and in what ways different socialization settings mediate different adult attributes. The work reported in this volume is a beginning in this direction.

A second need is for innovative and sophisticated research designs that will combine alternative methods for investigating and assessing socialization processes in the natural field settings where they occur and that will provide replicated findings. All of the chapters in this volume reflect this orientation. A third need is for comparative studies of socialization processes and outcomes mediated by various socialization resources in the community such as the family, the school, the peer group, community organizations, the mass media, etc. These studies would permit a mapping of the contributions of these settings and would establish the areas of minimal and maximal socializing efficiency of each. Finally, a related need is for comparative studies of socialization outcomes mediated by different high schools such as the work focusing on Wayne and Thurston High Schools. Such investigations will document the ways in which unique characteristics of the normative structure of each high school mediate and contribute to the development of special atrributes in the individual adolescent.

Returning to the original question of what is the relative standing of the high school as a socialization resource when compared to other socialization settings in the community, it is obvious that it is difficult to formulate a conclusive answer. The high school undoubtedly has an impact on the educational and occupational careers of adolescents as it affects their aspirations and provides them with skills necessary for future occupational accomplishment. It also has an impact on the adolescents' self-perceptions. However, as far as the acquisition of values, of social skills, and of social motivation is concerned, the impact of the high school is presently unknown.

A general disenchantment with high schools has led to considerable speculation among behavioral scientists about the present and future functioning of the high school as a socializing organization. For example, Coleman, a serious student of high schools, suggests that they should relegate their cognitive—educational functions to external organizations and restructure themselves to provide training for responsible adulthood and develop in the young abilities to utilize the rich, information-processing resources of the environment (1972). Given the lack of empirical support for such views, one could equally well argue the opposite, i.e., that the high school keep the cognitive—educational functions and allocate the social learning functions to outside community agencies, where adolescents will interact with other members of the community, be less isolated from the rest of the community, and receive training in autonomy and responsibility. Nevertheless, until more systematic empirical information about the various functions and contributions of the high school is collected, behavioral scientists have a very limited basis from which to make policy recommendations.

For all its present limitations and drawbacks, the future of research on high school socialization seems rather promising. Social psychological and sociological theory are brought increasingly to bear on the processes taking place in the high school. Increased sophistication in field research and quasiexperimental designs can facilitate investigations in high schools and other socialization settings. Educational reforms are increasingly accompanied by evaluative research, providing the social scientist with an excellent opportunity to gather information about the changes in the impact of the high school as a function of changes in the structure of the school and the roles of its participants. There is public concern over educational issues, which is bound to generate support for new types of research. Therefore, it is highly possible that in the near future, a considerable number of the questions about adolescent socialization in the high school that are presently unanswered will be clarified.

REFERENCES

Adelson, J., & Beall, L. Adolescent perspectives on law and government. *Law and Society Review,* 1970, *4*(4), 495–504.

Adelson, J., & O'Neil, R. Growth of political ideas in adolescence: The sense of community. *Journal of Personality and Social Psychology,* 1966, *4,* 295–306.

Alexander, C. N., Jr., & Campbell, E. Q. Peer influences on adolescent educational aspirations and attainments. *American Sociological Review,* 1964, *29,* 568–575.

Alexander, L., Epson, B., Means, R., & Means, G. Achievement as a function of teacher-initiated student–teacher personal interactions. *Psychological Reports,* 1971, *28,* 431–434.

Ausubel, D. P. *Theory and problems of adolescent development.* New York: Grune and Stratton, 1954.

Bachman, J. G. *Youth in transition* (Vol. 2). *The impact of family background and intelligence on tenth-grade boys.* Ann Arbor, Mich.: Institute for Social Research, 1970.

Bachman, J. G., Green, S., & Wirtanen, I. D. *Youth in transition* (Vol. 3). *Dropping out — Problem or symptom?* Ann Arbor, Mich.: Institute for Social Research, 1971.

Bachman, J. G., Kahn, R. L., Mednick, M. T., Davidson, T. N., & Johnston, L. D. *Youth in transition* (Vol. 1). *Blueprint for a nationwide longitudinal study of adolescent boys.* Ann Arbor, Mich.: Institute for Social Research, 1967.

Backman, C. W., & Secord, P. F. *A social psychological view of education.* New York: Harcourt, Brace and World, 1968.

Barker, R. G., & Gump, P. V. *Big school, small school: High school size and student behavior.* Stanford, Calif.: Stanford University Press, 1964.

Bennis, W. G. Beyond bureaucracy. In W. G. Bennis & P. E. Slater (Eds.), *The temporary society.* New York: Harper and Row, 1968.

Bidwell, C. E. The school as a formal organization. In J. March (Ed.), *Handbook of organizations.* Chicago: Rand–McNally, 1965.

Boocock, S. S. Toward a sociology of learning: A selective review of existing research. *Sociology of Education,* 1966, *39,* 1–45.

Boyle, R. P. The effect of the high school on students' aspirations. *The American Journal of Sociology,* 1966, *71,* 628–639.

Brim, O. G., Jr. Socialization through the life cycle. In O. G. Brim, Jr., & W. Stanton (Eds.), *Socialization after childhood: Two essays.* New York: Wiley, 1966.

Brittain, C. V. Adolescent choices and parent–peer cross pressures. *American Sociological Review,* 1962, *28*(3), 385–391.

Bronfenbrenner, U. Reaction to social pressure from adults versus peers among Soviet day school and boarding school pupils in the perspective of an American sample. *Journal of Personality and Social Psychology,* 1970, *15*(3), 179–189.

Brookover, W. B., & Erickson, E. L. *Society, schools and learning.* Boston: Allyn and Bacon, 1969.

Brookover, W. B., & Gottlieb, D. *A sociology of education.* New York: American Book Company, 1964.

Brookover, W. B., Paterson, A., & Shailer, T. Self-concept of ability and academic achievement of junior high school students. Report of Cooperative Research Project #845. East Lansing: Michigan State University, College of Education, 1962.

Brookover, W. B., Thomas, S., & Paterson, A. Self-concept of ability and school achievement. *Sociology of Education,* 1964, *37,* 271–279.

Bryan, R. C. High school students view classrooms control. In S. Frey (Ed.), *Adolescent behavior in school: Determinants and outcomes.* Chicago: Rand–McNally, 1970.

Clark, B. R. Sociology of education. In R. E. L. Faris (Ed.), *Handbook of modern sociology.* Chicago: Rand–McNally, 1964.

Cogan, M. L. The behavior of teachers and the productive behavior of their pupils. *Journal of Experimental Education,* 1958, *27,* 89–124.

Coleman, J. S. *The adolescent society.* New York: Free Press, 1961.

Coleman, J. S. *The adolescent and the schools.* New York: Basic Books, 1965.

Coleman, J. S. The children have outgrown the schools. *Psychology Today,* 1972, *5*(9), 72–75 ff.

Coleman, J. S., Campbell, E. Q., Hobson, C. J., McPartland, J., Mood, A. M., Weinfeld, F. D., & York, R. L. *Equality of educational opportunity.* Washington, D.C.: U.S. Government Printing Office, 1966.

Davidson, H., & Lang, G. Children's perceptions of teachers' feelings toward them. *Journal of Experimental Education,* 1960, *29*(2), 107–118.

Douvan, E., & Adelson, J. *The adolescent experience.* New York: Wiley, 1966.

Douvan, E., & Gold, M. Model patterns in American adolescence. In L. Hoffman & M. L. Hoffman (Eds.), *Review of child development research.* New York: Russel Sage Foundation, 1966.

Dreeben, R. *On what is learned in school.* Reading, Mass.: Addison–Wesley, 1968.

Dreeben, R. American schooling: Patterns and processes of stability and change. In B. Barber & A. Inkeles (Eds.), *Stability and social change.* Boston: Little, Brown and Company, 1971.

Duncan, O. D., Haller, A. O., & Portes, A. Peer influences on aspirations: A reinterpretation. *American Journal of Sociology,* 1968, *74,* 119–137.

Edwards, D. W. Exploration and the high school experience: A study of tenth-grade boys' perceptions of themselves, their peers, and their schools. Unpublished doctoral dissertation, The University of Michigan, Ann Arbor, Michigan, 1971.

Ehman, L. H. Normative discourse and attitude change in the social studies classroom. *The High School Journal,* 1970, *54*(2), 77–83.

Elkin, F., & Westley, W. A. The myth of adolescent culture. *American Sociological Review,* 1955, *20,* 680–684.

Elliot, D. S., Voss, H. L., & Wendling, A. Dropout and the social milieu of the high school: A preliminary analysis. *American Journal of Orthopsychiatry,* 1966, *36,* 808–817.

Epperson, D. C. A reassessment of indices of parental influences in "The Adolescent Society." *American Sociological Review,* 1964, *29,* 93–96.

Epps, E. G. Correlates of academic achievement among northern and southern urban Negro students. *Journal of Social Issues,* 1969, *25*(3), 55–70.

Friedenberg, E. Z. The modern high school: A profile. In F. Cordasco, M. Hillson, & H. A. Bullock (Eds.), *The school in the social order: A sociological introduction to educational understanding.* Scranton, Penn.: International Textbook Company, 1970.

Getzels, J. W. A social psychology of education. In G. Lindzey & E. Aronson, (Eds.), *The handbook of social psychology* (2nd ed., Vol. 5). Reading, Mass.: Addison–Wesley, 1969.

Goffman, E. *Asylums.* Garden City, N.Y.: Doubleday, Anchor Books, 1961.

Gold, M., & Mann, D. Delinquency as defense. Unpublished manuscript, Institute for Social Research, Ann Arbor, Michigan, 1970.

Gordon, C. W. The role of the teacher in the social structure of the high school. *Journal of Educational Sociology,* 1955, *29,* 21–29.

Gordon, C. W. *The social system of the high school.* Glencoe, Ill.: The Free Press, 1957.

Gordon, I. J., & Wood, P. C. The relationship between pupil self-evaluation, teacher evaluation of the pupil and scholastic achievement. *Journal of Educational Research,* 1963, *56,* 440–443.

Goslin, D. A. *The school in contemporary society.* Glenview, Ill.: Scott, Foresman and Company, 1965.

Goslin, D. A. The school in a changing society: Notes on the development of strategies for solving educational problems. *American Journal of Orthopsychiatry,* 1967, *37*(5), 843–858.

Goslin, D. A., & Glass, D. C. The social effects of standardized testing in American elementary and secondary schools. *Sociology of Education,* 1967, *40,* 115–131.

Gottlieb, D., & Ramsey, C. *The American adolescent.* Homewood, Ill.: Dorsey, 1964.

Gurin, P., & Katz, D. *Motivation and aspiration in the Negro college.* Ann Arbor, Mich.: Institute for Social Research, 1966.

Haller, A. O., & Butterworth, C. E. Peer influences on levels of occupational and educational aspiration. *Social Forces,* 1960, *38,* 289–295.

Havighurst, R. J., & Newgarten, B. L. *Society and education.* Boston: Allyn and Bacon, 1962.

Hess, R. D., & Torney, J. V. *The development of political attitudes in children.* Chicago: Aldine Publishing Company, 1967.

Inkeles, A. Social structure and the socialization of competence. *Harvard Educational Review,* 1966, *36*(3), 282.

Jenks, C., Smith, M., Acland, H., Bane, M. S., Cohen, D., Gintis, H., Heyns, B., & Michelson, S. *Inequality: A reassessment of the effect of family and schooling in America.* New York: Basic Books, 1972.

Jennings, M. K., & Langton, K. P. Mothers versus fathers: The formation of political orientations among young Americans. *Journal of Politics,* 1969, *31*(2), 329–359.

Jones, E. E., & Gerard, H. B. *Foundation of social psychology.* New York: Wiley, 1967.

Kandel, D. B., & Lesser, G. S. Parental and peer influences on educational plans of adolescents. *American Sociological Review,* 1969, *34*(2), 212–222.

Katz, D., & Kahn, R. L. *The social psychology of organization.* New York: Wiley, 1966.

Kelly, J. G. Towards an ecological conception of preventive interventions. In J. W. Carter, Jr. (Ed.), *Research contributions from psychology to community mental health.* New York: Behavioral Publications, 1968.

Kelly, J. G. Naturalistic observations in contrasting social environments. In E. P. Willems & H. L. Raush (Eds.), *Naturalistic viewpoints in psychological research.* New York: Holt, Rinehart and Winston, 1969.

Kelly, J. G. The coping process in varied high school environments. In M. J. Feldman (Ed.), *Studies in psychotherapy and behavioral change, No. 2, Theory and research in community mental health.* Buffalo, N.Y.: State University of New York at Buffalo, 1971.

Langton, K. P., & Jennings, M. K. Political socialization and the high school curriculum in the United States. *The American Political Science Review,* 1968, *42,* 852–867.

McClintock, S. M. K. The socialization experience of adolescents in two suburban high schools: Its quality, outcomes and correlates. Unpublished doctoral dissertation, The University of Michigan, 1972.

McDill, E. L., & Coleman, J. High school social status, college plans and interest in academic achievement: A panel analysis, *American Sociological Review,* 1963, *18,* 905–918.

McDill, E. L., & Coleman, J. Family and peer influences in college plans of high school students. *Sociology of Education,* 1965, *38,* 112–126.

McPartland, J. The relative influence of school and of classroom desegregation on the academic achievement of ninth-grade Negro students. *Journal of Social Issues,* 1969, *25*(3), 93–103.

Mead, M. Education as cultural growth. In C. S. Brembeck & M. Grandstaff (Eds.), *Social foundations of education: A book of readings.* New York: Wiley, 1969.

Meyer, J. W. High school effects on college intentions. *American Journal of Sociology,* 1970, *79*(1), 59–62.

Mutiner, D. D., & Rosemier, R. A. Behavioral problems of children as viewed by teachers and the children themselves. *Journal of Consulting Psychology,* 1967, *31*(6), 583–587.

Nelson, J. L., & Besag, F. P. *Sociological perspectives in education: Models for analysis.* London: Pitman, 1970.

Parsons, T. The school class as a social system: Some of its functions in American society. *Harvard Educational Review,* 1959, *29*(4), 297–318.

Pervin, L. Performance and satisfaction as a function of individual–environment fit. *Psychological Bulletin,* 1968, *69,* 56–68.

Pettigrew, T. F. Social evaluation theory. In D. Levine (Ed.), *Nebraska Symposium on Motivation.* Lincoln: University of Nebraska Press, 1967.

Ramsoy, V. R. *American high school of mid-century.* New York: Bureau of Applied Social Research, Columbia University, 1961.

Rosenberg, M. *Society and the adolescent self-image.* Princeton, N.J.: Princeton University Press, 1965.

Rosenthal, R., & Jacobson, L. Teacher's expectancies: Determinants of pupils' I.Q. gains. *Psychological Reports,* 1966, *19,* 115–118.

Sexton, P. *The American school: A sociological analysis.* Englewood Cliffs, N.J.: Prentice–Hall, 1967.

Sherif, M., & Sherif, C. W. *Social psychology.* New York: Harper and Row, 1969.

Slater, P. E. On social regression. *American Sociological Review,* 1963, *28*(3), 339–364.

Stern, G. G. Measuring noncognitive variables in research on teaching. In N. L. Gage (Ed.), *Handbook of research on teaching.* Chicago: Rand–McNally, 1963.

Strom, R. D. Comparison of adolescent and adult behavioral norm properties. *Journal of Educational Psychology,* 1963, *54,* 322–330.

Todd, D. M. Helping behavior for citizens and tribe: A case study of two adolescent subcultures of a high school. Unpublished doctoral dissertation, The University of Michigan, 1971.

Torney, J. V. Contemporary political socialization in elementary schools and beyond. *The High School Journal,* 1970, *54*(2), 153–163.

Trickett, E. J., Kelly, J. G., & Todd, D. M. The social environment of the high school: Guidelines for individual change and organizational redevelopment. In S. Golann & C. Eisdorfer (Eds.), *Handbook of community psychology.* New York: Appleton–Century–Crofts, 1972.

Turner, R. H. *The social context of ambition.* San Francisco: Chandler, 1964.

Utech, D. A., & Hoving, K. L. Parents and peers as competing influences in the decisions of children of differing ages. *Journal of Social Psychology,* 1969, *78*(1), 267–274.

Waller, W. *The sociology of teaching.* New York: Wiley, 1932.

Wicker, A. W. Undermanning performances and students' subjective experiences in behavior settings of large and small high schools. *Journal of Personality and Social Psychology,* 1968, *10*(3), 255–261.

Willems, E. P. Sense of obligation to high school activities as related to school size and marginality of student. *Child Development,* 1967, *38*(4), 1247–1260.

Wilson, A. B. Residential segregation of social classes and aspirations of high school boys. *American Sociological Review,* 1959, *24,* 836–845.

Zigler, E., & Phillips, L. Social competence and the process reactive distinction in psychopathology. *Journal of Abnormal Social Psychology,* 1962, *65,* 215–222.

4 The Social Environments of the Two High Schools: Background Data

Richard R. Rice
Marilyn Marsh[1]
Institute for Social Research
The University of Michigan

The purpose of this chapter is to describe characteristics of the two high schools and their communities.

In addition to questionnaire data collected from the faculty of the two high schools, statistics derived from the 1960 and 1970 census are used, along with self-reports obtained from a sample of male students in the eighth grade and again in the first semester of the 11th grade. A discussion of the general characteristics of the communities is presented, followed by descriptions of the physical and social environments of the schools and reports from the students.

THE COMMUNITIES

The Wayne School Community

Wayne Memorial High School is located in Wayne, Michigan, approximately 20 miles from Detroit. The town of Wayne dates back to the middle of the 19th century. It has a four-block downtown business district under urban renewal, stimulated by an upsurge of suburban shopping centers in the nearby area. The nature of the community changed greatly as a result of the growth of Detroit as a manufacturing center in the 1930s and 1940s and during World War II.

During World War II Wayne experienced a great influx of white laborers, largely from the South, who came to work in the defense plants. This expansion continued after the war; five large manufacturing plants are now located in

---

[1]Present address: Catholic Social Services, Ann Arbor, Michigan.

Wayne. The community has a large proportion of semi-skilled and skilled blue-collar workers as heads of households. Many families immigrated from other states and communities, and most of the students who transfer out of the Wayne school system move with their families to other industrial areas of Michigan or return to the South.

The Thurston School Community

Lee M. Thurston High School draws its students from the southern half of Redford Township, also located near the western edge of Wayne County, 15 to 20 miles from the center of Detroit and about 10 miles north of Wayne. This area is predominantly residential with less than 1% nonwhite population. Unlike Wayne, it has no "downtown," main street, or past history as a cohesive community. Most of the area has developed since World War II as the result of the suburban expansion of Detroit. Typically, the area has experienced immigration from Detroit as more upwardly mobile white citizens left the core city and moved to the suburbs. It has experienced rapid growth in new housing since 1950, although some sections contain homes dating back to 1920. A study conducted in recent years indicates a slowing of this growth trend. A report prepared by the Citizen's Committee on Economic Opportunity (1965) indicates that the area has a limited amount of industry but is generally considered as a residential community with most of its residents earning their livelihood in other areas.

Comparative Socioeconomic and Sociocultural Data

Data from the 1970 Census presented in Table 4.1 show these two communities to be similar in size and racial compositions. Both communities are almost entirely white. The Wayne community is somewhat larger than the Thurston

TABLE 4.1
1970 Census: General Characteristics
of the Populations

Characteristic	Wayne School Community	Thurston School Comunity
Population	42,441	33,048
Percent of population that is black	.009%	1.08%
Number of families	9,935	8,376
Percentage of families with own children under age 18	58%	60%
Mean number of children per family	2.82	2.39

TABLE 4.2
1960 Census: Education and Income of the Communities

Variable	Wayne School Community	Thurston School Community
Median family income	$6,880	$8,539
Percentage of low-income families (less than $3,000)	7.6%	3.7%
Percentage of high-income families (more than $10,000)	19.3%	33.0%
Median years of education	11.3	12.2

community and has families with a somewhat larger number of children under 18 years old. When the two communities are compared as to education and income from 1960 census data (see Table 4.2), a socioeconomic difference can be noted between the two communities.

The socioeconomic status (SES) difference between the two communities is a reflection of the distribution of the labor force. The Wayne community, being more highly industrialized, has a larger proportion of blue-collar workers, whereas the Thurston community has a larger proportion of white-collar workers, as shown in Table 4.3. The larger percentage of renter-occupied housing, lower median rent, and lower housing values reported by the data currently available from the 1970 census confirms that the Thurston community is of a somewhat higher socioeconomic level (SES) than the Wayne community (see Table 4.4).

In the spring of 1969, the Opinions of Youth Study administered questionnaires to over 95% of all the eighth-grade boys attending school in the four

TABLE 4.3
1960 Census: Employment by Occupation,
Percentage of Labor Force

Occupation	Wayne School Community	Thurston School Community
Professional, managerial and technical[a]	21.6%	27.4%
Clerical and sales[a]	22.1%	29.4%
Craftsmen and Foremen[b]	18.7%	15.7%
Operatives[b]	23.2%	16.6%
Service Workers[b]	8.7%	7.4%
Laborers[b]	3.1%	1.9%
No response	2.6%	1.6%

[a]The percentage of white-collar workers in the Wayne community is 43.7%; in the Thurston community, 56.8%.

[b]The percentage of blue-collar workers in the Wayne community is 53.7%; in the Thurston community, 41.6%.

TABLE 4.4
1970 Census: Characteristics of Housing Units
for the Communities

Characteristics	Wayne School Community	Thurston School Community
Number of housing units	11,246	9,263
Percentage renter occupied	25%	5%
Mean number of rooms per housing unit	5.1	5.4
Mean number of persons per housing unit	3.5	3.5
Median value of owner-occupied housing units	$18,199	$23,449
Median monthly rent	$114.50	$158.41

junior high schools that feed into the Wayne and Thurston High Schools. These data show many of the differences observed in the 1960 and 1970 census data. For these samples, Thurston students reported statistically significantly higher education and SES levels than Wayne students, as shown in Table 4.5. These data show that 23.2% of the Wayne boys' fathers have white-collar occupations and 76.8% blue-collar positions, whereas 52.1% of the Thurston boys' fathers have white-collar jobs and only 47.9% blue-collar jobs.

Family Composition

The number of children per family within the two communities is essentially the same, as reported both by the 1970 census data and the self-reports of the sample of eighth-grade boys. The Wayne students reported a mean of 2.7 siblings living at home with them and the Thurston boys reported 2.3 siblings when in the eighth grade.

There are no significant differences in the reports from students of both schools regarding parental absence from the home. The father was reported

TABLE 4.5
Eighth-Grade Boys: Mean Education and
Socioeconomic Status of Fathers

Variable	Wayne boys		Thurston boys		F	Sig.	eta^2
	$\bar{X}$	N	$\bar{X}$	N			
Education	11.0	250	12.7	274	46.3	<.000	.08
Duncan SES[a]	35.1	233	48.9	280	51.2	<.000	.09

[a]Duncan, O.D. A socioeconomic index for all occupations. In A. J. Reiss, Jr. (Ed.), *Occupations and social status.* New York: The Free Press, 1965.

missing from the home by 5% of the Wayne boys and 7% of the Thurston boys, whereas 3% of the Wayne boys and 2% of the Thurston boys reported no mother or stepmother in the home.

Mobility

There are differences revealed between these two groups of students in mobility variables obtained in their self-report data. The Wayne junior high school boys reported living in a greater number of homes and attending a greater number of schools than the Thurston boys. Proportionately three times as many Wayne junior high school boys (36%) reported having lived outside the Detroit area than did the Thurston junior high school boys (11%). These differences are presented in Table 4.6.

Summary of the Communities

In gross demographic terms, the two communities differ somewhat in their socioeconomic levels, background mobility, and family size. The Thurston community has a higher SES level than the Wayne community; the Wayne community has a higher geographic mobility level and slightly larger families. The differences between the two communities in SES, mobility, and family size account for 21% of the variances of these variables in a multivariate, one-way analysis of variance. The difference between the two communities in terms of family size is quite small. The difference between them in terms of geographic mobility is at most moderate. It can be noted that although three times as many of the Wayne junior high school boys reported living outside the Detroit area as did Thurston junior high school boys, 64% of the Wayne and 89% of the Thurston junior high school boys reported never having lived outside this geographic area.

The difference between the two communities in terms of SES level should also be characterized as moderate. The mean Duncan SES score for the fathers of the Thurston junior high school boys (48.9) corresponds to the Duncan score assigned to food store managers, airplane mechanics, plate printers and pressmen, and tool and die makers. The mean Duncan SES score for the fathers of the

TABLE 4.6
Eighth-Grade Boys: Past Mobility

| Variable | Wayne boys | | Thurston boys | | | | |
	$\overline{X}$	N	$\overline{X}$	N	F	Sig.	eta^2
Mean number of homes lived in	3.4	225	1.9	242	77.8	<000	.14
Mean number of schools attended	3.5	224	2.6	239	47.4	<000	.09

Wayne junior high school boys (35.1) corresponds to the Duncan SES score assigned to managers of automobile repair garages, jewelers and watchmakers, office machine repairmen, radio and TV repairmen, and structural metalworkers.

We can conclude that there are moderate differences between the two communities, but they are more similar than different. Both can be characterized as all-white, suburban, middle-class communities. The difference may be suggested best by characterizing the Thurston community as "middle-middle class" and the Wayne community as "lower-middle class," although the danger of such labeling is obvious.

THE HIGH SCHOOLS

The Physical Environment

Thurston High School.   Thurston has a very attractive, modern high school that was built in 1957. Its design consists of two large, connected squares with each square including an open courtyard in the center. Only one wing has a second level. The hallways have low ceilings, and the school feels warm, modern, and spacious. It has two large, comfortable teachers' lounges but no student lounge. Although the industrial arts building is separate, the school is quite contiguous and homogeneous.

Wayne High School.   Wayne High School was built in 1952. The main building has three stories, and to the visitor it looks quite functional. The long, high-ceilinged halls, although by no means unattractive, do not radiate the same warmth as the Thurston halls. It has two student cafeterias and a student lounge with couches and a TV set. The many small, teachers' lounges cannot be described as posh. The industrial arts building is separate but connected to the main building by a roofed walkway, as is another small, classroom building called the *annex*. In 1957, a modern, octagonal-shaped auditorium was constructed, and a swimming pool was added to the gym. This complex was considered the achievement of the school band director, who is now the principal of Wayne High School. All in all, the high school is architecturally fragmented and complex. Wayne students have mentioned a problem of getting from one place to another in the time allotted between classes more frequently than have Thurston students.

Characteristics of the Two High Schools

Enrollment.   The two schools have similar student enrollments. During the 1970–1971 academic year, Wayne High School had a student enrollment of 1,963 and Thurston, an enrollment of 2,126. A problem experienced by both Wayne and Thurston High Schools is the continuing increase in enrollment. This problem is felt more intensely at Thurston than at Wayne. From the 1965–1966 school year to the 1970–1971 school year, Wayne has experienced an enrollment increase of 10.6%; Thurston, 20.2%. Thurston students more frequently mention problems of overcrowding in their school than do Wayne students.

Curriculum.   Both high schools have similar course offerings. There are differences, however, in the structure and emphasis of curriculum. Wayne High School uses a three-tracked, ability grouping system and places a greater emphasis on business and vocational courses, with particular emphasis on commerce and business. The business and vocational departments at Wayne include 28% of the faculty with 15% in the commercial and business department. At Thurston, 17% of the faculty are in the business and vocational departments with 5% in the commercial and business department. Both schools have a cooperative work/study program, offering on-the-job training in addition to related school instruction. At Thurston, there is strong emphasis on college preparatory courses with 77% of the faculty in academic departments as compared to 64% at Wayne. A greater percentage of Thurston graduates go on to college or university than do Wayne graduates. Of the 1970 graduating class, 57% of the Thurston students went to college as compared to 42% of the Wayne students.

Sports and extracurricular activities.   Both high schools have an approximately equal number of sports activities. There are 13 different athletic organizations for male students at each school; and there are from three to five female sports teams in operation each year, depending on student interest. Both schools have extramural and intramural competitions. Wayne High School has 10 different music groups as compared to Thurston's four. The principal at Wayne, former band director of the school, encourages interest and involvement in music, and FM radio music flows through the hallways each day. Both schools have a student government body with class officers and faculty advisors for each grade. Election of class officers is held each year. The two schools offer a wide variety of other clubs and organizations. There are 35 different clubs at Thurston and 29 clubs at Wayne. As P. Newman (1971) has noted, the clubs at Wayne serve more social functions for the school, whereas at Thurston the clubs are more task oriented. Wayne also sponsors more informal social activities that involve both faculty and students.

Summary.   The size of enrollment at the two schools is similar. Wayne and Thurston are also similar in terms of the physical facilities provided for their student bodies. Thurston High School provides more attractive and coherent accommodations for its students than does Wayne High School; but Wayne, due to its greater physical size and the greater increase in enrollment experienced by Thurston in the past few years, provides slightly more adequate and less crowded physical facilities than does Thurston High School.

Curricular and extracurricular programs for students are also quite similar in both schools. The Thurston curriculum places slightly greater emphasis on college preparation, whereas the Wayne curriculum places slightly greater emphasis on commercial and business preparation. The Wayne extracurricular program places a slightly greater emphasis on serving social functions in that school, and the Thurston extracurricular program is slightly more task oriented. The differences in emphasis of the curricular and extracurricular programs at the two schools seem quite consistent with the socioeconomic and mobility differences noted within their communities earlier. In sum, we can conclude that these two schools are quite similar in these terms with apparent differences being minor. Both might be characterized as typical moderate-sized, middle-class suburban schools.

THE SOCIAL STRUCTURE

The Faculty

Number.   The quantity of faculty employed at the two schools is very similar. Wayne High School has 95 teaching faculty; Thurston has 99. Both have a classroom teacher/student ratio of 1:21. Wayne has five administrative staff members and Thurston, four. Thurston High School employs eight counselors; Wayne, six.

Educational background.   The educational backgrounds of these two faculty groups are almost identical. The highest degree earned by 55% of each staff is a BA, and 43% of each faculty have earned their MA. At Wayne, 38% of the staff are currently working on their MA degrees, and 37% of the Thurston staff are doing so.

Demographic characteristics.   During the spring of 1971, anonymous self-report questionnaires were distributed to the administrators, teaching staff, and counselors of both schools by P. Newman, who reports in detail on this data in Chapter 11. Of the questionnaires distributed, 84% were completed and returned from Wayne High School; 80% were completed and returned by the Thurston staff. Descriptive data obtained from this questionnaire show that the faculties are about half male and half female. From 75% to 80% of the faculty at each school are married, with 56% of each faculty reporting previous high school teaching experience.

There is a difference in age between the two faculties, however. On the average, Wayne staff are about 3 to 4 years older than Thurston staff. Wayne staff tend to have about 2 years more teaching experience and have been at their high school an average of about 2 ½ years longer than Thurston staff. The distributions between the two schools on the above variables are largely due to fewer Thurston faculty having more than 20 years of teaching experience. A small number of faculty at both schools report that they live within the school district. Eight percent of the Thurston staff report living within the Thurston school district, whereas 26% of the Wayne faculty report living within the Wayne community.

Involvement in school events. Data was obtained from this questionnaire regarding the frequency with which the staff members attended various kinds of school-related meetings and events. No differences are found between the faculty of the two schools in their reported attendance at school dances, P.T.A. meetings, and faculty social events. Moderate differences were noted, however, in terms of their reported attendance at school board meetings and school sports events. The Thurston staff report attending school board meetings more frequently than the Wayne staff, whereas the Wayne staff report attending school sports events more frequently. The more frequent attendance of the Thurston staff at school board meetings may be the result of greater teacher union activities at this school. Eleven members of the Wayne staff (only three at Thurston) report that they always attend these events whenever it is possible. The percentages of faculty of the two schools reporting occasional attendance at school sporting events are almost identical.

Age, experience, and staff longevity seem to be related to differences in involvement of the staffs at the two schools. Staff members 35 years or older are more apt to live within their school districts at both schools. Of this age group, 37.5% of the Wayne and 17% of the Thurston staff members report living within their school's district. Of the staff members under 35 years, 18% of the Wayne staff and only 3% of the Thurston staff report living within their school district. To a significant extent, the older members of both staffs report attending school board and P.T.A. meetings more frequently than the younger staff members.

Expectations of students. Of nine questions asked of the faculty of both schools regarding their expectations of students, only two questions revealed significant differences. Such topics as "plan to attend college," "be involved in school activities," "obey school rules," "bring an academic attitude to class," "be friendly and outgoing," "do their own thing," "talk to you," and "do what you say to do" show no significant mean differences between the schools.

The Thurston staff, however, do report that they expect their students "to think out work clearly and carefully" to a significantly greater extent than the Wayne staff; the Wayne staff expect their students "to obey school rules" to a significantly greater extent than do the Thurston staff. Neither of these differences is very strong, as can be noted on Table 4.7.

An examination of the variances for each school on these expectation items indicates a lesser amount of agreement among the staff at Thurston than at

TABLE 4.7
School Staffs: Their Expectations
of Their Students[a]

Variable	Wayne staff		Thurston staff				
	$\overline{X}$	N	$\overline{X}$	N	F	Sig.	eta^2
How much staffs expect their students to:							
Obey school rules	6.0	85	5.6	86	5.5	.02	.03
Think out work clearly							
and carefully	5.5	85	5.8	88	3.7	.05	.02
Do what you say to do	5.4	81	5.1	86	1.1	NS	NS
Talk to you	5.3	82	5.1	83	.5	NS	NS
Be friendly and							
outgoing	5.2	82	5.2	86	.1	NS	NS
Bring an academic							
attitude to class	4.9	84	4.9	87	.1	NS	NS
"Do their own thing"	4.3	82	4.3	84	0.0	NS	NS
Be involved in school							
activities	4.3	85	4.1	84	1.8	NS	NS
Plan to attend college	3.3	85	3.4	82	.1	NS	NS

[a]The expectations of students were reported by the staffs on 7-point scales, the end points being defined as "NOT AT ALL" (1) and "VERY MUCH" (7).

Wayne regarding expectations for student behavior. Of the nine items, the variance is greater for the Thurston staff than for the Wayne staff on all of them except "to think out work clearly and carefully." This would suggest that the Wayne faculty have more consensus than the faculty at Thurston and thus tend to transmit the same expectations to their students.

Classroom techniques.   No differences are found between the two staffs regarding the amount of structure they report that they provide their classes; the amount of discussion between them and their students in classes; nor the amount of discussion that they report goes on between the students in the classroom.

Perceptions of students.   No differences were found in the reports of the faculty regarding the proportion of the students in their schools whom they perceive as being "very friendly" toward them or the proportion of students whom they see as "interested in school and in getting an education." Moderate differences are noted between the proportion of students they perceive as "being unhappy with the way your school is run" and "like your school a lot." The Thurston staff report a larger proportion of their students as unhappy with the way their school is run than do the Wayne staff. The Wayne staff, on the other hand, report that a larger proportion of their students like their school. No difference is found between the two staffs as to "how comfortable" they report being when "joking around" and "rapping" with most of the students in their schools.

No differences are found in faculty reports of the friendliness or degree of educational interest of their respective student bodies. Nor is a difference reported in the ease of their informal interactions with the student bodies of their schools. They do, however, differ in their reports of the extent to which their student bodies are dissatisfied with their respective schools; the Thurston staff report more of their student body dissatisfied than do the Wayne staff.

Attitude toward student independence.   No difference is found between the two staffs on the question of the amount of independence that they feel the students in their school should have. The mean for both schools is near the mid-scale point. However, a significant degree of variance within the staffs of the two schools is observed again. The Thurston staff show a relative lack of agreement among themselves on this issue compared to the Wayne staff.

Perceptions of groups influencing school policy.   The faculty of the two schools were asked to report the amount of influence that they felt the school board, central administration, principal, teachers, students, and parents of students have in the way their respective schools are run. The mean amounts of influence reported for these groups by the respective staffs of the two schools are displayed in Table 4.8. The amount of influence reported for four of these six groups differs significantly between the two schools. The staff at Wayne report a significantly greater amount of influence for their principal and student body than the Thurston staff do for theirs. Conversely, more influence is reported for the school board and the parents of students at Thurston than is reported for these respective groups at Wayne.

TABLE 4.8
School Staffs: Amount of Influence that Various Groups
Are Seen as Having in the Operation of the School[a]

School Group	Wayne staff		Thurston staff		F	Sig.	eta^2
	$\bar{X}$	N	$\bar{X}$	N			
School board	3.6	83	4.0	89	7.4	.007	.04
Central administration	3.8	83	3.9	89	.7	NS	NS
The principal	4.6	84	3.8	89	54.6	<.000	.24
Teachers	3.0	83	3.0	89	.1	NS	NS
Students	2.8	83	2.4	88	11.0	.001	.06
Parents	2.7	83	3.1	89	10.6	.001	.06

[a]Reported on 5-point scales labeled "NONE AT ALL" (1), "VERY LITTLE" (2), "SOME" (3), "QUITE A BIT" (4), and "A LOT" (5).

TABLE 4.9
School Staffs: The Groups Rank-Ordered Within Each School
on the Mean Amount of Influence Reported for Them
by Their Staffs

	Wayne			Thurston	
Rank	Group	$\overline{X}$	Rank	Group	$\overline{X}$
1	Principal	4.6	1	School Board	4.0
	***				
2	Central Administration	3.8	2	Central Administration	3.9
3	School Board	3.6	3	Principal	3.8
	***			***	
4	Teachers	3.0	4	Parents of Students	3.1
5	Student body	2.8	5	Teachers	3.0
				***	
6	Parents of students	2.7	6	Student body	2.4

***A t test for dependent measures, computed between the mean amount of influence reported by the staff of this school for these two groups, is significant beyond the .05 level.

A clearer impression of the differences found between the influence structures of the two schools can be gained by analyzing these reports from the two staffs within each school. For this purpose, the six groups were rank-ordered within each school according to the mean amount of influence each respective staff reported for it. A t test for dependent measures was then computed to test whether the mean amount of influence reported for a group by its respective school staff differed significantly from the amount of influence reported by that staff for the group ranked above and below it in that school. The results of these data are shown in Table 4.9 and show considerable differences in the influence structures of the two schools. At Wayne, the amount of influence reported for the principal is significantly greater than the amount of influence that staff reports for any of the other five groups at their school. The Wayne staff report a significantly greater amount of influence for the central administration and the school board in their school than they do for teachers, students, or the parents of students.

The reports from the Thurston staff present a somewhat different picture. At Thurston there is no significant difference in the amount of influence reported for the principal, school board, or the central administration. A significantly greater amount of influence is reported by the Thurston staff for these three administrative groups, however, than for parents, teachers, and students. In addition, parents and teachers are perceived by the Thurston staff as having a significantly greater amount of influence than the students in that school. In sum, a number of differences are found among the influence structures of the two schools, the most notable being that:

1. At Wayne, the principal is perceived as having a significantly greater amount of influence than any of the other groups.

2. At Thurston, the students are perceived as having a significantly lesser amount of influence than any of the other five groups in that school.

The influence structures presented in Table 4.9 would suggest that Wayne is a high school directed by its principal, who enjoys a large degree of autonomy. At Thurston, although the principal by no means lacks influence, more decisions are likely to come down to the staff and students from the school board and central administration (i.e., from groups outside the school). Undoubtedly, the main reason for this observed difference in influence between the principals at the two schools can be attributed to the length of time they have held their respective positions. The Wayne principal, as mentioned previously, has been the principal of that school for over 8 years and has been in that school in other capacities for a good deal longer. The principal at Thurston, on the other hand, was just completing his first year as principal at the time this data was obtained.

The influence structures of the two schools presented in Table 4.9 further suggest that at Thurston High School, the students have relatively little say in the decision-making process. One of the consequences of this finding may be that the students at Thurston are less satisfied with their school than the students at Wayne, where the student body has a relatively greater amount of influence. As has already been noted, the reports from the staffs of the two schools indicate this to be true. Reports from students in the two schools also confirm this.

Faculty satisfactions.   The staffs of the two schools were asked to report their satisfaction with their professions and with their jobs. In addition, they were asked to report their satisfaction with the performance of the principal and the teaching faculty in their schools. The Wayne staff reported significantly greater satisfaction with their jobs, their professions, their principal, and their teaching faculty than did the Thurston staff.

Summary of the School Staffs

Reports from the staffs show many similarities between the two schools. In terms of the size, male/female ratio and educational background, they seem almost identical. Some small differences can be observed in the age, teaching experience, and length of time staff members have been at the school — the Wayne staff are slightly older, are more experienced, and have been at their school somewhat longer than the Thurston staff. A somewhat larger proportion of the Wayne staff live within their high school district and report attending school sports events. The staff at Thurston report attending school board meetings somewhat more frequently than the staff at Wayne.

The staffs of the two high schools report quite similar expectations for their students. Only two very small differences are found on the nine items relating to this issue, although differences in the variances for the staffs at the two schools suggest that there is greater consensus among the Wayne staff. Wayne teachers transmit their expectations to their students with more clarity than Thurston teachers. Although both staffs agree on the amount of independence they feel the students in their school should have, the staff at Thurston are more divided on this issue than the staff at Wayne. The reports from the two staffs show much more agreement in terms of the ease of their informal interactions with the students in their schools.

Perceptions of the student bodies in the two schools by the staffs show some similarities and differences. The staff at Thurston report that a smaller proportion of their student body likes their school and that a larger proportion is unhappy with how their school is run than the staff at Wayne report.

There are also large variations between the two staffs in terms of their own satisfactions. The Wayne staff report greater satisfaction with their professions, with their jobs, with their principal, and with the teaching faculty of their school than do the Thurston staff. The largest statistical differences relate to statements of satisfaction with the principal and teaching faculty of their schools.

The staffs' reports of the amount of influence that the school board, central administration, principal, teachers, students, and the parents of students have in determining how their schools are run indicate some different influence structures in the two schools. The principal and the students at Wayne are reported to have more influence in that school than the Thurston staff report regarding the influence of the principal and student body. The Thurston staff, however, report more influence for their school board and the parents of students than is reported for these groups at Wayne. The Wayne staff report significantly more influence for their principal than for any of the other groups in their school, whereas the Thurston staff report no large differences among the three administrative groups. The Thurston staff do report significantly more influence for all the faculty groups in that school than they do for their student body, whereas the Wayne staff report no significant differences between their student body and teachers or the parents in their school.

The Students

Selection of samples.   The present project administered questionnaires to 96% of the eighth-grade boys in four junior high schools in 1969. On the basis of these data, stratified and random samples of boys were selected for the longitudinal study. They were also administered questionnaires while in the ninth grade of junior high school, in the fall and spring semesters of their 10th grade, and again during the first semester of their 11th grade. The project continued to administer self-report questionnaires to these boys each semester they were in high school until they graduated in June of 1973.

Measures of individual characteristics.   Measures collected from these boys on the self-report questionnaires show that the boys at the two schools do not differ from each other in age, weight, or height; nor are there significant differences in the proportion reporting ever having had a job or in the frequency of dating girls.

The mean age of the boys in the two schools reported during the fall semester of the 10th grade was 15.20. The self-report measures of height and weight collected in the spring semester of that year show a mean height of 5'9" for the boys in each school, with the boys at Wayne reporting a mean weight of 152 pounds and the boys at Thurston, 145 pounds.

In the fall semester of that year, 64% of the Wayne students and 56% of the Thurston students reported having a full- or part-time job. The boys reported occasional dating for all three semesters, with the frequency reported increasing slightly each semester for both groups.

Standard psychological measures.   The boys from the two high schools do not differ in their scores on the Bachman version of the Rosenberg Self-Esteem Scale (Bachman, Kahn, Mednick, Davidson, & Johnston, 1967; Rosenberg, 1965) administered during the eighth, ninth, and 10th grades. Rotter's Internal–External Control Scale (Rotter, 1966) and the Marlowe–Crowne Social Desirability Scale (Crowne & Marlowe, 1964), which were administered during the ninth and 10th grades, also reveal no significant differences between students in the two schools. The scores from the Progressive Matrices I.Q. Test (U.S. Employment Service, 1971), a nonverbal measure of IQ that was administered during the boys' eighth-grade year, also showed no significant difference. Very little variation is found in the means of these measures at different time periods for either group of boys.

Reports of school satisfaction and rating of school excellence.   Measures of personal characteristics of the boys do not indicate significant differences between the two schools. However, differences can be observed in measures of students' perceptions and evaluations of the social environments of their schools. The largest difference observed in the reports from the boys at the two schools relates to their attitudes toward their schools. In the eighth grade, in both semesters of the 10th grade, and again in the 11th grade, the boys at the two schools were first asked to report, on 11-point scales, how much they liked going to school (School Satisfaction). There are no differences in terms of School Satisfaction between the two groups of boys in the eighth grade, either when they were attending junior high school or during either semester of the 10th

TABLE 4.10
High School Boys: Longitudinal Reports of School Satisfaction
and Evaluations of Their Schools

Variable/time	Wayne boys		Thurston boys				
	$\overline{X}$	N	$\overline{X}$	N	F	Sig.	eta^2
School Satisfaction							
8th grade	5.7	48	6.1	47	.6	NS	NS
10th grade							
1st semester	6.9	40	6.6	44	.5	NS	NS
2nd semester	6.7	39	5.9	42	.5	NS	NS
11th grade							
1st semester	6.8	73	5.7	81	7.8	.005	.05
School Evaluation							
8th grade	6.8	48	6.5	47	.5	NS	NS
10th grade							
1st semester	7.0	40	5.7	44	10.0	.002	.11
2nd semester	6.7	39	5.1	43	11.8	<001	.13
11th grade							
1st semester	7.7	74	5.5	80	44.5	<001	.23

grade in high school. However, in the 11th grade there is a small difference. The boys at Wayne reported somewhat greater satisfaction with school than did the boys at Thurston.

Additionally, students were asked to rate their schools in relation to the worst and best schools they could imagine (School Evaluation). These ratings show moderate differences between the two groups of boys in both semesters of the 10th grade and a relatively large difference in the 11th grade. On all three occasions, during the 10th grade and twice during 11th grade, the Wayne High School boys rated their school higher than the Thurston boys rated their school. These differences are noted in Table 4.10.

Positiveness toward school authorities. In the questionnaire administered to the boys while they were in the 10th and the 11th grades, they were asked to rate both their principal and teachers on five 7-point, semantic differential scales. The word pairs used were STRICT/EASYGOING, UNFAIR/FAIR, CLOSED-MINDED/OPEN-MINDED, HELPFUL/UNHELPFUL, and FRIENDLY/UNFRIENDLY. The scales were assigned scores from 1 to 7 with the negative ends scored 1. The five scales for the principal and the five for the teachers in the school were summed to generate measures of students' positive or negative feelings toward each. Although the amount of positive feelings reported by the boys was not very large at either school for either the principal or the teachers, the boys at Wayne reported more positive feelings than the boys at Thurston.

Involvement with classes and perceived opportunity for independence and growth.   The Wayne High School boys reported feeling more involved with their classes and having more chance for personal development in their school than the Thurston boys. These differences are small, however. The mean scores reported by the boys are neither extremely high nor extremely low at either school.

The importance to the students of changing their schools.   A measure of the extent to which the boys wished to change their schools was generated from eight questionnaire items on which they reported how important it was for them to change certain aspects of their school in order to make it better (School Change). There is no significant difference between the amounts of importance the boys at the two schools reported attaching to changing their schools in the 10th grade. In the 11th grade a small difference can be observed; the boys at Thurston reported a significantly greater amount of importance to changing their school than did the boys at Wayne. The way they felt they were treated and the way they felt their schools were run seemed to be the most saliently different aspects of the two school environments to these boys at this time.

The amount of independence students want.   A question concerning the amount of independence students should have in the school, which was asked of the staff members, was also asked of the students. No school differences can be observed in the reports from the boys at the two schools in either their 10th or 11th grades. However, the means for the students suggest that a trend may be developing. The reports from the students at Thurston show a greater increase in

TABLE 4.11
High School Boys: School Evalutaion by School
and Amount of Independence Desired

| Variable | Wayne boys | | Thurston boys | | F | Sig. | eta^2 |
	$\overline{X}$	N	$\overline{X}$	N			
Amount of independence desired							
Less or same							
as now	7.5	37	6.5	34			
More than now	7.9	34	4.9	44			
Source of variation							
By school					39.8	<.001	.27
By amount of							
independent							
groups					14.2	.05	.03
By interaction					10.5	.01	.07
Total							.37

the amount of independence wanted than do the reports from the Wayne students. This suggestion of a trend can also be noticed in the boys' reports concerning their desire that their schools change and is quite pronounced in their evaluations of their school. These trends may indicate that important school differences are emerging as the students spend more time in their schools. Some verification for this trend is presented in Table 4.11. This table shows the mean evaluations of their schools by 11th-grade boys. The sample at each school is divided into two groups according to the amount of independence desired for the students in their school. The boys at Wayne who desire more independence give slightly higher evaluations of their school than do the boys who desire less or the same amount of independence. The boys at Thurston who desire more independence, however, give a significantly lower evaluation of their school than do the boys who wish less or the same amount of independence.

Summary of the Student Reports

The data from student reports show no significant differences between the boys at the two schools as to physical characteristics, standard psychological measures obtained over time, or variables related to behavior and experiences outside school. Significant differences between the two groups of boys have emerged, however, on variables related to their school environments.

CONCLUSIONS

A comparison of the communities surrounding Wayne and Thurston High Schools, from which these schools draw their enrollments, shows moderate differences in socioeconomic levels, background mobility, and size of families. The Thurston community is of higher SES level than the Wayne community, whereas the population of the Wayne community has more mobility and slightly larger families. Although these differences should not be ignored, they seem to be differences of degree; so that both communities could be characterized as all-white, middle-class, and suburban, with the Thurston school community characterized as a more middle-class community than Wayne.

In contrast to the differences in the communities at large, the two high schools seem very similar. For such criteria as physical facilities and educational resources, age of the physical plants, size of student enrollment, size, composition, and educational preparation of faculty; both schools seem very much alike. Slight differences can be noted in their curricular and extracurricular programs, which seem consistent with the differences noted in the socioeconomic levels of the communities. The importance of other small differences that can be observed — a difference in design and appearance of the physical plant, a small difference in the age, experience, and seniority of the staffs; a difference in the proportion of staff who live within the school district — is difficult to assess.

More important differences between the two schools become apparent in the reports from staff and students. These reports indicate that although these schools do not outwardly differ, they do have different social structures. Reports from the staffs of the schools show quite clear differences in their influence structures, particularly in terms of the role of the principal at Wayne and the relationship of the student body at Thurston to the decision-making process in their respective schools. The principal at Wayne seems to have a large amount of influence at his school, whereas the student body at Thurston seems to have very little in theirs. The Wayne principal seems to have a great deal of autonomy, yet students share some of the decision making. At Thurston, the school board and the parents have larger amounts of influence, and the students seem to be left out. Some of this difference may be due to the difference in the length of time the principals at the two schools have held their positions as well as to the middle-class socioeconomic level of the Thurston community.

Other differences between the social environments of the two schools can be noted from the reports of the staffs. The staff at Thurston report less satisfaction than the Wayne staff. Less consensus is found among the Thurston staff in terms of their expectations for students and in terms of other issues concerning students than is reported by the Wayne staff. These differences observed in the staff responses appear to be transmitted to the environment of the school as perceived by the students. We can speculate that the students at Thurston perceive a more arbitrary social environment, one that is more difficult to come to grips with than that perceived by the Wayne students.

The reports from the students in the two schools confirm much of what was noted in the staff reports. Outwardly, in terms of individual characteristics and standard psychological measures, the boys at the two schools seem very similar. The most salient differences between the two groups of students are their evaluations of the schools and their feelings of positiveness toward school adults. The Thurston students evaluate their school less favorably than the Wayne students and report less positive feelings toward their principal and teachers than do the Wayne students.

The differences in the reports from the students at the two schools relating to more differentiated aspects of their social environments during the 10th grade do not appear large enough to be statistically significant, although the students at Wayne do report more involvement with their classes than the students at Thurston. However, in the 11th grade, their perceptions of the school environment have developed to a greater degree; and the differences in the boys' reports of the opportunities their schools provide for independence and growth, as well as the extent to which they report they wish to change the environment, show small yet statistically significant differences between them. In the fall semester of the 11th grade, the difference found in their evaluations of their schools has strengthened; and the Thurston students report significantly less satisfaction with school than the Wayne students.

Although these two schools seem outwardly to be very similar, in actuality there are important differences in their social environments. These differences, which may be due to differences in the communities, the roles of the two principals in their schools, and the differences observed in the faculties of the schools, seem to have an increasing impact on the reports from the students as they progress through their high school careers. To the extent that this is true, important school differences and person–environment interactions are expected to emerge with greater clarity in the reports from the students during the latter part of the 11th grade and during their senior year of high school.

REFERENCES

Bachman, J. G., Kahn, R. L., Mednick, M. T., Davidson, T. N., & Johnson, L. D. *Youth in transition* (Vol. 1). *Blueprint for a nationwide longitudinal study of adolescent boys.* Ann Arbor, Mich.: Institute for Social Research, 1967.

Citizen's Committee on Economic Opportunity for the Township of Redford. Development, operating grant for the administration and operating grant for fiscal year July 1, 1965– June 30, 1966, of a community action program. Proposal for a grant to continue Redford Township Community Action Program, 1965.

Crowne, D. P., & Marlowe, D. *The approval motive: Studies in evaluative dependence.* New York: John Wiley, 1964.

Newman, P. R. Person and settings: A comparative analysis of the quality and range of social interaction in two suburban high schools. Unpublished doctoral dissertation, The University of Michigan, 1971.

Rosenberg, M. *Society and the adolescent self-image.* Princeton, New Jersey: University of Princeton Press, 1965.

Rotter, J. B. Generalized expectancies for internal versus external control of reinforcement. *Psychological Monographs,* 1966, *80* (Whole No. 609), 1–28.

United States Employment Service. *Manual for the U.S. Employment Service (U.S.E.S.) non-reading aptitude battery, Form A.* Washington, D.C.: U.S. Department of Labor, 1971.

THE BOYS AND THEIR CONTEXT: FIVE APPROACHES TO RESEARCH

5 Coping Preference, Adaptive Roles, and Varied High School Environments: A Search for Person-Environment Transactions

Daniel W. Edwards[1]

Institute for Social Research
The University of Michigan

In this chapter, results of a self-report study of 10th- and 11th-grade boys are reported. The guiding framework of the research reported in this chapter is that the high school is viewed as a distinct community that has differential effects on the behavior and direction of development of adolescent boys.

PERSON—ENVIRONMENT TRANSACTIONS

The basic framework for analysis is a conception of person—environment transactions (Edwards, 1971; Pervin, 1968) or person—environment interaction (Endler & Hunt, 1968; Lazarus, Averill, & Opton, 1969; Sonquist, 1970; Trickett, Kelly, & Todd, 1972).

Adaptation and Person—Environment Fit

Any sustained participation in a social environment elicits the expression of personal qualities that meet minimal environmental demands. Every person is expected to develop some adaptation or fit to an environment. A high school provides a highly structured network of opportunities for socialization. A student can develop a "passive" adaptation, where he/she meets minimal environmental demands and develops few personal qualities. This passive adaptation is expected to represent a poorer fit to the environment than an active engagement

---

[1]Present address: The University of California, Davis, Sacramento Medical Center, Sacramento, California.

of the environment where there is seeking out of opportunities to allow for personal growth. Adaptations can be viewed, then, as a continuum of person–environment fit. Pervin (1968), in a review of the literature, provides evidence showing that degree of performance and degree of satisfaction are a joint function of the degree of fit between the person and the environment. In this study, it is hypothesized that degree of fit can be obtained by assessing personal qualities such as self-esteem and initiative in conjunction with perceptions of the environment, such as perceived positiveness of authorities or identification with school. The intent is to understand person–environment fit via the analysis of self-reports of perceptions of both selves and the school environment. Students are also asked to report their adaptive role in high school to further elaborate the topic of person–environment fit.

Preventive Interventions and Person—Environment Fit

The overall goal of the study is to help increase understanding of how boys adapt to school. It is also hoped that the research will contribute to concepts of preventive intervention that will help schools better meet the psychological needs of their clients. Trickett, Kelly, and Todd (1972) have reviewed and discussed the unmet mental health needs of high school students. Their review clearly shows the need for preventive rather than remedial solutions for mental health problems of students, and they suggest ecological principles that may be the first step toward a theory of preventive intervention for high schools. The ecological approach to person–environment relationships presented by Trickett, Kelly, and Todd views mental health problems as a function of a poor fit between individuals and their environment. They propose that increased knowledge of how the individual and the high school interact can lead to the redesign of schools so that all individuals can achieve a maximal fit with their environment. Increased understanding of how individuals relate to their environment or increased understanding of person–environment transactions are basic ingredients in suggesting preventive interventions for high schools.

Two different studies are described in this chapter that seek to test person–environment fit. The first study is about boys with distinctive coping preferences for exploration who were selected in the eighth grade and observed in 10th grade after they had entered the high schools described in Chapter 4. Three different levels of exploration were "fixed" by selecting boys on the basis of eighth-grade scores of the Exploration Preference Scale (Edwards, 1969, 1970, 1971). The second study is more descriptive. Boys were asked to identify the role they had adopted in high school. An empirical search was carried out for the differential correlates of these roles and is reported here. The author predicts that different adaptive roles will systematically be related to different perceptions of self and the school environment.

A GUESS AT CAUSALITY

Previous work has indicated that students who vary in their preference for exploration have different adaptations to their high school and that students with similar preferences in different high schools also have varied adaptations (Kelly, 1968, 1969). In 1969 a version of the exploration questionnaire was administered to the male eighth-grade population at four junior high schools that provide students for the two study high schools. As a result of this testing, it was possible to select a stratified sample of 20 high, 20 moderate, and 20 low exploration-preference students who would later enter each high school.

The exploration questionnaire was designed to assess a student's preference for exploration of the school environment and contains items such as "I often have new ideas for class projects" and "I go out of my way to take part in different activities." (See Edwards, 1971, for discussion of the development of the instrument.) It was hypothesized that exploration preferences as measured in the eighth grade would affect adaptation in high school.

A person who is very satisfied with school, who sees a lot of opportunity in school, or who has high self-esteem is assumed to have a better person—environment fit than a person scoring low on these variables. It was expected

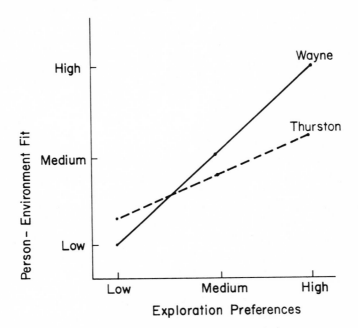

FIG. 5.1.   Expected relationship between person—environment fit and exploration preference at the two schools.

that students with high exploration scores would fit best in any school environment but that they would be more favored in an environment like Wayne High School than like Thurston High School. Students with low exploration scores were expected to have the most difficulty in adapting and the poorest fit in Wayne. Figure 5.1 shows the expected relationship for the means of high, moderate, and low persons at the two schools. Significant school, person, and school—person interactions also were expected. Significant person and environment main effects in the absence of statistical interactions would be interpreted as indications of the possible validity of the person—environment transaction hypothesis.

The general hypotheses for the 18 dependent measures reported here concerning levels of exploration are: High exploration-preference students should feel more positive about themselves (self-esteem) and desire less change of aspects of self (dissatisfaction with self); will have higher initiative scores and lower social problems scores; will feel more personal control over their lives (Rotter's I.E. measure); will have higher need for social approval scores (Marlowe—Crowne S.D. variable); and, as a validity check, will have higher scores on an alternative measure of exploration preferences. On the perception of school variables, high explorers are expected to have a more positive view of their peers and school authorities, to perceive less control exercised by school authorities, to perceive more opportunity in school, to feel more identified with school, to be more satisfied with school and more involved in classes, to want less change in school, and to report less deviant behavior.

The hypotheses about the environmental effects of the two schools predict a *better* fit for *high explorers* at Wayne than at Thurston and a *poorer* fit for *low explorers* at Wayne than at Thurston.

Adaptive Roles

In the second study, the same conception of person—environment transaction is assumed to hold. This study, however, is descriptive and not predictive. The boys are asked to indicate their adaptation to high school, and a search is carried out for the correlates of these roles. Differential patterns of relationships are expected for the two high schools because of the varied environmental demands. This study also serves as a partial validity check on the assumption that the dependent measures are indicators of person—environment fit.

The five adaptive role categories were originally suggested by Carlson (1964) in a paper discussing the relationship between organizational structure, personal characteristics, and behavior. Carlson posited a continuum ranging from "receptive" adaptation to "dropout" adaptation. The receptive person enjoys classes and activities, whereas the dropout finds the situation so negative that he has to leave the community. In between these extremes, Carlson suggested that there

Different students have different feelings about school. Which one of the attitudes below describes best how you feel about school? (CHECK ONE BOX BELOW)

---

1   I am very involved in classes and school activities.

2   I don't like classes but like school because of athletics, extracurricular, or other school activities.

3   I don't like classes or activities but I am trying to change school.

4   I don't care about school but just come to see friends.

5   I don't like school much and only come because I have to.

FIG. 5.2.   Questionnaire item to ascertain respondent's adaptive role group.

was a "side-payment" adaptation in which the person comes for extracurricular reasons; a "rebellious" adaptation where the individual challenges the high school system; a "social" adaptation where the person comes to school mainly to be with friends; and a "passive" or "withdrawn" adaptation where the person is physically present but mentally absent. Figure 5.2 shows the author's measure of the roles suggested by Carlson.

In previous research with an earlier version of this adaptive role variable, evidence was found that seemed to support the person—environment transaction hypothesis. Within each high school, there were significant and meaningful mean differences between the various role categories for different variables. In these analyses, the rebel groups had 10-point differences in mean scores between schools, whereas the other groups had almost identical mean scores between schools. Those data suggested that the schools had similar effects on the majority of students in the different groups but that they had widely divergent effects on the "rebel" groups. In this earlier research, the role groups at Wayne seemed to be differentiated more on perception of self-variables; at Thurston, the groups seemed to be differentiated on perception of school variables. Sampling problems and the small number of subjects in some cells offered only tentative hints to follow up. The results, however, did indicate some fruitful future directions and the need for a larger sample of subjects. The adaptive role variable was revised to that shown in Figure 5.2, and this revised version was administered to the students in the research sample at each school in the students' first semester of 11th grade (fall of 1971). Some of the results of these analyses are presented here.

METHOD

Two 1-hour self-report instruments have been developed by Richard Rice and the author. One form is given in the fall of the academic year and collects data on students' perceptions of self, peers, and school. The second form is administered in the spring of the academic year and contains additional items on perceptions along with global personality measures such as the Marlowe–Crowne Need for Social Approval Scale (Crowne & Marlowe, 1964) and Rotter's Internal–External Scale (Rotter, 1966).

The cohort at each school is made up of a random sample of 75 boys and a stratified sample of 60 boys (20 students with high, 20 with moderate, and 20 with low exploration-preference scores). This chapter reports analyses of data collected in the fall and spring of the 10th-grade year and in the fall of the boys' 11th-grade school year. In all administrations the boys are read standard instructions and fill out the questionnaire in groups of 20 to 25.

DEPENDENT MEASURES

The analyses reported here involve 18 different measures. There are 7 dependent measures for personal variables and 11 for perception of school variables. The variables at the personal level are Self-Esteem, Dissatisfaction with Self, Initiative, Social Problems, the Marlowe-Crowne, Rotter's I.E., and the Thematic Measure of Exploration Preferences.

The *Self-Esteem Scale* (Bachman, 1970) is composed of 10 items with 5-point scales and contains 6 of Rosenberg's (1965) item stems. The subject is asked to check a scale point on a continuum from "never true" to "almost always true" for items such as "I am a helpful guy to have around" or "I feel that my life is not very useful." The *Dissatisfaction with Self Scale* composite contains 10 change-self items where the subject is asked questions such as "How important is it to change myself as a student?" The 7-point scales range from "not at all important" to "very important." *Initiative and Social Problems* uses the same 7-point frequency scale (from "never true" to "often true"). Initiative is made up of six items such as "I take risks where I might fail" or "I suggest better ways to do things." The Social Problems composite is made up of five items concerning difficulty in making friends, working with others, or following instructions. The *Thematic Measure of Exploration* is described in detail by McClintock and Rice (1971) and was developed as an alternative measure of exploration preferences. It consists of short stories with 30 multiple-choice items.

The 11 perception of school variables deal with perception of peers and authorities, perceived control by school authorities, perceived opportunity in school, identification with school, satisfaction with school, class involvement, desired school change, and deviant behavior in school. Four 7-point semantic differential items make up the *Perceived Positiveness of Peers* composite. The anchoring adjectives are dimensions such as helpful—unhelpful or friendly—unfriendly. Three similar composites assess *Perceived Positiveness of the Principal*, the *Teachers*, and the *Counselors*. Each of the positiveness of authorities items is made up of the same five sementic differential items. The *Perceived Control of Principal and Teachers* cluster is composed of seven 7-point scales with anchor points of "never true" to "always true." Examples of items are, "The principal is very strict" or "You are watched and told what to do all the time."

Perceived Opportunity is assessed by six 5-point scales such as, "How much chance do you have to be with your friends?" or "How much chance does this school give you to improve yourself?" The *Identification* composite asks the student to indicate how much he feels a part of aspects of the school such as his classes or the student body. *Satisfaction with School* is an 11-point scale in the form of a ladder that ranges from "I don't like school at all" to "I like school a lot." The respondent is asked to indicate the rung of the ladder that best describes his position. *Class Involvement* is composed of four 7-point frequency items that ask, "How often do you ask a question in class?" *Desired School Change* is composed of nine change items (7-point scales) that ask, "How important is it to change the way teachers teach?" and similar items. The anchor points range from "not at all" to "very important." *Deviant Behavior* is another set of 7-point frequency items that ask about smoking, cutting classes, and hitting a teacher.

ANALYSIS OF THE DATA

Analysis of variance (ANOVA) is used for both studies to test for differences in mean scores. A two-way analysis of variance model with exploration preferences (three levels) and schools (two levels) as the independent variables is used for the first study. In the analyses for the second study, the unequal numbers of subjects in each group and the lack of matching across schools make it impossible to use the two-way design; and one-way ANOVAs are carried out for the role groups at each school.

Three criteria are seen as essential for interpreting the results. In this study, two of these criteria are met. One criterion is that significant differences are found by obtaining a statistic for nonchance differences at or beyond the .05 level. Meaningfulness, the second criterion, is assessed by estimating the strength of the relationship between the independent and dependent measures. Third, to

TABLE 5.1
F Ratios and Proportion of Variance Accounted for (ω^2)
by School and Exploration Group in Eighth,
Ninth, 10th, and 11th Grades

Variable name	df within	Statistic	School	Explor.	S × E
8th grade explor.	94	F	NS	559.29	NS
		ω^2	–	.914	–
9th grade explor.	94	F	NS	67.65	NS
		ω^2	–	.578	–
10th grade explor.	97	F	NS	37.67	NS
		ω^2	–	.423	–
11th grade explor.	90	F	NS	31.74	NS
(first semester)		ω^2	–	.389	–

be considered meaningful, a significant result must account for at least 5% of the variance in the dependent measure.[2]

In this paper, F tests are presented only for those tests significant at or beyond the .05 level of significance. Meaningfulness or the proportion of variance accounted for is reported for all significant F ratios. In addition, coefficient alpha is estimated and reported for all composite variables (Cronbach, 1951; Nunnally, 1967).[3]

RESULTS

The exploration questionnaire is composed of two 30-item parallel forms that correlate .77. The internal consistency for the 60 items is .85 (KR-20), whereas 2-week test—retest reliabilities average .823. In the following sections, the sta-

---

[2]Hays (1963), Vaughan and Corballis (1969), and Peters and Van Voorhis (1940) describe a statistic called *omega squared* that allows for estimation of the strength of the relationship between variables in analysis of variance designs. A more general version of omega squared — eta squared — is discussed by Nunnally (1967) and Andrews, Morgan, and Sonquist (1967). Omega squared and eta squared are interpreted in a manner similar to the square of the correlation coefficient. Realness is also seen as an essential feature of results and is assessed by a replication of previously found significant and meaningful differences. Realness or replication will not be obtained for most of the results presented here for another 6 months.

[3]Coefficient alpha is a generalized version of the Kuder—Richardson Formula 20 and is the mean of all possible split-half reliability coefficients. Cronbach (1951) has shown that coefficient alpha is the upper limit of single-factor variance and the lower limit of reliable common factors variance in a set of items. It is often instructive to compare eta squared or omega squared to coefficient alpha to estimate the strength of the predictors given the reliable variation present in the dependent measures.

bility of the exploration groupings are reported over a 2½year time span; the predictive utility of the person—environment transaction hypothesis is examined using eighth-grade exploration groupings in the two high schools. Results also are presented for the adaptive role variable.

The Stability of Exploration Preferences

Subjects were originally selected for the stratified sample on the basis of their responses to a 102-item exploration questionnaire. This questionnaire was then revised by item deletion to yield the two 30-item parallel forms. Table 5.1 contains the results of two-way analysis of variance for eighth-, ninth-, 10th-, and 11th-grade scores of the boys in the stratified sample. As can be seen, there is a significant and meaningful relationship between the original eighth-grade groupings and subsequent scores, although the strength of the relationship decreases with time. Figure 3 graphically depicts the mean scores of the stratified groups over the years. The 10th- and 11th-grade means are estimated from the scores on one of the 30-item parallel forms.

Although the strength of the relationship has decreased from 91% common variance to 39% common variance by the first semester of 11th grade, this is still a fairly strong relationship for psychological research. An omega squared of

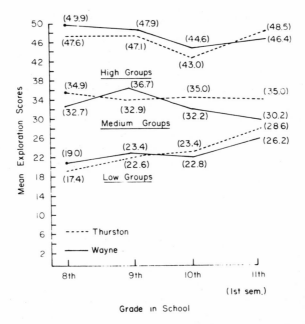

FIG. 5.3.   Mean exploration scores over time for high, medium, and low groups at the two schools.

.389, for example, is similar to a correlation of .63 between eighth- and 11th-grade scores.

As can be seen in Figure 5.3, there is some fluctuation in mean scores over time, but the matched groups at each school remain fairly similar.

Tests of the Person—Environment Transaction Hypothesis

Table 5.2 contains the *F* tests for school, exploration, and school—exploration interaction effects for the 18 dependent measures collected in the fall and spring of the 10th-grade year (1970—1971). As can be seen from the tables, there are no statistically significant interaction effects. In addition, only one variable — the thematic measure of exploration — shows significant school and exploration effects.

Significant school differences are found only for the thematic measure of exploration and perceived positiveness of the principal variable.

Significant exploration effects are found for self-esteem, initiative, thematic measures of exploration, social problems, identification, satisfaction with school, and involvement in class. These exploration effects are all in the expected direc-

TABLE 5.2
F Ratios for Dependent Measures Collected
in the 10th Grade

Variable	School	Exploration	S x E	df Within
Self				
Self-esteem (L1)	—	6.17	—	85
Dissatisfaction with self #2 (L2)	—	—	—	96
Initiative (L1)	—	8.74	—	92
Themes (L1)	11.05	10.68	—	83
Rotter's I.E. (L2)	—	—	—	97
Marlowe—Crowne S.D. (L2)	—	6.49	—	96
Social Problems (L1)	—	5.45	—	92
School				
Positiveness — other students (L2)	—	—	—	96
Positiveness — principal (1)	18.69	—	—	92
Positiveness — counselors (L1)	—	—	—	88
Positiveness — teachers (L1)	—	—	—	98
Perceived control (P & T) (L2)	—	—	—	93
Opportunity (L1)	—	—	—	98
Identification (L1)	—	5.32	—	98
Satisfaction (L1)	—	4.34	—	99
Satisfaction (L2)	—	4.71	—	96
Involvement in classes (L2)	—	7.41	—	91
Change school (L1)	—	—	—	100
Deviance (L2)	—	—	—	91

TABLE 5.3
Proportion of Variance Accounted for by School and Exploration
Factors for the Significant 10-Grade Results

Variable	School	Exploration	S × E	α*
Self				
Self-esteem (L2)	—	.114	—	.285
Dissatisfaction with self #2	—	—	—	.885
Initiative	—	.077	—	.756
Themes (L2)	.084	.162	—	1.000**
Rotter's I.E.	—	—	—	.610**
Marlowe-Crowne S.D.	—	.099	—	.712**
Social problems	—	.083	—	.664
School				
Positiveness — principal	.152	—	—	.829
Positiveness — other students	—	—	—	.739
Positiveness — counselors	—	—	—	.845
Positiveness — teachers	—	—	—	.691
Perceived control (P & T) (L2)	—	—	—	.625
Opportunity	—	—	—	.792
Identification	—	.077	—	.732
Satisfaction (L1)	—	.059	—	NC
Satisfaction (L2)	—	.069	—	NC
Involvement (L2)	—	.118	—	.728
Change school	—	—	—	.855*
Deviance (L2)	—	—	—	.624

*Computed from combined random samples.
**Computed from earlier data.

tion, indicating a better fit with the environment for high exploration-preference subjects.

Table 5.3 contains omega squared for these significant results. As can be seen, though all are strong enough to be considered meaningful, the strongest relationship accounts for only 16% of the variance in the dependent measure. Eighth-grade exploration preferences are not strong predictors of 10th-grade scores. When assessing exploration in the eighth grade, however, we can predict to a limited degree for a number of variables. Thus, high scorers on the exploration questionnaire have slightly but significantly higher self-esteem and initiative, identify more with school, are more satisfied and involved with school and classes, and have a lower social problems index.

Analysis of Adaptive Roles

The analyses reported here do not include large random samples, so that the analyses were carried out with the random samples and then with the total subjects (the random plus the stratified samples). Table 5.4 shows the number

TABLE 5.4
Distribution of Number of Subjects and Percentage of Sample Across the Five Adaptive Role Groups at the Two Schools

Adaptive role	Stratified		Random		Total	
	N	%	N	%	N	%
Wayne High School						
Receptive	17	35.4	29	40.3	46	38.3
Side-payment	13	27.1	25	34.7	38	31.7
Rebellious	7	14.6	8	11.1	15	12.5
Social	2	4.2	6	8.3	8	6.7
Passive	9	18.7	4	5.6	13	10.8
Total	48	100.0	72	100.0	120	100.0
Thurston High School						
Receptive	13	31.0	26	33.3	39	32.5
Side-payment	12	28.6	18	23.1	30	25.0
Rebellious	9	21.4	13	16.7	22	18.3
Social	5	11.9	7	9.0	12	10.0
Passive	3	7.1	14	17.9	17	14.2
Total	42	100.0	78	100.0	120	100.0

TABLE 5.5
Mean and F Tests for Adaptive Role Groups at Each School on the Exploration Questionnaire (L3)

Wayne			*Thurston*		
Adaptive role Group	Exploration Means	N	Adaptive role Group	Exploration Means	N
Receptive	20.2	46	Receptive	21.3	39
Side-payment	17.3	38	Side-payment	16.7	30
Rebellious	18.4	15	Rebellious	19.5	22
Social	14.3	8	Social	15.9	12
Passive	13.8	13	Passive	14.4	17
Total	18.0	120	Total	18.3	120

$F(4, 115) = 4.951$
$p < .05$
$eta^2 = .144$

$F(4, 115) = 7.326$
$p < .05$
$eta^2 = .203$

and percentage of subjects in each adaptive role category for the stratified, the random, and the total samples at each school. The analyses reported here must be interpreted as only descriptive of the particular subjects tested. Generalization and conclusions will have to await improved sampling or 100% testing of high school populations.

These results are presented because of the potential utility of this adaptive role variable for validating the dependent measures as indicators of degree of fit to the environment. The adaptive role variable can also make an important contribution to the understanding of the determinants of varied adaptations developed by high school boys.

Table 5.5 contains the mean exploration scores and F ratios for the role groups at each school. There are significant mean differences on exploration for this particular sample. The adaptive role variable accounts for 14% of the variance in exploration scores at Wayne and 20% of the variance in exploration scores at Thurston. In the analysis of the random sample, the results were similar; but the F test for Thurston did not quite reach the .05 level of significance. For the variables shown in Table 6, the F test generally increased when the stratified sample was added to the analysis, but the proportion of variance usually remained the same.

TABLE 5.6
Significant F Tests and Proportion of Variance Accounted for
by the Adaptive Role Categories on Measures Collected
in the First Semester of 11th Grade

Variable	Wayne			Thurston		
	df	F	eta²	df	F	eta²
Perceptions of Self						
Self-esteem	118	6.87	.194	117	8.19	.221
Initiative	118			118	N.S.	
Social problems	118	3.38	.102	118	3.78	.116
Perceptions of School						
Positiveness of students	117	3.49	.109	116	N.S.	
Positiveness of principal	116	11.91	.293	115	6.20	.186
Positiveness of counselors	117	N.S.		115	N.S.	
Positiveness of teachers	117	4.40	.137	116	6.38	.185
Opportunity	116	11.23	.280	116	6.82	.194
Identification	117	7.60	.212	116	8.40	.231
Satisfaction	116	30.77	.518	118	17.27	.372
Change school	118	2.78	.090	117	3.74	.116

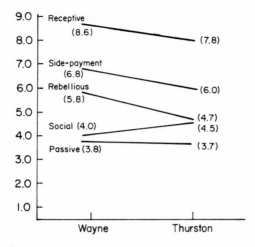

FIG. 5.4. Means for adaptive role groups on the satisfaction with schools ladder of the two schools.

Table 5.6 contains the significant F tests by school for the variables of interest. Only two of the variables assessed — Initiative and Positiveness of the Counselors — do not differentiate the varied role groups. Table 5.6 shows these mean differences to be fairly strong with the proportion of variance accounted for ranging from 9% to 52%. The relationship between the five adaptive role categories and dependent measures is almost always linear. The role categories account for 37% of the variance in School Satisfaction at Thurston and 52% of the variance in School Satisfaction at Wayne.

Figure 5.4 depicts the relationship between the mean scores in the five role categories at each school for the school satisfaction variable, and Figure 5.5 does

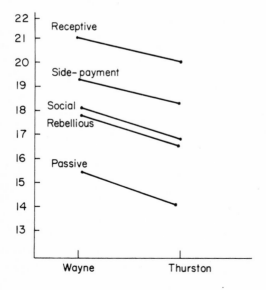

FIG. 5.5. Means for adaptive role groups on the identification with school composite.

the same for the identification variable. There does not seem to be any evidence at the present time for the person–environment transaction hypothesis using global school environments as a measure.

DISCUSSION

A large number of composite variables have been developed to assess the degree of fit with the environment for boys in the longitudinal study. The internal consistency or coefficient alpha reported in Table 5.2 generally indicates a high proportion of reliable variance in these composite scores (24% to 90%). The hypothesis that exploration preferences in the eighth grade and school environment effects will determine the degree of fit with the environment is modestly supported for these variables at this time. There is a general lack of school differences on the dependent measures. Though eighth-grade exploration groups have some predictive utility for 10th-grade scores, the relationships are not strong.

The literature on person–environment interactions yields many strong findings (Endler & Hunt, 1968; Pervin, 1968). The use of "global" school environment measure in this case precludes finding support for the person–environment transaction hypothesis. More specification is needed in defining varied environmental situations.

The exploration measure during the eighth grade is a tentative predictor of preferences for exploration at the 10th-grade level. It is surprising that any relationships are found at this age level, given the rapid changes that take place during adolescence and the small but important role thought to be played by exploratory behavior in everyday life. If an adult introspects and asks, "How much social exploring did I do yesterday?" one quickly becomes aware of the highly structured pattern of daily life, the lack of multiplicity of opportunities to explore, and the failure to take advantage of some of the few opportunities that did occur. Perhaps it is too much to ask of a 10th-grade student to expect a manifest and strong expression of such preferences. In spite of this, the exploration variable does have some predictive utility over a 2-year time span. This is considered to be a partial success of the longitudinal self-report study and indicates that the concept of exploration is worthy of further refinement.

The adaptive role variable has empirical utility for thinking about preventive interventions in a high school community. It is a simple descriptive variable that provides a very powerful classification of the varied fit of student to the environment. There is a lack of supporting evidence, however, for the person–environment transaction hypothesis. Although this lack is disappointing in some ways, it is heartening in others. In most cases, the role variable is strongly, linearly related to the various dependent measures. Also, the lack of school differences allows us to look at the schools as replications of each other and gives further support to the conclusion drawn about the adaptive role variable. This variable provides classifications that are relevant to the school staffs and that allow selection of target groups and ease of reassessment. The relevance to the school staffs allows this variable to be used by teachers, counselors, and peers in assigning independent ratings to students.

CONCLUSION

In evaluating the accomplishments to date of the longitudinal self-report study, a good set of procedures has been evolved for statistical analysis of data to allow assessment of the primary variables in terms of significance, meaningfulness, and realness. Evidence has been accumulated that shows the exploration variable to be interesting theoretically and predictively and that suggests its potential for further work. A new variable concerned with adaptive roles has been developed and found to differentiate groups of students.

The utility of this research for community mental health services must still be demonstrated, but there are several possibilities that should be mentioned:

1. The comparison of the analyses of exploration and the adaptive role variables indicates that the more concrete and contextual the variable, the more likelihood there is for significant and meaningful findings.

2. The author considers the criteria of meaningfulness and realness to have potential for understanding and using research findings. The use of these criteria can help evaluate and apply research findings for the design of social and community interventions.

3. The adaptive role variable provides a simple method of assessing high school students in terms of their involvement with school. It is a flexible variable that could be used for self-reports or ratings by peers or observers and as baseline measures for designing preventive programs.

4. The design of preventive interventions requires more detailed specification of environmental variables. Increased understanding of environmental effects and person—environmental transactions in field settings involves more detailed elaboration than has been developed in this particular study.

REFERENCES

Andrews, F., Morgan, J., & Sonquist, J. *Multiple classification analysis: A report on a computer program for multiple regression using categorical predictors.* Ann Arbor, Mich.: Institute for Social Research, 1967.

Bachman, J. G. *Youth in transition* (Vol. 2). *The impact of family background and intelligence on tenth-grade boys.* Ann Arbor, Mich.: Institute for Social Research, 1970.

Carlson, R. O. Environmental constraints and organizational consequences: The public school and its clients. *National Society for the Study of Education Yearbook,* 1964, *63,* (pt. 2), 262–276.

Cronbach, L. J. Coefficient alpha and the internal structure of tests. *Psychometrika,* 1951, *16,* 297–334.

Crowne, D. P., & Marlowe, D. *The approval motive: Studies in evaluative dependence.* New York: John Wiley, 1964.

Edwards, D. W. A questionnaire for the assessment of exploration preferences: Development and preliminary results of a measure of coping styles. Unpublished manuscript, The University of Michigan, May 1969.

Edwards, D. W. A questionnaire method of measuring exploration preferences. In M. J. Feldman (Ed.), *Studies in psychotherapy and behavioral change* (No. 2), *Theory and research in community mental health.* Buffalo, N.Y.: State University of New York at Buffalo, 1971.

Endler, N. S., & Hunt, J. M. S–R inventories of hostility and comparisons of the proportions of variance from persons, responses, and situations for hostility and anxiousness. *Journal of Personality and Social Psychology,* 1968, *9,* 309–315.

Hays, W. L. *Statistics for psychologists.* New York: Holt, Rinehart and Winston, 1963.

Kelly, J. G. Towards an ecological conception of preventive interventions. In J. W. Carter, Jr. (Ed.), *Research contributions from psychology to community mental health.* New York: Behavioral Publications, 1968.

Kelly, J. G. Naturalistic observations in contrasting social environments. In E. P. Willems & H. L. Raush (Eds.), *Naturalistic viewpoints in psychological research.* New York: Holt, Rinehart and Winston, 1969.

Lazarus, R. S., Averill, J. R., & Opton, E. M., Jr. Psychology of coping: Issues of research and assessment. Paper presented at Conference on Coping and Adaptation, Stanford, California, 1969.

McClintock, S. K., & Rice, R. The development of a thematic measure of preferences for exploration. In M. J. Feldman (Ed.), *Studies in psychotherapy and behavioral change* (No. 2), *Theory and research in community mental health.* Buffalo, N.Y.: State University of New York at Buffalo, 1971.

Nunnally, J. C. *Psychometric theory.* New York: McGraw–Hill, 1967.

Pervin, L. Performance and satisfaction as a function of individual–environment fit. *Psychological Bulletin,* 1968, *69,* 56–68.

Peters, C. C., & Van Voorhis, W. R. *Statistical procedures and their mathematical bases.* New York: McGraw–Hill, 1940.

Rosenberg, M. *Society and the adolescent self-image.* Princeton, New Jersey: University of Princeton Press, 1965.

Rotter, J. B. Generalized expectancies for internal versus external control of reinforcement. *Psychological Monographs,* 1966, *80* (Whole No. 609), 1–28.

Sonquist, J. A. *Multivariate model building.* Ann Arbor, Mich. Institute for Social Research, 1970.

Trickett, E. J., Kelly, J. G., & Todd, D. M. The social environment of the high school: Guidelines for individual change and organizational redevelopment. In S. Golann & C. Eisdorfer (Eds.), *Handbook of community psychology.* New York: Appleton–Century–Crofts, 1972.

Vaughn, G. M., & Corballis, M. C. Beyond tests of significance: Estimating strength of effects in selected ANOVA designs. *Psychological Bulletin,* 1969, *72,* 204–213.

6 Persons and Environments

Daniel W. Edwards[1]

Institute for Social Research
The University of Michigan

The previous chapter reported the framework used by the author to identify person—environment transactions. The present chapter examines some hypotheses drawn from the literature on high school students. The chapter also suggests an alternative method of studying coping strategies and adaptive roles using case studies.

A total of 195 10th-grade boys filled out the self-report questionnaire in their first semester of high school, 98 boys at Wayne High School and 97 boys at Thurston. The random samples contained 44 boys at Wayne and 43 boys at Thurston. The remainder of the sample includes boys who varied in their level of exploration preferences. To help make the text more readable, the results of Wayne Memorial High School are presented first (W), followed by the results for Thurston High School (T).

DESCRIPTIVE INFORMATION

Slightly over half the boys (61%) report having had a full- or part-time job. Twenty-one percent of the boys have never dated; 54% have dated "a few times," and 25% say they have dated girls "often."

To better understand the modal perceptions the boys have of themselves, each respondent was asked to check five positive and five negative adjectives that best described himself. The adjective checklists (each containing 15 adjectives) were taken from a procedure developed by Gergen and Morse (1967) as

---

[1]Present address: The University of California, Davis, Sacramento Medical Center, Sacramento, California.

TABLE 6.1
Modal Responses to Positive and
Negative Adjectives

Wayne		Thurston	
Positive Adjectives	*%*	*Positive Adjectives*	*%*
Friendly	62	Friendly	67
Happy	43	Happy	42
Honest	41	Honest	55
Adventurous	33	Reliable	34
Kind	32	Independent	34
Wayne		*Thurston*	
Negative Adjectives	*%*	*Negative Adjectives*	*%*
Often feel		Impatient	57
misunderstood	38	Stubborn	43
Quick-tempered	37	Lazy	38
Impatient	37	Often feel	
Worrier	34	misunderstood	37
Stubborn	32	Moody	33

described in Robinson and Shaver (1969). The following percentages are based on 98 subjects at Wayne and 97 subjects at Thurston. Table 6.1 reveals that there are marked similarities between the boys at the two schools. Being friendly is the attribute most frequently mentioned by both groups of boys. Looking at these responses as representing desired characteristics, there is a very positive picture of developing adolescents — honest, happy, reliable, kind, independent, and adventurous. On the negative side, the responses are in keeping with a striving for adulthood and with problems of impulse control. Being impatient, quick-tempered, stubborn, moody, and "feeling misunderstood" validates the usual picture of adolescents in a time of development.

In sketching a purely normative picture of 10th-grade boys, mean and modal responses are presented, evaporating large variations between the boys. The low modal percentages on the adjective checklist indicate this large variation. Another example of the variation is found in the responses to the open-ended question that asked boys to list their best and worst class this semester. At Wayne, 48 boys listed 24 different types of classes (English, math, auto shop, etc.) as their "best class," and 47 of these boys listed 16 types of classes as their worst, Ten, or 63%, of the worst types of classes are listed as "best" by other boys. The same picture is found at Thurston, where 48 boys listed 17 types of classes as best, and 45 of these boys listed 17 types of classes as their worst. Here 12, or 71%, of the worst types of classes are listed by other boys as their best.

GENERAL IMPRESSIONS OF THE ADOLESCENT IN THE LITERATURE

1. It has been suggested that the adolescent of today does not desire self-change, does not develop much, and forfeits his true adolescent development for a mixture of childishness and false adulthood that then leaves the adolescent dependent, shallow, and undeveloped (Douvan & Adelson, 1966, pp. 351–354).

2. Other studies have found that athletic prowess for boys is one of the most important determinants of peer status in high school (Coleman, 1961).

3. Informal conversation with high school teachers and counselors suggests that cars are a major and even detrimental interest of boys in high school.

4. It has been hypothesized that the importance of informal peer groups determines what school settings boys will take part in to be with friends in their free time.

These impressions provided the framework for the analysis of self-report data presented on the following pages.

Change and Blandness in Adolescence

Mean scores on the personality measures (described in Chapter 5) are near the midpoints for boys at each school (Edwards, 1971). The overall means indicate a lack of extreme personality characteristics for these high school boys. They are not defensively high or low on measures of self-esteem or depression. There are few signs of acting out that might be indicated by very high initiative scores. Social problems are not denied, nor are they seen as overwhelming.

How much do these boys want to change themselves? Two composite items and four additional items provide information on desired self-change. The physical change composite (desired change of height, weight, strength, etc.) shows significant school effects with means of 20.3 for Wayne Memorial High School (W) and 17.6 for Lee M. Thurston High School (T). The possible range for this scale is from 5 to 35. On changing social roles (student, son, boyfriend, etc.), the group at Wayne reports a mean of 28.2 (W), and the Thurston boys have a mean of 25.2 (T). A trend emerges for boys at Wayne to express a desire for more change than boys at Thurston. Four additional items show no significant school or exploration effects but reveal some interesting trends (see Table 6.2).

These four additional items indicate that it is slightly but significantly more important for these boys to change how much they are liked than it is to change their beliefs or what they think of themselves. This comparison reveals the desire for change in adolescents with an attempt to hold constant one's beliefs and self-conception — surely a difficult task but perhaps the generic task of adolescent development. The data in Table 6.2 show that the mean change scores on these four items are all significantly different from each other ($p < .05$). At

TABLE 6.2
Statistics on Four 7-point
Change-Self Items

Variable No.	Item	*Means* Wayne	Thurston	Total
11.89	Change my beliefs	3.2	2.6	2.9
11:94	Change what I think of myself	3.2	3.4	3.3
11:96	Change how much I am liked	3.6	3.4	3.5
11:91	Change my personality	3.9	3.9	3.9

Significant t tests for dependent measures (N = 180)

	Beliefs	Think of Self	How Liked
Think of self	−2.12*		
How liked	−3.83*	−2.32*	
Personality	−6.03*	4.67*	−2.96*

Correlations Between the Four Items:

	Beliefs	Think of Self	How Liked
Think of self	.486*		
How liked	.450*	.689*	
Personality	.474*	.648*	.702*

*(p < .05)

the same time, scores on each scale are significantly and positively correlated. These scales can be said to possess between 20% and 50% common variance, but each scale is responded to in a significantly different fashion.

In addition to the expression of moderate self-esteem, initiative, depression, etc., there is also a moderate amount of change desired by these boys as a group. The developmental stress of adolescence is reflected in part by negative responses to some of the adjective checklists versus positive responses to other adjective checklists. The picture of the average 10th-grade boy, based on the data presented here, is a delicate balance between desired change and constancy.

The final normative item dealing with self-perception has to do with the roles the boys see themselves adopting in their friendship groups. Seven types of roles were presented along with a "something else" category. The boys were asked to check whether they are seen as a leader, a second in command, a joker, a regular guy, a different type, a quiet type, or a resource person (see Table 6.3). As might be expected, the most preferred category is a "regular guy." The large number of responses for joker (26.8% [W] ; 25.0% [T]) is interesting and indicates that over one-fourth of the boys try to mediate social interaction and fit into their group by adopting a role where banter, humor, and wit are important skills.

TABLE 6.3
Percentage of Subjects Responding to Each Role
in Friendship Group Category
(Total *N* = 162)

School	Leader	Second in Command	Joker	Regular Guy	Different Type	Quiet Type	Resource Person
Thurston	7.3%	4.9%	26.8%	37.8%	6.1%	6.1%	6.1%
Wayne	6.3%	11.3%	25.0%	36.3%	3.8%	7.5%	2.5%
Total	6.8%	8.0%	26.9%	37.0%	4.9%	6.8%	4.3%

The data on self-conception yields a picture of the average adolescent that might be described as bland but delicately balanced. This picture is similar to Douvan and Adelson's (1966) conclusions about the contemporary adolescent. After Douvan and Adelson discarded the extreme respondents, they found the normative response of the adolescent population — of the silent majority — to be one of avoidance of conflict, of premature identity foreclosure, of general intellectual constriction, and an unwillingness to risk change (Douvan & Adelson, 1966, pp. 341–354). Douvan and Adelson's conclusion was that the adolescent of today, in general, does not develop much and forfeits his adolescence for a mixture of childishness and false adulthood that leaves the individual adolescent dependent, shallow, and undeveloped.

The results here are in agreement with some of Douvan and Adelson's findings. There is an emphasis on moderate change in restricted areas, but there is just as much effort expended to preserve past gains so as not to lose the foothold already attained on adulthood. These data do not refute Douvan and Adelson's conclusion that the majority of these adolescents may develop into shallow, dependent, childish, and undeveloped adults. The indications of moderate change desired by these boys suggest that there is a willingness to risk some change. A major task for the longitudinal study is to ascertain the varied stages of development of adolescents.

The Determinants of Peer Status

The boys were asked whether they would be "looked down on" or "looked up to" by other students according to eight attributes (Table 6.4). As with Coleman's study (1961), being an athlete is one of the most important determinants of peer status among the items. However, athletic prowess is reported to be not significantly different from "knowing a lot of girls" for this sample. These two items are significantly different from the other six (Table 6.4). The only item that is reported as a negative determinant is "being friends with teachers." Because no school or subject differences were found with these eight items, only the grand mean is presented in Table 6.4.

TABLE 6.4
Statistics for Eight Status Items
(1 = looked down on, 3 = neutral, 5 = looked up to)

Grand means (both schools combined, N = 187)

Variable	Item	Means
V5	Being an athlete	4.01
V8	Knowing a lot of girls	3.98
V7	Being a leader of school activities	3.65
V3	Knowing the right kind of people	3.61
V2	Getting good grades	3.51
V6	Coming from the right family	3.35
V4	Having money	3.23
V1	Being friends with teachers	2.81

T - tests for dependent measures and correlations (N = 187)

Variable	V1	V2	V3	V4	V5	V6	V7	V8
T tests for V5	−13.7*	−7.00*	−5.50*	−5.89*	–	−9.21*	4.53*	N.S.
r for V5	.183	.415*	.462*	.282*	–	.316*	.483*	.362*
T tests for V8	−12.3*	−4.99*	−3.86*	−5.31*	N.S.	−8.02*	−2.96*	–
r for V8	.147	.290*	.361*	.424*	.362*	.282*	.293*	–

*$p < .05$

TABLE 6.5
"What Do You and Your Friends Mostly Talk About?"

Category	Wayne %	Thurston %	Total %
1. Sports	22.9	25.0	23.9
2. Cars	8.6	6.9	7.7
3. Girls	28.9	19.4	23.9
4. Classes and school work	5.7	1.4	3.5
5. School activities	10.0	6.9	8.5
6. Intellectual ideas	2.9	0.0	1.4
7. Last weekend	2.9	9.7	6.3
8. Other[a]	18.6	30.6	24.6

[a]Other responses were generally combinations of the other categories or a special case such as "planning for next weekend."

The Importance of Cars to 10th-Grade Boys

Boys were asked to check the item that they and their friends talked about when they got together. The eight categories are shown in Table 6.5. Twenty-four percent talk mostly about sports, another 24% talk mostly about girls, and 9% talk about school activities. Cars as a topic of conversation is listed by only 8% of the respondents and is ranked fourth in order of frequency.

Where Do 10th-Grade Boys Go in Their Free Time?

The L1 form (Longitudinal Data Form) contained a section that asked boys where they would go if they could go anywhere during the school day, if they went there, and what they did. Responses from both schools were very similar. Combining both school responses gives the following results: Fifty-four percent said they would seek out a place on the school grounds, 29% said they would journey off the grounds, and 17% indicated they did not have a place to go. Of those who said they had a place to go (83%), 70% said they would go there to be with friends, 17% said they would go there to be alone, and the balance (13%) said they would engage in some other unique activity.

To get an idea of how often these places are used, the boys were asked how often they went there during the day and how much time they normally spent on each occasion. These items were converted to approximate frequencies per day and minutes per day to allow computation of means. Students at both schools say on the average that they go to this "free time place" about 1.5 times per day and that they spend between 40 and 45 minutes there. The responses range from 15 minutes to more than 3 hours. As might be expected, the lunch hour is the most mentioned time period for free time (33%). Four other times were checked with lower and almost equal frequency. Seventeen percent said they go to this place after school, 11% said they go there when they cut classes, 10% said they go there during free hours of the day, and 9% said they stop there between classes.

A significant school difference was found for whether or not adults are present at the "free time place" ($X^2 = 11.02; df = 2; P$ .05). at Wayne, 26% said adults are usually present at this place, 28% said sometimes, and 47% checked not usually. At Thurston, 8% said adults are usually present, 26% checked sometimes present, and 58% said adults are not usually present in this "free time place."

Where are these places, and why do the boys go there? For these responses, only the data from the stratified sample are presented. Table 6.6 contains the list of places and the frequency and percentages for boys in the stratified sample at each school. At Wayne, seven categories of places were listed by more than one boy, and 65% of those places mentioned are school related. At Thurston, more settings off the school grounds are listed. It is not clear whether this difference is due mainly to the availability of a student lounge at Wayne or to class scheduling or some other factor.

TABLE 6.6
Places Boys Go to in "Free Time"

Place	Frequency	%
Wayne High School		
1. Band room	3	6.1
2. Library	4	8.2
3. Gym	3	6.1
4. Student lounge	9	18.4
5. Walk halls or place in halls	6	8.2
6. In front of school	3	6.1
7. McDonald's or Burger King	4	8.2
8. Nowhere	4	8.2
9. Other (mentioned only once)	14	28.6
Thurston High School		
1. Gym	2	3.9
2. Cafeteria	5	9.8
3. Johns	2	3.9
4. Walk halls	13	25.5
5. Outside school building (on grounds)	6	11.8
6. McDonald's, Burger King, Palace	3	5.9
7. Friend's house	5	9.8
8. Other (mentioned only once)	15	29.4

An analysis of what it is that makes this place special shows generally that it is because one can meet friends and talk (53% [W] ; 66% [T]). Many boys also said that the place was safe or free from adult influence or constraints.

DISCUSSION

The first impression from the literature was partially supported. Adolescents in this study could be described as presenting a "moderate" and somewhat "bland" picture. Contrary to Douvan and Adelson's conclusions, however, these boys desire a moderate amount of personal change; and 25% of them describe themselves as "jokers" in social situations, which certainly does not suggest a "bland" picture.

Coleman's finding of the importance of athletic prowess was confirmed for these boys, but "knowing a lot of girls" was equally important. The importance of cars (Impression 3) was not supported. It may be that these boys are still too young to be very interested in cars, given the mean age of 15.2; or it could be that teachers and counselors over-emphasize the importance of this topic for high school students. The fourth impression about the importance of informal peer groups was supported, with 70% of the respondents seeking out a place where they could be with their friends.

None of these impressions was subjected to a rigorous, controlled test, so these findings should be viewed cautiously. The data do provide some interesting baseline data, however, and suggest a future framework for the longitudinal study. The next section of this chapter presents information on two boys. It illustrates how the "case study" method might be used to develop a taxonomy of coping strategies and adaptive roles.

A CLOSER LOOK AT TWO BOYS

This presentation illustrates the utility of the data for understanding individual boys and lays the comparative base for the presentations by George Gilmore in Chapter 7 and Barbara Newman in Chapter 8. They report complementary data on these same two boys. "Harold" is a boy with medium exploration preferences at Thurston; "Dave" is a Wayne student with high preferences for exploration. Tables 6.7 and 6.8 present the individual data on "Harold" and "Dave." The individual's score is presented first, followed by the group mean at the school (individual score/school mean).

"Harold"

On the self-report measures, "Harold" differs from the "average student" in that he wants more school change; he sees less opportunity; he sees the counselors and principal as less positive; and though he generally likes school more than

TABLE 6.7
Information on "Harold":
A Medium Exploration-Preference Person

Who Am I?	What Am I Like?	

Who Am I?		
1. Kind	*Positive*	*Negative*
2. Gentle	Optimistic	Moody
3. Understanding	Honest	Quick-tempered
4. Affectionate	Kind	Envious
5. Quiet	Practical	Often feel
6. Shy		misunderstood
7. Moody	Sensitive	Stubborn
8. Quick-tempered sometimes		
9. Nice		
10. Loyal		

Factor I – *School Evaluation*		Factor II – *Exploration*	
School change	50/35	Exploration questionnaire eighth grade	39/33
Perceived opportunity	10/18		
Positiveness – teachers	19/21	Exploration questionnaire ninth grade	29/34
Positiveness – counselors	8/30		
Positiveness – principal	8/17	Exploration – themes 8th	41/52
School satisfaction	9/6	Exploration – themes 9th	70/62
School excellence	3/5	Initiative	33/26

Factor III – *Change self*		Factor IV – *Self esteem*	
Change physical self	16/18	Social problems	18/17
Change social self	12/25	Self-esteem – 8th grade	40/37
Depression	16/29	Self-esteem – 9th grade	46/36
		Rotter's I.E. – 9th grade	11/11
		Marlowe–Crowne S.D. – 9th	21/15

Factor V		Factor VI	
Identification	16/18	Positiveness – students	10/21

most, he says his particular school is lower on the excellence dimension than the average school. His exploration scores are near the mean, but his initiative score is much higher than average. "Harold" does not want to change his social self as much as most boys; he has a low depression score and much higher self-esteem and need for social approval than his peers. "Harold" also sees other students as much less positive than the average student. Thus, here is a picture of a boy who likes school but not the high school he is in. Although he is high on initiative and self-esteem, he is low on changing himself and on his evaluation of other students.

"Harold" is an unusual boy, for he still maintains ties with his junior high school. To open-ended questions, he says he tries to go back there at least every other week to watch sports events and argue with his friends. He says his friends see him as a "different type" of guy that they do not understand. "Harold" spends much of his time with them, trying to explain the way he thinks. An important setting for social interaction for "Harold" is just outside of school. He goes there just about every day to be alone and "think about things he does not have time for in school."

"Harold" is happiest when meeting new people and being in high school, but he is unhappiest about the way his high school is run and "some of the people in the school." The best thing that could happen next semester would be for the school to change for the better. "Harold's" best class was a science course that was open to everyone and provided a lot of freedom. His worst class was history because of his poor grade.

"Harold" presents a picture of general dissatisfaction with his school but one softened by some active involvement with school. "Harold's" style of coping with high school seems to be one of not-too-active involvement while expanding effort in other areas — back at his junior high or sitting by himself outside of school. It does not look as though "Harold" is going to run into any major problems in getting through school, but one does not get the feeling that he will get a lot out of the three years he is there.

"Dave"

"Dave," a high-exploration-preference subject, is described by Gilmore (1971) as a thin boy who was cooperative, courteous, especially friendly, but very anxious during the interview. "Dave" obtained a curious pattern of scores on the variables in Table 6.8. He obtained the lowest possible school change score; he gave counselors and his school the highest possible ratings. His exploration and initiative scores were above average, and he gave other students the highest possible positiveness rating.

"Dave" says he is happiest about the teachers and the students in school. He does not list anything he is unhappy about, and the only problem he sees with the school is "hard-grading teachers." Dave says the most important place for him is at the end of the first-floor halls near an outside door, because "you can have a cigarette there." There are usually about 10 friends present who see "Dave" as the "joker" of the group. "Dave's" best class is journalism, because he can write, talk with friends, and do new things there.

In contrast to "Harold," "Dave" mentions more active involvement with school; and he has much more positive scores on many variables. The extremely high scores and the unanswered questions on the questionnaire give rise to doubts about how good things really are for "Dave"; but on the basis of the data presented here, he seems to be coping with high school most directly by getting actively involved in the school.

TABLE 6.8
Information on "Dave":
A High Exploration-Preference Person

Who Am I?		What Am I Like?	
		Positive	*Negative*
1. Friendly		Honest	Impatient
2. Honest		Independent	Disorganized
3. Clean		Happy	Noisy
4. Optimistic		Sensitive	
5. Concerned for others		Adventurous	
6.			
7.			
8.			
9.			
10.			

Factor I – *School Evaluation*		Factor II – *Exploration*	
School change	8/31	Exploration questionnaire Eighth grade	51/34
Perceived opportunity	22/20		
Positiveness – teachers	18/23	Exploration questionnaire Ninth grade	57/35
Positiveness – counselor	35/28		
Positiveness – principal	–/25	Exploration – themes 8th	94/56
School satisfaction	8/7	Exploration – themes 9th	70/53
School excellence	10/7	Initiative	

Factor III – *Change self*		Factor IV – *Self Esteem*	
Change physical self	21/20	Social problems	21/18
Change social self	31/28	Self-esteem – 8th grade	– – –
Depression	31/30	Self-esteem – 10th grade	32/35
		Rotter's I.E. – 9th grade	9/10
		Marlowe–Crowne – 9th grade	19/16

Factor V		Factor VI	
Identification	18/19	Positiveness – students	28/21

IMPLICATIONS OF RESULTS FOR THE DESIGN OF COMMUNITY SERVICES

The use of self-report measures makes it possible to accumulate data at a relatively inexpensive cost. This chapter illustrates some of the many ways self-report data can be used to obtain a better picture of the respondents and their environments. The ecological perspective for the longitudinal study requires that the social environment and its members be surveyed so that the investigator can begin to understand the complex forces that determine individual behavior in a specific environment. This chapter summarizes some of the study's initial attempts at such a survey. The age, work experience, dating experience, and self-descriptions provide some basic baseline measures that serve as anchor points for the longitudinal study.

An attempt was made to go beyond self-concept and the effect of informal peer groups on behavior. Boys were asked initially to indicate those factors leading to high or low peer status, their role in their information group, and the topics they discussed in informal meetings of a peer group. The study also surveyed use of the environment by the boys' informal groupings. Barker and Gump (1964) have detailed a set of exacting procedures for assessing the formal "behavior settings" in high schools. This study tried to elaborate the location, use, and function of informal "behavior settings" within the high school. Finally, all available self-report data were brought together for two participants. From this data, some indications were obtained about the types of adaptation and modes of coping with the environment.

What are the implications for the field of community psychology? Though only a crude beginning has been made, there are some implications that can be stated. The following questions seem apt:

1. What are the self-perceptions of different groups served by a community mental health program? Although the two high schools and their students are very similar, some differences between students have been found. This study to date has been able to examine the topic of desired change. It is often observed that community workers may believe that the local residents do not desire change, whereas the empirical data from such a procedure may indicate that the population does desire a moderate amount of change. Another "contradictory" finding was the relative unimportance of cars as a topic of conversation for this sample. The popular literature and the opinions of school authorities suggest that this is an overriding concern of 10th-graders. The data indicate otherwise. One might expect similar "myths" to be found in any community. Through systematic collection of self-report data and other perceptions from inhabitants, a more accurate picture of the various communities can be obtained.

2. What are the status determinants for subgroups within a population? The low priority of "good grades" or of "being friends with teachers" could be viewed as a negative factor for a high school environment. Coleman (1961) was severely critical of the importance of athletics in his earlier study. If one tries to understand the status forces operating for a given group, deviant behavior may be able to be explained. By understanding the pressures for status differences in a community, it also may be possible to serve the "deviant" subgroups in a community. This understanding can lead to the design of different preventive interventions to achieve organizational or community objectives. In the school setting, for example, it has been proposed that academic objectives could be better met by eliminating the distracting influence of athletics. Understanding of the importance of sports, both for social status and for the development of competence — as revealed in Gilmore's work in Chapter 7 — can lead to a radi-

cally different proposal. If athletics are centrally important to adolescent social and cognitive development, then academic objectives might be better achieved by integrating physical activity into the academic program.

Similar preventive interventions in communities can take account of the unique needs of special population groups and insure that these needs are met in achieving program objectives. Certainly much more needs to be learned about the cultural, social, and interpersonal forces operative for different subgroupings in a community.

3. What are the important social settings in a community, and for what purpose are they used? Studies have been done on the use of mental health facilities related to distance and location. Increased understanding of formal and informal behavior settings can improve the effectiveness of crisis services, outpatient clinics, aftercare services, etc. Data from this study, for example, suggest that a student lounge or several chairs in a hallway at both schools (away from the principal's office) would be a good spot for counselors who wished to provide "crisis intervention" to many of these high school boys.

Analysis of informal social settings in natural communities may reveal much about the needs and activities of citizens. Preventive intervention efforts, whether for educational, treatment, or crisis intervention purposes, often lose much of their effectiveness by inappropriate location. The choice of setting for the intervention is as important as the choice of the media for the intervention.

The case studies have attempted to utilize both normative and standardized items in conjunction with responses to open-ended questions in a structured interview to develop a comprehensive portrait of modes of coping and types of adaptations to the high school. Although these case studies represent just a beginning, systematic development of such studies for all students can create a comprehensive taxonomy of coping styles and adaptive roles for high school boys. The case study method prevented here may provide a multidimensional typology of coping styles and caried adaptations.

These are some of the implications of the present data for the field of community psychology. Germane to all four examples and to the longitudinal study is the concept that a better understanding of persons and environments will encourage the design of preventive interventions for varied groups in diverse communities.

REFERENCES

Barker, R. G., & Gump, P. *Big school, small school.* Stanford, Calif.: Stanford University Press, 1964.

Coleman, J. S. *The adolescent society.* New York: The Free Press of Glencoe, 1961.

Douvan, E., & Adelson, J. *The adolescent experience.* New York: John Wiley, 1966.

Edwards, D. W. Exploration and the high school experience: A study of tenth-grade boys' perceptions of themselves, their peers, and their schools. Unpublished doctoral dissertation, The University of Michigan, 1971.

Gergen, K. J., & Morse, S. J. Self-consistency: Measurement and validation. *Proceedings, 75th Annual Convention, APA,* 1967, 207–208.

Gilmore, G. E., Jr. Exploration, identity development, and the sense of competency: A case study of high school boys. Unpuulished doctoral dissertation, The University of Michigan, 1971.

Robinson, J. P., & Shaver, P. R. *Measures of social psychological attitudes.* Ann Arbor, Mich.: Survey Research Center, Institute for Social Research, 1969.

7 Exploration, Identity Development, and the Sense of Competency: A Case Study

George E. Gilmore, Jr.
Institute for Social Research
The University of Michigan

The development of the field of community psychology has called for a re-newal of the conception of person–environment relationships. Kelly (1966, 1968, 1970; Mills & Kelly, 1972; Trickett, Kelly, & Todd, 1972), utilizing a point of view stimulated by concepts from biological ecology, has developed a framework for viewing psychosocial events for the research reported here. One of four principles related to this theoretical perspective, the principle of inter-dependence, affirms that a social environment be viewed as having a variety of resources, that individuals can be considered as varying in adaptative strengths, and that psychological development depends on the relationship between the person and his various social settings.

To examine the application of this point of view, the research reported in this chapter examines how male adolescents who vary in their coping styles adapt to different high school environments. The coping style of choice is ex-ploratory behavior. Previous studies have developed a questionnaire for assessing students' preferences for exploratory behavior (Edwards, 1970, 1971) as re-ported in Chapters 5 and 6 in this volume. Other work has provided an initial evaluation of the school environment (Stillman, 1969) and examined specific social processes such as the experience of the new student (Fatke, 1970) and help-giving behavior (Todd, 1971) in the two schools, reported in Chapter 10.

A THEORETICAL FORMULATION

The work reported in this chapter shares with the work reported in the other chapters the common goal of increasing our understanding of adolescent devel-opment as a function of person–environment interaction. However, the work reported in this chapter differs in elaborating the rationale for individual dif-ferences and in the methodology employed. In the present study, three concepts are considered central for the adolescent experience: identity, competence, and exploration preferences. The study represents an effort to relate each of those concepts via the assessment of students' behavior in the two schools at the 10th grade.

Identity

Identity is a universal term used with diverse connotations; it retains little specific meaning. Its status as a psychological concept is barely intact. An empirical concept central to Erikson's writings, as a term it can signify: (a) a conscious sense of individuality; (b) an unconscious process that helps one maintain a continuity of personal character; (c) a process of ego synthesis; and (d) establishing communion with a group. The diffuseness of these descriptions reflects the confusion of the concept and illustrates the difficulties confronted when attempting any empirical investigation.

Both theoretical discussions and a limited number of empirical studies offer some direction, however. Blos (1962), White (1963), Sanford (1964, 1965), and Erikson (1968), though using varied terms, offer two consistent themes: that identity depends on (a) one's mastery of the environment and (b) on the development of life styles or roles that the self and others similarly perceive. Miller (1963), speaking specifically to the problem of measurement, suggests that one index of identity development is the congruence between one's self-perception and another's perception of the individual. A series of empirical studies (Constantinople, 1969; Donovan, 1970; Marcia, 1966, 1967, 1968; Podd, 1969, 1970) have developed experimental indices of identity and have established some validity for the concept. Such studies generally examine the consequences rather than the process of identity development.

As suggested by Miller's (1963) formulation, identity is defined in the current work as the degree of congruence between the individual's self-perceptions and his perception of how others see him. Such self—other congruence is important in respect to both the individual's actual performance in a variety of roles (here labeled "current role identity") and his ideal of such roles (the "ideal role identity"). Thus, in the present study, two factors are used to assess identity development: (a) current role identity, which is determined by the congruence between the individual's evaluation of his own role performance and his perception of how others evaluate such behaviors; and (b) ideal role identity — the degree to which the individual perceives that others agree with his ideal conception of these roles.

Exploration

Exploration, too, suffers definitional ambiguity. One frequently encounters concrete examples of exploratory behavior (e.g., Dashiell, 1925). Piaget (1952), Mittleman (1954), Peller (1954), Berlyne (1960), and Rapaport (1960), working from a variety of theoretical models, suggest several behavioral correlates of exploration that focus either on cognitive factors or emotional meanings of the term *exploration*. Edwards (1970), summarizing such conceptualizations, argues that exploration may be manifested in at least three dimensions: (a) the cognitive (receptivity to and active search for new ideas); (b) the behavioral (engaging in diverse activities); and (c) the innovative (manipulation of existing situations or the creation of new ones that allow for novel experiences). The present work attempts to clarify the functional meaning of these concepts by developing and examining the validity of a theoretical schema that suggests a direct relationship between identity development and exploratory behavior.

Exploration is defined by Edwards's (1970) questionnaire, which attempts to measure the degree to which students prefer to interact with various segments of the environment. Previous studies by Edwards (1970, 1971) and the preceding two chapters suggest this questionnaire moderately assesses preferences for *social* exploration.

Competency

White's delineation of competency as a product of one's effective dealings with reality begins to describe measurable factors that may affect identity development (White, 1963). The present writer proposes that identity is a direct consequence of the development of a variety of competences. This proposal is congruent with White's proposition that self-esteem is the direct product of the experiences of competency, though admittedly the present formulation views competency as having a more extensive effect than White suggests. It is perhaps merely coincidental that White chose exploratory behavior as an example of human (and animal) behavior for which standard motivational theories were unable to account. Yet one cannot fail to recognize that the variable, exploration, responds well to the principal characteristic of theories of identity development — that identity is somehow the consequence of person—environment interaction.

Exploration, at least when viewed from the transactional perspective, is specifically that — a variable that determines one aspect of an individual's style of relating to the environment. Thus, we propose a schema describing the process of identity development, with exploration, as a product of effectance motivation leading to the experience of competency, which in turn affects the development of identity (see Figure 7.1). To test this formulation, this study examines the relationship between two independent variables (degree of preference for exploratory behavior and school attended) and two dependent variables (identity and the sense of competency). The school attended is included as an independent variable in order to assess potential differences between effects of exploration preferences on identity development in boys functioning in the two school environments — Wayne and Thurston High Schools.

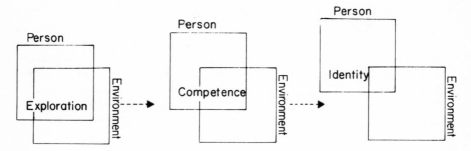

FIG. 7.1   Transactional view of identity development.

Sense of competency is defined simply as the individual's self-report experience of being able to do something well. A competency is any behavior or set of behaviors that constitutes a perceived skill. This study deals specifically with the sense of competency, with those skills that the person reports. In assessing the sense of competency, both the number and diversity of such skills are recognized as factors that reflect the degree to which the person experiences himself as competent.

METHODOLOGY

The methodology chosen to examine this theoretical formulation is the "case study." It is important to recognize that this method is significantly distinct from the traditional clinical case study, where the aim is to describe an individual comprehensively with particular attention to intrapsychic processes. Nor does this method correspond directly to the social case report, which frequently focuses on the careful examination of a person's life history. Rather, the case study in this instance is a method to generate a high degree of personal information via a structured interview in which the individual is the primary unit of analysis. This particular definition of the case study does not limit itself to an examination of intrapsychic phenomena or historical happenings, but includes consideration of developmental processes derived from a person's interactions with family, school, and peer environments.

We are as interested in a person's perception of significant other persons and the effects of the environment as in the person's self-perception. The focus of the research is directed to the individual's identity as a function of his interaction with significant segments of the contemporary environment. Further, the persons under study have been clustered into six groups: low, moderate, and high preferences for exploration in each of the two schools. An important part of the present work is the comparison of these groups. The findings are presented as guides for two individuals, "Harold" and "Dave," who are discussed in detail.

The Interview

The concepts under examination encourage the use of an interviewing procedure. Two other factors influence the selection of this methodology. First, it complements the procedures of data collection employed in concurrent studies. The population study conducted by Edwards (Chapters 5 and 6) and the assessment of the environment (P. Newman, Chapter 11) derive from self-reports of students and faculty. The group process study of students (B. Newman, Chapter 8) relies on observational techniques. Selection of a distinct methodology for the present research supports the development of multiple-method, construct-validational procedures as recommended by Campbell and Fiske (1959). Second, the present investigation directs itself to an intensive assessment of the individuals under study. The data are thus subject to considerable interpretation. Since the interview situation allows for clarification of an individual's response — which in a paper-and-pencil self-report might always remain ambiguous — collection of information through interviewing can be designed in such a way that interpretation of the data is to a greater degree determined by the subjects' responses. Viewed in this fashion, the interview method can serve to highlight an elaboration of the individual.

With these criteria in mind, a highly structured interview protocol was developed for the case study. A good proportion of questions asked of respondents were highly specified and yet allowed for a wide range of responses. Highly structured aspects of the interview were followed by a series of more open stimuli, which allowed the respondent to clarify, define, or even nullify his responses to highly structured questions. The questions that made up the interview protocol are for the most part unique to the present study. A few items were adopted from an interviewing procedure developed for a nationwide study of adolescents (Bachman, Kahn, Mednick, Davidson, & Johnston, 1967). The procedures for the interview are discussed in more detail in Gilmore (1971).

Several versions of the interview were pretested, using a small sample of high school sophomores who were not part of the experimental sample. Results from the pretest interviews indicated that although it was generally a coherent, functional instrument, it suffered from some deficiencies: The specific language was sometimes misunderstood by 15-year-old boys; the organizational format of the interview protocol occasionally confused the interviewer; and the interview was too lengthy. Each of these deficiencies was attended to in subsequent revisions of the interview protocol. In its final form, the interview met several criteria:

1. From a theoretical point of view it was judged to assess the central variables.
2. Its form and language were such that respondents varying in level of intellectual functioning and personality style were able to respond with little difficulty.

3. The protocol was free enough to encourage an actual interview, rather than merely an oral questionnaire.

4. The interview could be conducted within a 2-hour period.

The interviews were conducted by four trained interviewers, including this author. To reduce interviewer variance, considerable attention was given to the selection and training of interviewers. Three criteria guided interviewer selection: (a) formal training in psychology, (b) previous interviewing experience, and (c) research experience. The author and two assistants were advanced graduate students with considerable training in psychology. The third assistant was a recent undergraduate majoring in psychology. All interviewers had previous experience with adolescents in counseling or therapeutic situations and had conducted interviews for research purposes. All interviewers were young males, reasonably similar in dress and appearance.

The interviewers as a group undertook a training program designed to assure optimal and standard use of the interview protocol as an assessment procedure. Interviewers familiarized themselves with the *Manual for Interviewers* (Survey Research Center, 1969), which defines standard interviewing procedures. Particular care was taken to insure that interviewers used identical introductions and standardized probing and closure procedures. Each interviewer conducted a pretest interview in the selected schools with a volunteer high school subject who was not part of the selected sample. In a final group training session, areas of procedural ambiguity were clarified.

RESULTS

Three levels of analysis are employed to test the study's hypothesis. A two-way analysis of variance provides a formal test for assessing the effects of students' preferences for exploration, the school environment, and the interaction effect of these two independent variables on students' sense of competency and identity. Content analyses of the types of competences and identities offer considerable direction to the interpretation of the statistical findings, and two examples from a series of case reports illustrate the significance of such findings as reflected in the real-life world of students. Interviews were conducted during both the fall and spring semesters of the boys' 10th-grade year.

Statistical analysis indicates that although students generally report a large number of actual competences, those attending Thurston reported significantly more skills than their peers at Wayne (see Figure 7.2). Similar results emerge when examining the number of competences students hope to acquire in the future. Again, students at Thurston report more competences than those at Wayne (see Figure 7.3). High, moderate, and low explorers were not distinguished on either of these measures; however, high explorers did report a greater confi-

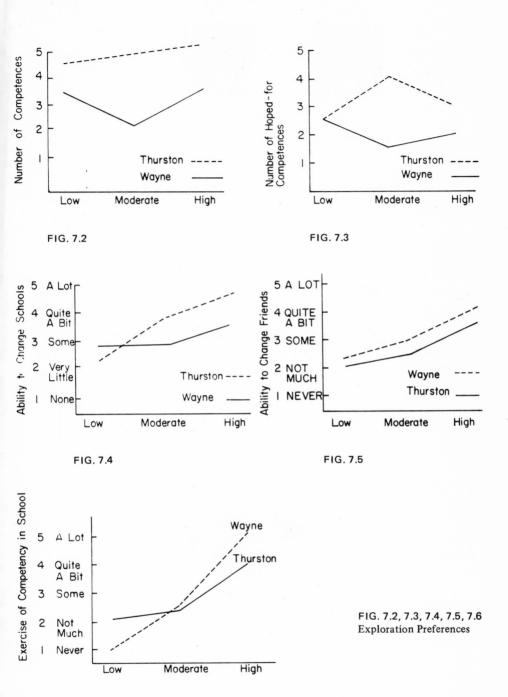

FIG. 7.2

FIG. 7.3

FIG. 7.4

FIG. 7.5

FIG. 7.6

FIG. 7.2, 7.3, 7.4, 7.5, 7.6
Exploration Preferences

dence in their ability to change their schools and their friends than did low explorers (see Figures 7.4 and 7.5). Significant for the overall study is the finding that although all students reported exercising the competences to about the same degree in both environments, it was found that exploration is positively related to the use of competences in school or school-related activities (see Figure 7.6). Content analysis suggests that neither the environment nor the variable of exploration alone affects the types of competences students enjoy. Approximately 80% of the actual competences reported by students were athletic or recreational. In summary, the school environments seem to differentiate students in respect to the general indices of competency. Exploration, on the other hand, is related to more concrete expression of how the boys use their competences in the school environment.

Statistical analyses of the measure of current role identity — the degree to which students felt that others perceived them as they perceived themselves — are summarized in Table 7.1. Students at Thurston reported less self–other congruence. This result is significant in terms of the general measures: the number and size of self–other discrepancies, and in terms of three specific roles: student, son, and boyfriend. There is very limited evidence that exploration is related to this index of identity.

Results that emerge from an analysis of students' ideal role identity are quite different (see Table 7.2). Exploration is found to be positively related to how

TABLE 7.1
Analysis of Variance: Identity Variables

Variable Label	df	F (School)	F (Exploration)	F (Interaction)
Number of discrepancies between self-and others' perception	1,2,2	18.20**	1.36	0.54
Discrepancies: self–others' perceptions as student	1,2,2	6.40*	0.30	1.30
Discrepancies: self–others' perceptions as son	1,2,2	8.26**	3.78*	2.14
Discrepancies: self–others' perceptions as friend	1,2,2	1.43	0.27	0.09
Discrepancies: self–others' perceptions as boyfriend	1,2,2	4.28*	0.83	1.07
Discrepancies: self–others' perceptions as athlete	1,2,2	2.69	0.16	0.06
Discrepancies: self–others' perceptions as worker	1,2,2	1.79	0.28	0.28
Largest discrepancy: self–others' perception	1,2,2	9.41**	1.03	1.03

*$p < .05$
**$p < .01$

TABLE 7.2
Analysis of Variance: Agreement with Ideals

Variable Label	df	F (School)	F (Exploration)	F (Interaction)
$\overline{X}$ Parental agreement	1,2,2	0.48	8.44**	1.13
Parental agreement − student	1,2,2	0.50	9.49**	1.18
Parental agreement − son	1,2,2	0.14	2.74	2.53
Parental agreement − friend	1,2,2	0.04	2.11	0.65
Parental agreement − boyfriend	1,2,2	1.07	4.74*	3.38*
Parental agreement − athlete	1,2,2	0.32	4.15*	0.32
Parental agreement − worker	1,2,2			
$\overline{X}$ Teacher agreement	1,2,2	0.07	3.36*	0.89
Teacher agreement − student	1,2,2	0.72	6.45**	0.20
Teacher agreement − son	1,2,2	2.13	3.30	0.17
Teacher agreement − friend	1,2,2	0.32	2.41	2.91
Teacher agreement − boyfriend	1,2,2	0.84	0.23	1.04
Teacher agreement − athlete	1,2,2	0.03	3.62*	0.57
Teacher agreement − worker	1,2,2	0.34	1.41	0.11
$\overline{X}$ Student agreement	1,2,2	0.54	3.43*	1.63
Student agreement − student	1,2,2	0.51	1.50	0.14
Student agreement − son	1,2,2	1.45	2.16	0.38
Student agreement − friend	1,2,2	0.20	5.15*	1.55
Student agreement − boyfriend	1,2,2	0.37	1.78	2.60
Student agreement − athlete	1,2,2	0.03	1.05	0.12
Student agreement − worker	1,2,2	2.05	0.90	1.62

*$p < .05$
**$p < .01$

much parents, teachers, and fellow students agree with respondents' ideals. This general finding is most striking in terms of high explorers reporting greater agreement with their parents' ideal of three roles: student, boyfriend, and athlete. There is no indication of school attended being related to this measure of identity.

Students' descriptions of ideal role behaviors were classified according to six categories: personal success, moral qualities, social qualities, commitment, skill, and attitudes. It is found that regardless of exploration preferences or school attended, students: (a) agree on the specific meaning of each role, and (b) distinguish among the several roles. Friend and boyfriend are described as social roles; son as a moral role; athlete and worker as roles requiring skill and commitment; and student as a role that requires a little of everything.

These analyses indicate that both the factor of exploration and the school attended differentiate students on the measures of identity. The fact that both independent factors do not simultaneously affect the indices of identity suggests two different and unrelated determinants: School and home factors affect general self—other perceptions, and exploration preferences are related more to future orientations and the more advanced developmental level of the student.

In a third level of analysis, a case was selected from each of the six groups under study. Both tape and verbatim recordings of the students' interviews rendered a comprehensive picture of the individual students. A summary report on two such cases illustrates this process.

"Harold," A Moderate Explorer at Thurston

"Harold," a moderate explorer at Thurston High School, is a handsome youngster who looks older than his 15 years. Like many low and moderate explorers at Thurston, he has a multitude of competences but only rarely does he use these in school. He feels that others see him quite differently than he really is and that his peers will not agree with his ideals, though parents and teachers will. In a variety of ways, he reports a closer relationship to adults than to peers: Adults but not peers will help him solve problems, help him change the school, and encourage him to use his competences. He has some friends but fewer than most students. "Harold" relates to the school in a highly restricted fashion — as a vehicle that will allow him to achieve academic and career goals rather than as a community with varied resources, opportunities, and demands, including a social life.

Certain traditional psychological factors are apparent as one studies "Harold." He manifests a very high need for achievement coupled with a fear that others will recognize his failings, not his accomplishments. This may in part account for his avoidance of the peer culture. Such avoidance in turn helps one understand the minimal degree to which he uses his competences in school as well as his apparent identity confusion. An ecological interpretation suggests that there is congruence between "Harold's" hesitancy to engage much of the surrounding environment and the school's norms and reward system that encourages only limited involvement. Optimistically, "Harold's" narrow but successful attachment to the academic aspect of Thurston may provide a secure anchor point from which he can eventually explore more diverse segments of the school.

"Dave," A High Explorer at Wayne

On objective indices, "Dave," a high explorer at Wayne, appears only moderately competent. But in contrast to "Harold," Dave very often uses his competences in school. He scores high on all indices of identity, feeling that all groups of others agree with his ideals and see him much as he perceives himself. In almost a direct reflection of his high preference for exploration, "Dave" appears to have engaged multiple segments of the school. He appears to think, behave, and engage the environment with a particular limiting style. Reminding one of the hysteric who is carefully oblivious of and only superficially in contact with reality, "Dave" bounces from scene to scene, from group to group, just touching upon them without becoming genuinely involved in any setting. This style is reflected in "Dave's" descriptions of his friendships — "I really don't have best friends, just ones I hang around with, go to football games, just go places" — and in the fact that he seems unable to differentiate parts of the school. He can speak of and apparently only think of students, teachers, and classes in a very global fashion. Whereas "Harold" has a single anchor point at Thurston, "Dave" has none at Wayne. It may be fortuitous that his school is a fairly well demarcated environment with respect to both activities and norms for behavior. With such boundaries provided for him, "Dave's" apparent scattering style may be functional; at least the school offers him multiple and obvious opportunities for engagement.

The Follow-Up Study

A follow-up study (Gilmore, 1971) using an abbreviated form of the interview was conducted six months after the initial interview. Special attention was given to two topics: (a) the stability of initial findings and (b) the degree to which students' development of identity and a sense of competency may reflect the types of relationships the boys enjoy with parents, fellow students, and educational personnel. The general findings concerning identity and the sense of competency were partially replicated in the second study. Students at Wayne again scored higher on the index of identity. Also, preference for exploratory behavior is found to be positively related to students' sense of competency. There is, however, minimal evidence that exploration is significantly related to students' identity development in interviews conducted toward the end of the 10th grade. Results from this follow-up study, however, again indicate that high-exploring students relate more effectively and in more diverse ways to significant others in their environment than do low explorers. In addition, the follow-up study provides ample evidence that boys at Wayne have more positive relationships with school personnel than their peers at Thurston.

DISCUSSION

The studies encourage some commentary on three types of issues: (a) the apparent significance of the principal dependent and independent variables; (b) the relevance of the general and specific theoretical schemata that underlie the present work; and (c) the "case study" methodology.

Exploration

As this work was initiated, each of the principal variables — exploration, school environment, identity, and sense of competency — had definitional deficiencies. The independent variable of exploration at least benefited from some operational definition: scores on an experimental questionnaire. The degree to which such scores corresponded to either personality characteristics or actual behaviors was undetermined. Are such behaviors, attitudes, or traits cohesive enough to constitute a single dimension, or does the term *exploration* refer to a series of underlying behaviors? One theme that appears to characterize the several findings is that exploration is a variable that does distinguish groups of students. In each case, the student's behavior or attitude involves some interaction with other people and/or the social institution of the school (e.g., changing school and friends, using competences *in school*, whether or not others agree with ideals). Such findings suggest that the research is working with an individual difference variable that does relate to *social* exploration. The fact that the follow-up study consistently illustrates that high explorers interact with others more than low explorers offers support for the validity of this construct.

The School Environment

The results of the present study confirm the general hypothesis that the school environments distinguish between students on several dependent measures, but not as predicted. It was expected that the vague, undifferentiated world of Thurston High School would be less nurturant of students in developing a sense of competency and identity. In contrast, we find that boys at Thurston consistently score higher on the indices of competence, whereas those at Wayne with equal regularity score higher on the measures of identity. Thus, it seems clear that although the schools may represent significantly different social environments, they are not distinguished as originally had been expected. It may be that the reports of greater competences at Thurston are related to a greater value for education in the Thurston community, whereas the greater identity scores for the students at Wayne reflect the strong compensating school environment at Wayne.

The stability of the original findings over a time period of one school year cautions against a conclusion that the school environment changes students' sense of competency or their identity development. Taken together, the findings that emerge from the interviews at two points in time suggest two complementary hypotheses. First, what has been labeled "school effect" may in fact represent more general cultural or community effects or effects of the home environment. Second, the school environments may simply nurture previously learned patterns of behavior.

Measures of Competency

In assessing students' sense of competency, it was found that the direct measure of number of competences distinguished between different groups of students, whereas an indirect measure of this concept (number of improvements) did not. In an apparently contradictory fashion, the indirect measure of the diversity of students' competences produced significant results; the direct measure did not. The fact that students who reported different numbers of competences indicated no difference in the number of things they wanted to improve about themselves challenges the assumption that students with more competences will be less defensive about needed improvements. However, as the qualitative analyses have suggested, the different results that emerge from the direct and indirect measures seem not contradictory but instead complementary.

These findings suggest that although groups of high-, moderate-, or low-explorer students experience a different number of competences, the kinds of competences reported by students are quite similar and largely represent skill in recreational activities. The competences reported by the students could be considered baseline for each level of exploration group under study. Viewed in this way, the fact that the groups differ in the diversity of desired competences assumes added significance. The results seem to indicate that high explorers, especially those at Thurston, are able to consider acquiring more diverse competences (and perhaps to consider more diverse goals) than their peers, even though at present they manifest competences very similar to those of other students. The differences between direct and indirect measures imply some validity for the salience of the concept of diversity of competences; the significant differences found between groups could hardly be seen as reflecting the tendency of some students to respond with greater diversity to any stimulus question. Furthermore, it can be suggested that the question that refers to the future ("In what ways would you like to improve?") is a more open stimulus that imposes fewer constraints on respondents than a question that asks them to report facts ("What are you good at and like to do?"). The results indicate, in assessing students' sense of competence, that utilization of both direct and indirect measures is likely to render more useful information than the separate use of either single probe.

The fact that high, moderate, and low explorers were differentiated in terms of the degree to which they exercised their competences in school, rather than in terms of the degree to which they used such skills in general, indicates that the school environment does have a significant effect on students' sense of competency. It was rather surprising, then, to find that students with high preferences for exploration use their competences in school to a similar degree at both schools. Such findings encourage the argument that the two schools are important as functional environments but are not as different as expected — at least in respect to the major dependent variables of the present study. The evidence that high explorers are more able to find ways in which to utilize their skills within the school environment than other students, despite the fact that all students report the same types of competences, suggests that exploration may affect students' sense of competency precisely because students with high preferences for exploration are likely in fact to engage diverse and multiple aspects of the environments. This finding also adds additional support to the validity of the exploration concept.

Measures of Identity

Despite a moderate correlation between the two measures of identity, students at the two schools were differentiated only in terms of their current role identities (Wayne > Thurston); whereas students with differing levels of preference for exploration were differentiated by the measure of ideal role identity (high explorers greater than low explorers). These findings question the degree to which these measures assess the same general concept of identity. However, the differences in results are quite consonant with the present writer's conceptualization of identity, where ideals and current behaviors are expected to represent distinct aspects of a single but general factor.

In examining the specific variables used to assess students' identity, it is found that only a subset of the six roles differentiates the experimental groups. For current identity, students at the two schools respond in significantly different ways to the roles of student, son, and boyfriend but only somewhat differently to roles of friend, athlete, and worker. These apparent differences may confirm the impression gained from the content analysis that the role of worker is novel to 10th graders and that the roles of friend and athlete are acquiring new connotations for these boys.

In respect to the measure of ideal identity, the boys responded in significantly different ways to the roles of student, friend, boyfriend, and athlete, but not to the roles of son and worker. Neither the principal findings nor the qualitative analyses suggest any reasons why these latter two roles are not significantly related to the factor of ideal identity.

The study has developed a very concrete, measurable definition of identity but provides little evidence by which one can evaluate the degree to which this measure actually assesses identity as described by Erikson (1959). That these measures of identity are, as predicted, related to students' preferences for exploration is evidence for the construct validity of these measures. The case studies (Gilmore, 1971) suggest that these measures reflect the individual's identity status to some degree, but this level of data analysis also illustrates the limitations of the measures. For instance, the measures do not indicate whether a student manifests a negative or positive identity. This limitation suggests that, as measured in this study, identity refers to a somewhat more general concept than is reflected in much of the literature. This use of the term *identity* has two significant advantages: It is essentially value free, and it does not say whether the person is satisfied or dissatisfied with himself. Further, it is a concrete, rather objective measure to which 15-year-old boys are able to respond appropriately and with minimal difficulty.

THEORETICAL FORMULATIONS

The general theory directing the present work, frequently labeled "transactional," generates the hypothesis that significant differences in human functioning are the consequence of person—environment interaction. Although idiographic case study data do illustrate such interaction effects, statistical analyses provide minimal evidence in support of this general hypothesis. Such findings may reflect theoretical limitations. However, the untested nature of the dependent variables and the limited differences between schools suggest the present work may not have genuinely examined the transactional perspective.

Similar criticism can be offered in terms of the theoretical formulation of identity development, which suggested that exploration affects the degree to which students acquire a sense of competency and thus indirectly affects identity development. The findings presented here do not contradict such a formulation, but they do provide evidence suggesting a more economical conception of the interrelationship of these variables. It can be concluded on the basis of these studies that exploration affects both students' sense of competency and their identity. However, there is very limited evidence that an individual's sense of competency serves as a mediating link between exploration and identity.

IMPLICATIONS

These results offer implications both for the high schools and for future research. For the schools, as might easily have been predicted, these findings suggest neither that all is well nor that all is bad. In terms of psychological development, we find that the bulk of students are surviving and a few are excelling. One problematic issue is highlighted — the difficulties students experience in engaging the environments. Though this difficulty is reflected in various ways, the present data emphasize the limited degree to which students exercise their competences in schools. Low and moderate explorers are unable to use their competences as a channel of engagement with either school environment. This limitation may be due to the fact that most students perceive their self-competences as athletic in nature. As with most high schools, the athletic programs at Wayne and Thurston focus on varsity sports that allow for only a few direct participants. The expansion of strong intramural athletic programs would offer many more students the opportunity to become active members of the school environment.

A second implication for the schools suggests that the factor of exploration, though in need of continued validation, may provide a new dimension for viewing individual differences between students. A plethora of studies indicates that the dimension constituted by measures of achievement and intelligence offers only limited information about students. Exploration may be found to represent a distinct dimension that will help the schools detect and respond to significant differences within their populations.

The present study holds implications for two methodological issues. First, it suggests that the "case study" methodology need not limit itself to the study of isolated individuals. Useful information may more readily be gained about a single case if it is examined within the perspective of immediate relevant group data. This is particularly so if the group data do not refer to a general normative population but to some subpopulation about which more definitive information is available. Second, the present work encourages the use of a structured interview as an assessment procedure, which allows high school boys to respond in considerable detail about very complex personal issues.

REFERENCES

Bachman, J. G., Kahn, R. L., Mednick, M. T., Davidson, T. N., & Johnston, L. D. *Youth in transition* (Vol. 1). Ann Arbor, Mich.: Institute for Social Research, 1967.

Berlyne, D. E. *Conflict, arousal, and curiosity.* New York: McGraw—Hill, 1960.

Blos, P. *On adolescence: A psychoanalytic interpretation.* New York: The Free Press, 1962.

Campbell, D. T., & Fiske, D. W. Convergent and discriminant validation by the multi-trait multi-method matrix. *Psychological Bulletin, 1959, 56,* 91—105.

Constantinople, A. An Eriksonian measure of personality development in college students. *Developmental Psychology, 1969, 1,* 47—58.

Dashiell, J. F. A quantitative demonstration of animal drive. *Journal of Comparative Psychology, 1925, 5,* 205—208.

Donovan, J. M. A study of ego identity formation. Unpublished doctoral dissertation, The University of Michigan, 1970.

Edwards, D. W. The development of a questionnaire method of measuring exploration preferences. In G. V. Coelho (Chair), *Coping styles and the high school: Multiple methods for studying varied environments.* Paper presented at the annual meeting of the American Psychological Association, Miami Beach, September 1970.

Edwards, D. W. Exploration and the high school experience: A study of tenth grade boys' perceptions of themselves, their peers, and their schools. Unpublished doctoral dissertation, The University of Michigan, 1971.

Erikson, E. H. The problem of ego identity. *Psychological Issues, 1959, 1,* 101—173.

Erikson, E. H. *Identity: Youth and crisis.* New York: W. W. Norton, 1968.

Fatke, R. The adaptation process of new students in two suburban high schools. In G. V. Coelho (Chair), *Copying styles and the high school: Multiple methods for studying varied environments.* Paper presented at the annual meeting of the American Psychological Association, Miami Beach, September 1970.

Gilmore, G. E. Exploration, identity development, and the sense of competency: A case study of high school boys. Unpublished doctoral dissertation, The University of Michigan, 1971.

Kelly, J. G. Social adaptation to varied environments. In B. Bloom (Chair), *Community mental health: A challenge to traditional diagnostic methods.* Paper presented at the annual meeting of the American Psychological Association, New York, September 1966.

Kelly, J. G. Towards an ecological conception of preventive interventions. In J. W. Carter, Jr. (Ed.), *Research contributions from psychology to community mental health.* New York: Behavioral Publications, 1968.

Kelly, J. G. The quest for valid preventive interventions. In C. D. Spielberger (Ed.), *Current topics in clinical and community psychology* (Vol. 2). New York: Academic Press, 1970.

Marcia, J. E. Development and validation of ego identity status. *Journal of Personality and Social Psychology,* 1966, *3,* 551–558.

Marcia, J. E. Ego identity status: Relationship to change in self-esteem, general maladjustment, and authoritarianism. *Journal of Personality,* 1967, *35,* 118–133.

Marcia, J. E. The case-history of a construct: Ego identity status. In E. Vinacke (Ed.), *Readings in general psychology.* New York: American Book Co., 1968.

Miller, D. R. The study of social relationships: Situation identity and social interaction. In S. Koch (Ed.), *Psychology: The study of a science* (Vol. 1). New York: McGraw–Hill, 1963.

Mills, R. C., & Kelly, J. G. Cultural and social adaptations to change: A case example and critique. In S. Golann & C. Eisdorfer (Eds.), *Handbook of community psychology.* New York: Appleton–Century–Crofts, 1972.

Mittleman, B. Motility in infants, children, and adults. *Psychoanalytic Study of the Child,* 1954, *9,* 142–177.

Peller, L. E. Libidinal phases, ego development, and play. *Psychoanalytic Study of the Child,* 1954, *19,* 178–198.

Piaget, J. *The origins of intelligence in children.* New York: International Universities Press, 1952.

Podd, N. H. The relationship between ego identity status and two measures of morality. Unpublished doctoral dissertation, University of New York at Buffalo, 1969.

Podd, N. H., Marcia, J. E., & Rubin, B. M. The effects of ego identity status and partner perception on a prisoner's dilemma game. Unpublished paper, University of New York at Buffalo, 1970.

Rapaport, D. On the psychoanalytic theory of motivation. *Nebraska Symposium on Motivation,* 1960, *8,* 173–247.

Sanford, R. N. *College and character.* New York: Wiley, 1964.

Sanford, R. N. Ego process in learning. In *The Protection and Promotion of Mental Health in Schools,* Mental Health Monograph No. 5. Washington, D.C.: U.S. Department of Health, Education, and Welfare, 1965.

Stillman, H. An exploratory study of two high school environments. Unpublished paper, The University of Michigan, 1969.

Survey Research Center. *Manual for interviewers.* Ann Arbor, Mich.: Institute for Social Research, 1969.

Todd, D. M. Peer structure and help-giving for adolescent boys: A case study of social processes in a high school. In M. J. Feldman (Ed.), *Studies in psychotherapy and behavioral change, No. 2, Theory and research in community mental health.* Buffalo, N.Y.: State University of New York at Buffalo, 1971.

Trickett, E. J., Kelly, J. G., & Todd, D. M. The social environment of the high school: Guidelines for individual change and organizational redevelopment. In S. Golann & C. Eisdorder (Eds.), *Handbook of community psychology.* New York: Appleton–Century–Crofts, 1972.

White, R. W. *The study of lives.* Englewood Cliffs, N.J.: Prentice-Hall, 1963.

8 Interpersonal Behavior and Preferences for Exploration in Adolescent Boys: A Small Group Study

Barbara M. Newman[1]

Institute for Social Research
The University of Michigan

The present study is an attempt to describe the interpersonal behavior of boys with high, moderate, and low preferences for exploration in a social situation not highly school related. Subjects were selected from Gilmore's sample, described in Chapter 7, in an effort to add a behavioral dimension to an already broad range of self-report data collected from the boys who had participated in studies reported in Chapters 5 and 6. It was believed that the findings about school involvement, personality characteristics, and identity development reported in Chapters 5 and 6 could be amplified by observing the boys in an ongoing social situation with their peers. It was also believed that a group setting would present an opportunity for the boys to modify and expand upon the type of information that is often very stylized in a one—to—one, student—adult interaction.

There were three specific goals for the present study: first, to compare the interpersonal styles of boys who differ in exploration preferences; second, to consider the characteristics of social interaction for 10th-grade boys; third, to capture the social climate of the two study schools in the discussion groups.

THE DISCUSSION GROUP METHOD

The discussion group situation deserves some mention. There are several reasons for choosing this particular method of observing the boys. The group setting straddles the line between naturalistic observation — where little or no interven-

---

[1] Present address: Russell Sage College, Troy, New York.

tion is made by the experimenter into the ongoing life of the persons — and a more tightly controlled experimental design in which all but one or two parameters of the subject's behavior are controlled. The group discussion was a relatively unique situation for boys at both schools. It was controlled to the extent that similar topics and the same group leader were part of both groups. Yet the manner in which the boys chose to interact with each other or to exploit the resources of that setting was not manipulated or motivated by any specific experimental technique. A central question was whether or not the detailed observation of group behavior would be useful as a means of highlighting unique personality characteristics.

The author had an opportunity to observe a large sample of verbal and nonverbal behavior in a relatively small group of boys. The data allowed us to examine interpersonal style as it is related to three interdependent characteristics of the sample. On the most global level, we considered the subjects as young adolescent males, specifically 10th graders. Taking this as the point of departure, the group was designed to raise topics that were considered relevant for adolescents and to allow the boys to react and share their points of view. It was designed to give each boy a chance to see that his peers were experiencing some of his feelings and were puzzling over some of his issues.

Secondly, the group was designed to focus on the different responses of high, moderate, and low explorers to the situation. The group situation provided unique data about the ways the boys responded to a novel situation, their manners of organizing and expressing their opinions and feelings, and their styles of engaging a comparatively nonthreatening adult authority. These three elements are at the core of the interpersonal components of a coping strategy. It was anticipated that the behavioral data from the groups would provide some validation for the notion that social exploration unfolds and develops differently, depending on the environmental supports or restraints for its expression.

Finally, because the group was a miniature of the school culture, the norms for "play" in the school setting, the style of responding to adults, the patterns of dealing with outsiders, and the strategies for handling stressful or novel situations that might be characteristic of the school cultures were reenacted in the group setting. Even though the boys had only been at these two schools for 5 months, they were participants in the two school environments and expressed whatever cultures were present in the group.

METHODOLOGY

The data reported are based on observations and coding of verbal behavior in a discussion group at each of the study schools. The sample for the group discussions and the coding scheme are described in detail elsewhere (B. Newman, 1971).

TABLE 8.1
Discussion Topics for Each Group Session

Session	Topic
1	What is it like to be a student at _____?
2	What do you think of teaching as a profession? Other ideas about future occupations?
3	How have you changed in the last few years?
4	How has your relationship with your parents changed?
5	What kinds of things do you and your friends do together?
6	What sorts of skills would you like to develop if you had the opportunity?
7	Do you see yourself as part of a revolution or period of change?
8	What is it like to grow up in the community of _____?

The boys who were selected to participate in the group were three boys with high preferences for exploration, three boys with moderate preferences for exploration, and three boys with low preferences for exploration from the 10th grade at each school who had participated in other parts of the research program and in Gilmore's interview study described in Chapter 7. The boys in the present study were similar in intelligence, yet were not known to be close friends.

The group met for eight 1-hour sessions, scheduled twice a week for a month during school hours. The meetings were timed so as to prevent any boy from missing too many sessions of any one class.

The present author, the group leader at both schools, did not know which boys had high, moderate, or low preferences for exploration. The role of the group leader was to suggest a topic for discussion at the beginning of each session and then to permit the discussion to evolve. A list of topics for each session is presented in Table 8.1. The leader supported the expression of a diversity of opinions and tried to generate further discussions when there was a silence but did not encourage any specific group members to participate except in trying to allow everyone an opportunity to talk.

At each group session, the chairs were arranged in a circle. Two observers were present who sat at a table where they could watch and hear the group discussion. All the group members were aware of the presence of the observers. Both verbal and nonverbal behavior was coded for every session. In addition, a questionnaire regarding events of the session was filled out by each boy after every session. Each group session was tape-recorded, a fact made known to the participants at the start. Finally, at both schools a videotape was made of the group during session number six, primarily to preserve a visual record of the group.

Procedure for Coding Verbal Behavior

During each group session, one observer kept a record of who has talking to whom, including side conversations that might not be audible on the tape

TABLE 8.2
Verbal Category System

Codes	Category	Example
	1. Acting supportive and friendly	Hi. Have a doughnut.
	2. Acting hostile and unfriendly	Why should we tell you? That's our business.
Affective codes	3. Expressing anxiety	Why doesn't somebody say something?
	4. Expressing discouragement	It just wouldn't matter. Nothing would change.
	5. Dramatizing and denial	That guy was so mean he had the teacher doing errands for him.
	6. Agreeing	I know what you mean.
	7. Disagreeing	No, let's meet 3rd hour so I can miss biology.
Cognitive codes	8. Giving opinions, suggestions, or orientations	The food in the cafeteria is lousy.
	9. Asking for opinions, suggestions, or orientations	What did you do last Friday night?

recording. After the session, this observer used the observation record to follow the tape and to code verbal interaction. The category system was intended to capture the range of affect that was expressed, as well as to follow the more task-oriented behaviors characteristic of most discussion groups. There are nine categories representing a blend of codes used by Bales (1970) and Mann (1967). The categories in both of these systems have been used with high coder reliability. However, each system by itself is more complex than seemed appropriate for a high school group. The strength of Mann's system is to elaborate expressions of affect, whereas the strength of the Bales system is to generate categories to describe task-oriented behavior. Because the type of group under study was neither a task group nor a training group, the composite coding system was believed to capture a broad range of behaviors. A list of the coding categories and a behavioral example is presented in Table 8.2.

The composite coding scheme was based on acts of behavior. The definition of an act follows Mann's use of this concept (1967).

> We define an act as a single speech or burst of sentences within which the expressed feelings are uniform. One of two events signals the end of an act: (1) the speaker is interrupted by another member of the group or by the leader, or (2) the speaker shifts from expressing one set of feelings to expressing feelings which call for a different array of scored categories [p. 61].

This definition differs from other interaction systems that identify an act with a simple sentence. The former definition was selected, because it was well suited to the boys' style of verbal expression. This definition also takes into account the fact that even a simple sentence may have more than one meaning. If within a single sentence, it seemed that the meaning shifted, the coder would give a separate code to each section of the sentence that had a different meaning. If an individual spoke for longer than 5 seconds and continued in the same meaning, another act would be coded for each 5 seconds of talking. This procedure, which is suggested by Bales (1970), allows the coding system to reflect the extent to which any single individual dominates the group session. Each act was identified by who was speaking and to whom the act was addressed, and only one code was permitted for each act. Many expressions, of course, have multiple meanings; but for the purpose of analysis and clarity, it was decided to force the coder to make a single decision on each act.

Because only one code was allowed for each act, and because the cognitive codes are assumed to be affect free, a hierarchy of coding emerged. Any act that was judged to have any affective message was coded in an affect category (1–5) and not a task category. This hierarchy was further elaborated in that within the affective codes, anxiety, discouragement, and dramatizing were coded before support and hostility. This scheme insured that the codes that were intended to reflect one's position toward another (support and hostility) were relatively free from expressions of one's own ego state. Further, the codes that were intended to be affectively neutral were not confounded by expressions of feelings.

Coding Reliability

The overall percent agreement between coders for 138 acts was 77%. Table 8.3 presents the reliability for each verbal category. Category 7 (disagreeing) is omitted from this table, because in two separate efforts to establish reliability no acts were coded in this category.

TABLE 8.3
Reliability Based on Percent Agreement
for the Verbal Coding Categories

Code	Category	Percent Agreement
1	Acting supportive or friendly	57
2	Acting hostile and unfriendly	20
3	Expressing anxiety	90
4	Expressing discouragement	25
5	Dramatizing and denial	45
6	Agreeing	57
8	Giving opinions, suggestions, and orientation	69
9	Asking for opinions, suggestions, and orientation	77

From this table, it is concluded that considerable confidence can be placed in findings between the two groups that are related to categories 3, 8, and 9; somewhat less confidence in results related to categories 1, 5, and 6; and very little confidence in results related to categories 2, 4, and 7. One reason the coder reliability for these last three categories is so low is that the behaviors — conflict or discouragement — were infrequently observed in the group.

TABLE 8.4
The Operational Definitions of 10 Dependent Variables

Interaction Style	*Definition*
Participation:	Total number of acts
	Number of group sessions attended
Initiation:	Acts not preceded by Category 9 in verbal coding system, "asks for opinions, suggestions, or orientation"
Range of affective expression:	Proportion of total acts coded in each affective category (1–5) of the verbal coding system
Responses to the Leader	
Interaction with the leader:	The number of acts directed to the leader
Affect expressed to the leader:	The proportion and range of affective acts (Categories 1–5) directed by each member to the leader
Use of the leader as a resource:	The proportion of acts coded 9, "asks for opinions, suggestions, and orientation," directed to the leader
Conflict in the Group	
The amount of conflict in the group:	The number of conflicts coded
	The number of group members involved in the conflicts
The perception of conflict:	Reports on the amount of disagreement that took place during each session
	Reports on disagreements each boy had with every other group member
Exploration Within the Group Context	
Involvement with other group members:	The number of boys each group member spoke to during each session
	The number of boys each member reports having gotten to be better friends with from the group
Ideas for change:	Ideas about change suggested during group sessions and in the postgroup evaluation

Critical Variables

The effects of level of exploratory preference, school differences, and the particular group session were measured for 10 dependent variables: participation, initiation, range of affective expression, interaction with the group leader, affect expressed to the leader, use of the leader as a resource, the amount of conflict in the group, the perception of conflict in the group, involvement with other group members, and ideas for change. The operational definitions for each variable are summarized in Table 8.4.

Hypotheses were raised with respect to exploration and school effects. In general, high explorers were expected to be active group members at both schools. They were expected to participate more, to initiate more often, to be involved in conflict, to interact more with other group members, and to express more ideas for change than others. Moderate explorers were expected to be unique in expressing the widest range of affect. The differences between schools were predicted to be in the direction of a more active, affect-laden group at Wayne High School and at Thurston High School, a restrained group that focused on the leader.

RESULTS

Before discussing the data about the specific study variables, a more general description of the interpersonal behavior of two boys, "Harold" and "Dave," who were described earlier by Edwards in Chapter 5 and Gilmore in Chapter 7, is presented. The case studies that follow are intended to demonstrate the value of using both self-report and behavioral observation in the study of coping behavior.

"Harold:" A Moderate Explorer at Thurston

"Harold" was quite self-confident for a boy his age. He assumed a leadership role in the group, particularly in the absence of the more verbal high explorers. It was almost as if he felt that it was his duty to help the group along, something of a noblesse oblige.

"Harold" was more varied in his expressions than many of the other group members, and he was willing to discuss his personal involvement with sports. He also had a variety of opinions about teachers, students, politics, etc. Usually these opinions conveyed something of a discouraged or cynical note. He did not have much faith that people, in whatever capacity, were trying their hardest or being entirely honest. He also did not seem to feel that there was much he or anyone else could do about it. Themes of discouragement and self-righteous anger were strongly interwoven in his comments.

The important features of "Harold's" interpersonal style were his relatively high score for participation, his high cognitive expression, and his extremely high focus on the leader. In spite of these signs that might be interpreted as evidence of serious involvement with the group, "Harold" only attended four group sessions.

The data confirm that "Harold" was something of a group leader, particularly in the fact that more boys talked to him than the reverse. The other characteristic of "Harold's" style captured by the data is his focus on the group leader. "Harold" respected or cared more for the leader's attention than for the other group members. In fact, one might deduce that "Harold" was scornful of the leader, perhaps because of the group's lack of focus in keeping with "Harold's" energy, perhaps because of the leader's failure to respond positively to his remarks.

"Harold" was described by Edwards in Chapter 6 and Gilmore in Chapter 7 as a boy who has confidence, high self-esteem, and competences in both athletic and academic areas. Nonetheless, he is not highly identified with the school and is quite critical of the way the school is run. "Harold" also has a very negative view of his peers. These responses to the school and to his peers appear to be a defensive projection of the deficiencies or inadequacies "Harold" may fear in himself.

In the group, "Harold's" confidence as well as his scorn for others were expressed. He appeared to be somewhat more involved in the school than is evident from the interview data. However, this involvement in school varsity sports may have been more an expression of "Harold's" personal needs than an expression of identification with the school. One additional aspect of the picture, provided via the data reported by Gilmore and Edwards, was "Harold's" persistent focus on the group leader. In "Harold's" case, this concentration on the leader was also a rejection of group members.

"Dave": A High Explorer at Wayne

During the first four group sessions, "Dave" said very little. He sat looking down at his hands. His remarks were directed most specifically to the group leader. However, session five brought a dramatic change in his behavior. During that hour, he was energetic, animated, eager to be noticed. He spoke quickly and loudly as if competing with the group for the leader's ear.

After that session, "Dave" remained an active but unpredictable member. He would move quickly from withdrawal to high energy involvement. In the middle of a conversation, he might burst in with, "Do you know what happened to me yesterday?" His tales usually involved a certain bravado and little concern for others' reactions to him. At one moment, he could be cutting and sarcastic; then

TABLE 8.5
A Comparison of Two Group Members
on Six Dependent Variables

Dependent Variable	"Dave" High Explorer at Wayne	"Harold" Moderate Explorer at Thurston
Participation		
Number of sessions	7	5
Total acts	607	572
Mean number of acts	87	143
Rank within group	5	3
Initiation		
Number of acts	369	239
Percent of total	61%	42%
Rank within group	1	4
Affective Expression		
Number of acts	300	258
Percent of total	49%	45%
Rank within group	6	7
Rank on friendly acts	6	8
Rank on anxious acts	9	9
Rank on dramatizing acts	4	4
Cognitive Expression		
Number of acts	307	314
Percent of total	51%	55%
Rank within group	4	3
Interaction with Leader		
Number of acts	339	382
Percent of total	56%	67%
Rank within group	2	1
Involvement with Others		
Number of acts sent	191	94
To number of people	4	3
Number of acts received	238	108
From number of people	4	4

he would turn quickly to seek emotional support. "Dave" seemed torn between needing to lash out at the leader and to be reassured by her approval and attention.

Table 8.5 summarizes the data for "Harold" and "Dave" on six of the dependent variables measured in the study.

The outstanding features of "Dave's" interpersonal style were his high rate of initiation, the great frequency of acts directed to the leader, and his extremely low rank on expressing anxiety. "Dave" was keenly tuned in to the leader. It

TABLE 8.6
A Summary of Trends for Exploration and School Differences

Dependent Variable	Exploration	School
Participation	High explorers at Wayne participate more than moderates and lows. Low explorers at Thurston participate more than moderate and highs	Extreme high and low amounts of participation at Wayne. More homogeneous participation at Thurston.
Initiation		More initiation at Wayne than at Thurston.
Affective expression	Moderate explorers exhibit a wider range of affect. Low explorers at Wayne express the most hostility.	More affective expression at Wayne, particularly dramatizing and denial.
Interaction with the leader	High explorers at Wayne interact more than moderates or lows. Moderate explorers at Thurston interact more than highs or lows.	Somewhat more acts directed toward the leader at Thurston.
Affect expressed toward the leader		More total affective behavior directed toward the leader at Wayne. More hostility expressed toward the leader at Thurston.
Use of the leader as a resource		More use of the leader as a resource at Wayne.
Amount of conflict	High explorers at Wayne and low explorers at Thurston engage in the greatest number of conflict situations.	More conflict at Wayne than at Thurston.
Perceptions of conflict	Moderate explorers perceive more conflict than high or low explorers.	
Involvement with other group members	High explorers at Wayne and low explorers at Thurston	

(continued)

TABLE 8.6 *(continued)*
A Summary of Trends for Exploration and School Differences

Dependent Variable	Exploration	School
	were most involved with other group members. Moderate explorers at Thurston were particularly uninvolved with other group members.	
Ideas for change		Ideas for change more clearly conceptualized at Thurston than at Wayne.

was he who suggested that she might save time by buying doughnuts near the school. On the other hand, "Dave" appeared to be quite immature in his ability to respond to the other boys in the group.

Gilmore found "Dave" to be "totally unreflective." "Dave's" responses to many of the interview questions appeared to be global and undifferentiated (Chapter 7, p. 125). Looking at his participation in the group, it was clear that "Dave" was initially quite suspicious and defensive in his responses to the group leader. His early group behavior was both flippant and hostile. As the group continued to meet, however, "Dave's" suspiciousness was replaced by genuine warmth and eagerness to be a group member. In these later meetings, he made some insightful comments about himself and his relationship to others. At the source of these remarks, however, there appeared a quality of cynicism, mistaken as expressing low introspection.

"Dave's" scores on several of Edwards' factors are clearly supported by his participation in the group (Chapter 6, p. 109). "Dave" had a high initiative score on Edwards' questionnaire. His initiation score in the group was also very high. "Dave" expressed a relatively high need for social approval. This need may have been expressed in "Dave's" persistent efforts to gain the group leader's attention and approval. His varied scores on ratings of school, teachers, and his ability to change the school reflect some of his mistrust of the environment. His defensive technique of dealing with the anxiety and mistrust he feels is to respond in a clearly positive or clearly negative manner.

Observations From The Groups

The main trend for exploration and school differences with respect to the dependent variables is summarized in Table 8.6. This table highlights patterns in the data regardless of their statistical significance. Using these data, the quality of the group interaction at the two schools and the differences in coping styles between high, moderate, and low explorers are now characterized.

School Differences In Interpersonal Behavior.   The group at Wayne was characterized by two subgroups — an active subgroup that participated frequently and initiated much of the interaction, and a quiet subgroup that directed most of its acts to the group leader. There was a high level of affective behavior, joking and teasing, in the group. This resulted in a greater amount of observed conflict in the group at Wayne than in the group at Thurston. With respect to the group leader, the boys at Wayne were likely to direct their affective expressions toward her in a teasing, bragging, or anxious manner. They were also likely to respond to her as a personal resource, asking questions about her role, her experiences as a graduate student, and her expectation of the group.

The group at Thurston tended to respond rather homogeneously to the group situation. There was a much more restricted range in participation and initiation than at Wayne. One group member who might have proven to be an extremely active participant only attended two of the seven recorded group sessions. Thus, his potentially active responses were not evidenced through most of the sessions. In general, there was a more even balance between affective and task-related interaction in the Thurston group. The affective behavior in this group was dominated by expressions of anxiety. The boys tended to be more preoccupied with the group leader and more selfconscious in their interaction with her than were the boys in the Wayne group. More of their hostile responses were directed to her than to the other group members. In general, the Thurston group's response to the situation was cooperative but skeptical. This reaction is well summarized by the response of one group member at Thurston to the question of whether the group experience should be included as a regular part of high school. He answered, "Yes, if somebody thinks it will change something." In general, the boys at Thurston were more reserved about the group and somewhat more sophisticated in differentiating it from their other daily experiences than the boys at Wayne.

The Relationship Between Preference For Exploration And Interpersonal Behavior.   The variability of behaviors within each exploration subgroup was usually too great to allow any clear differentiation by exploration groupings. The data did tend to suggest an interaction between exploration and school with respect to the group situation. The high explorers at Wayne and the low explorers at Thurston responded most enthusiastically to the group.

At Wayne, high explorers tended to be high participators. They also tended to be high initiators. Their affective style was characterized by a great deal of dramatizing and joking. During the videotape session, one high explorer asked, "Will we be on Channel 11? Can I wave to my mother?" They were the highest group in directing their remarks to the group leader.

The moderate explorers at Wayne took a middle position on these variables. They were unique in that they expressed more friendly acts and more discouraged acts than the other two groups. They appeared to be least involved in conflict. In fact, the moderate boys at Wayne tended to be the most work-oriented group members, trying to stick to the topic and keep the discussion moving along. In a discussion about families, one moderate explorer reminisced with the group about his trips to his uncle's orchard as a small child.

Low explorers tended to be low participators, low initiators, and low in their affective expression. They were highest in expressing hostility and joined the high explorers in engaging in conflict. Considering their lower level of participation, the quality of contentiousness appeared to be a strong characteristic of their style.

The pattern was quite different at Thurston. The high explorers appeared to be minimally involved in the group. They were low participators, low initiators, and low in expressing affect. They were also unlikely to get involved in conflict, and they made minimal contact with other group members.

The moderate explorers were moderate in participation, initiation, and affective expression. They tended to communicate hostility and discouragement more than the other two groups. One moderate explorer said that the most exciting thing he did last year was to "sit on the bench" for the baseball team. Moderates tended to direct the highest proportion of their acts to the leader. The moderates at Thurston were somewhat ambivalent about the group. They expressed more discomfort and hostility about their situation and about the group in general than did the other group members.

The low explorers appeared to be most involved with the group. They were high participators, high initiators, and high in affective expression. Their affective style was characterized by more friendliness and anxiety than the other two groups. During a discussion about the family, one low explorer told an elaborate story about his father. He raised the possibility that his father's identity had been hidden from him by his foster parents. In contrast to the high explorers at Wayne, the low explorers at Thurston were more focused on the other group members than on the leader. In many ways, the low explorers at Thurston were like the moderates at Wayne, except that they did not express as much discouragement.

The Usefulness Of The Discussion Group As A Source Of Data

The group situation provided data that reflected the developmental level of the boys, the social climate of the study schools, and the exploration preferences of the individual members. With respect to developmental level, the boys demonstrated very limited skills in group interaction. It was difficult, no matter what the subject matter, for them to maintain a conversation in which there was continuity between one person's comments and the next. The most frequently coded behaviors were Giving Opinions, Suggestions, and Orientation; and Dramatizing and Denial. Both of these types of behavior have an egocentric quality. The boys rarely demonstrated their ability to give support or encouragement to a peer or, for that matter, to criticize or disagree with a peer. The little hostility that was expressed in the group was directed at the group leader. The group was an opportunity for each boy to "grab the spotlight." If the boy was admired by others, he could continue or get others to join in. If his tale was too personal or if his status was low, he was interrupted or ignored.

The attempt to apply the same group method and observational techniques at both schools highlighted some unique qualities of the social climate at the two study schools. At Wayne, the techniques of group observation were more difficult to apply. Interactions happened rapidly; subgroup conversations competed with the mainstream of interaction; boys moved around the room, etc. The difficulty in using the observation techniques came about, primarily because the boys denied their existence or responded to them in a very counterphobic manner. One might even suggest that the boys' behaviors in the group were at a particularly high level as a defense against their feelings of being observed.

At Thurston, the methods were considerably easier to apply. The coders agreed that they had less difficulty following and coding interaction at Thurston. The difference may have been due in part to the fact that the method itself more seriously inhibited the boys at Thurston. Their response to the videotaped session suggests that their general reaction as a group may have been to hold back, to remain aloof and maintain their "cool" by focusing on the cognitive, rather than the affective, dimensions of the interaction. Stated more directly, at Wayne the group was involving and fun, but the observational methods were clumsy and difficult to apply. At Thurston, the observation went smoothly, and the group methodology worked well; but the group experience itself was not so satisfying for the members.

Finally, with respect to preferences for exploration, the data suggest that the boys with high preferences for exploration at Wayne and the boys with low preferences for exploration at Thurston responded most positively to the group situation. This outcome raises questions about the variable of exploration and its meaning in the two school environments. The two high explorers at Wayne who were particularly active group members tended to use the group as an opportunity to voice their own opinions and to attract attention and approval either from the leader or the other group members. The third explorer was a quiet and serious boy who seemed to be disappointed that the group took such a playful direction. His independence and more mature style may have caused him some discomfort in the group at Wayne. He would probably have been more comfortable and more active in the group at Thurston.

The behavior of these three boys in the group at Wayne suggests that the two active explorers may fit easily into the atmosphere of a school that invites involvement and high participation. The isolation of the third explorer suggests that boys who are more comfortable in an individual, private, low-display situation may feel passed by or devalued at Wayne. In a sense, the dominant culture at Wayne exerts a strong pressure to be "one of the gang." This pressure includes a strong element of denial and a facade of invulnerability that is often the sign of a premature resolution of an identity crisis. The two high explorers who participated in the group were not eager to question themselves but rather to display themselves. They were really looking not for close interaction with the other boys but rather for their public admiration.

At Thurston, the three low explorers shared the quality of enjoying the spotlight but in a far less intrusive manner than the two high explorers at Wayne. It was as if the group experience was unique for the low explorers at Thurston in that someone was really interested in them. These three boys were not particularly successful academically. They tended to be anxious about their difficulties in this domain. The group, because of its nonevaluating nature, was a place for them to share something of themselves and to be valued for who they were, rather than to be criticized for their limitations.

At Thurston, no strong effort is exerted to engage students in a visible role in the school life. Those students who want to participate can do so, but there do not appear to be many public rewards or sanctions for involvement. For the low explorers, Thurston may be a comfortable environment where they can remain on the sidelines as long as they want. On the other hand, their response to the group suggests that they would react favorably to some directed efforts to engage them.

IMPLICATIONS FOR PREVENTIVE INTERVENTIONS AND RESEARCH ON COPING STYLES

In general, the boys in both groups were just beginning to see themselves as adults. They had very little ability to envision themselves in any other situation than their present state. If there were no school, they thought they would probably enjoy lying around all day. They were not skilled in the art of group interaction. They had trouble listening to someone else's ideas and responding appropriately. They could not challenge or criticize each other in a nonpersonal way, nor could they offer each other much support or encouragement in their thoughts. In other words, they could not act in a facilitative role with one another. This limitation resulted in a continuing distance between the boys. Each boys's efforts to identify and solidify his ideas about maturity kept him somewhat isolated from his peers. In part, this distance may be due to the threat that intimacy with another male poses to an adolescent's fable of masculinity. Another explanation is that the boys did not have the skills or access to role models for engaging in the kind of communication that would give them an intimate view of another boy's world.

A Small Group Intervention

The response to the group at the two schools suggests that some kind of group setting to enhance self-esteem would be a valuable addition to the 10th-grade year at both schools, but that the group setting would have to be uniquely designed. The general success of the group at Wayne suggests that the boys would be highly motivated to participate in such a group, particularly if girls were included. At Wayne, the active, dramatic style of some of the boys tended to prevent other boys from participating. A discussion group at Wayne might easily be focused around the task of learning interpersonal skills. This might involve exercises in role playing, in expressing feelings of hostility and warmth directly, and in learning to listen and respond appropriately to another person's point of view.

The group would provide some continuous contact with a school adult in a nonacademic setting during the 1st year of high school. This contact would help those students who are less likely to actively engage adults in the school to feel accepted and valued by them. This setting would also provide an opportunity for students to voice their complaints and problems about school within a context that might allow for the expression of constructive solutions. Finally, the group would provide the students with a core of friends during the 1st year with whom they could develop their interpersonal skills and shed some of the artificiality of a pretense of maturity.

At Thurston, the suspicion and threat of intrusiveness was much greater than at Wayne. It took a much longer time for boys at Thurston to admit any of the other group members into their life space. A group experience at Thurston would probably need to be highly structured and nonevaluative. It might involve a group project like leveling the field, painting houses, or building toys for children at an orphanage. The focus for these groups would be on cooperation and interdependence. The interpersonal focus would be added after the group members began to know each other on an experiential level. An example of a group experience might be a 10th-grade year, 2 week wilderness camping trip where boys and girls learned about skills for survival in small groups of 10 or 12. This type of experience could provide the beginning for an identification with a small group of peers. Discussion sessions would profit from the authenticity of the contacts that took place in that first experience.

The group situation is a legitimate setting for social and emotional development. At both schools, these areas of personality development are influenced either deliberately or inadvertently by the norms for social interaction that function in each setting. The group provides a focus for these concerns both by students and faculty. The group could offer a bridge between the school's goals for intellectual development and for the growth of social responsibility and the student's needs for personal satisfaction.

Research In Adolescent Coping Styles

An unanticipated characteristic of the interaction in the two study groups was the frequent use of the dramatizing category. Joking, mimicking, and fantasizing were predominant in the boys' responses to one another and to the group leader. At both schools, the boys enjoyed entertaining each other with stories and tales that were clearly exaggerated or completely independent of reality. This quality of interpersonal behavior suggests that fantasy may have a critical function in the psychological development of adolescents. Caught as they are a long way from the experiences that society associates with adulthood, they use their imaginations to create images of themselves that replace infantile idealizations. Through fantasy, perhaps even more than through peer contacts, adolescents fight out the struggle between childhood and adulthood. It is the preoccupation with this fantasy world that is identified as immaturity. The present research suggests that a key to the development of an effective adaptive style is the ability to use fantasy as a tool for the resolution of one's ambivalences about growing up.

Another theme that was persistent in the group was the conflict between demonstrating one's autonomy and maintaining meaningful relationships with adults. On one hand, the boys respond very eagerly to teachers or other adults (the group is one example) who show an interest in them. They resent being pressured into a relationship, but they enjoy talking about themselves to a sympathetic adult. On the other hand, they perceive their parents and many of their teachers as adults from whom they hide most of the meaningful experiences in their lives. Their parents do not know where they go, what they do, or what they think. Their teachers do not know them. In general, they do not want to be with adults.

For some of the boys at Wayne, their relationships with their parents seem to have dwindled to almost no communication and very little time spent together. For these boys, the idea of autonomy is really irrelevant. They are independent because of circumstance, not because of a directed effort on their part to loosen the bonds of childhood. They are eager for attention and yet suspicious of rejection. Their relationships with adults are highly personalized.

At Thurston, the boys report their parents expect them to do chores, to baby-sit, or to spend time with them. What is missing in this interaction is the positive end of communication. The boys do not talk to their parents about their pleasures and pains. Their parents do not seem to balance their demands with concessions to their sons' increasing maturity. The boys at Thurston see their parents as intruders into their privacy. Their push for independence is a direct confrontation against very concrete demands. Consequently, they protect their independence more fervently. They keep their distance from adults by maintaining role relationships that have clearly structured prescriptions for behavior.

One implication of this expressed ambivalence about adults is a study of the evolution of student–adult relationships within the school setting. This aspect of adaptation might be particularly relevant for differentiating the strategies of persons with high, moderate, and low preferences of exploration within their school environments. There is a good deal of evidence from the present study and from other work that 10th-grade boys do not frequently conceptualize or bring about change. The link between exploration and change-oriented behaviors might, at best, begin to be observed by the 11th or 12th grade.

One direction for tracing the adaptive histories of high, moderate, and low explorers might be to describe the use they make of the human resources in their environments. The pattern of relationships the boys establish with the adults in the school, for example, could serve to highlight the active, independent quality of the high explorers or the reserved ambivalence of the moderate explorers. Which boys make friends with the school administration? Which boys know the cafeteria staff? Which boys have a relationship with the bus driver? How structured or informal are these relationships, and what needs or ends do they serve?

This line of investigation makes the notion of adaptation quite concrete within the school context. The quality of relationships and the specific school adults involved might easily change as the 3 years of high school go by. Tracing this change would provide some insight into the functions adults serve for different students. Following the changing pattern of relationships with school adults would also help to identify the evolving character of the boys' coping styles. The particular behavior of seeking out and interacting with school adults may be more compatible with all levels in the life of high school students than is the path toward innovation and change.

REFERENCES

Bales, F. F. *Personality and interpersonal behavior.* New York: Holt, Rinehart and Winston, 1970.

Mann, R. D., Gibbard, G. S., & Hartman, J. J. *Interpersonal styles and group development.* New York: Wiley, 1967.

Newman, B. M. *Interpersonal behavior and preferences for exploration in adolescent boys: A small group study.* Unpublished doctoral dissertation, the University of Michigan, 1971.

9 Exploratory Behavior of Adolescents in a Dyadic, Problem-Solving Situation

William H. Jones[1]

Institute for Social Research
The University of Michigan

INTRODUCTION

The present study investigates the relationship between preference for social exploration (Edwards, 1970) and actual exploratory behavior. Pairs of high school boys were asked in a seminatural school situation to prepare solutions to realistic school problems. Their recorded verbal interaction in the preparation of the solutions was rated in terms of social exploration. For example, a person with high preference for social exploration would be expected to propose relatively more solutions and solution elaborations. He might also be expected to be more receptive to input from the other pair member.

In this study there are four types of variables.

1. Exploration preference, as measured by questionnaire, is a predisposition to certain types of behavior and as such is a *personality construct*.
2. Exploratory behavior, as measured by verbal interaction ratings, is a *behavioral construct*. These dependent variables were derived from the situation itself via pilot testing.
3. The pair composition variables are on the *interpersonal—situational level*.
4. The school variable is a *cultural—organizational* or macroenvironmental level.

Probably as important as, or more important than, any of these variables in isolation are the interactions that occur between them. Structuring this study in terms of these levels of analysis is more than hedging one's bets; it is more than

---

[1]Present address: Desert Community Mental Health Center, Palm Springs, California.

avoiding the narrow perspective dilemma of the blind men and the elephant. It allows an ecological perspective of the problem. Appreciation is given to the variety of determinants of human behavior and the complexity of their interactions. Kelly (1967, 1969, 1971); Trickett, Kelly, and Todd (1972); Pervin (1968), and Yinger (1965) have all made good cases for the usefulness and illumination of this multideterminant, interactive approach.

Rationale for the present study: Most of the research in this volume utilizes survey or interview methods and, accordingly, suffers the biases and limitations of self-report methods. Only Barbara Newman in Chapter 8 actually deals directly with behavior (small group discussion), and her work is limited by small sample size. The present study thus attempts to fill a gap in this body of research dealing with social exploration by focusing on "real" behavior in a controlled situation. This approach allows us to examine the relationship between preference for exploration as a coping style and actual exploratory behavior, in this case the behavior occurring in the verbal interaction of subject pairs. Use of the dyad allows us to closely examine the interpersonal aspects of exploration without introducing the almost hopeless complexity brought about by the use of larger groups. The present study investigates the possible interactive effects of exploration preference; for example, will a high explorer interact differently in relevant ways with a low explorer than he will with another high explorer? And will the school environment influence the type and amount of exploratory behavior manifested in the problem-solving situation?

CONCEPTS

Social exploration has been the phenomenon studied in this volume in order to get at the person—environment interface. Edwards (1971, and in this volume) has discussed the meaning of social exploration as measured by his questionnaire. This concept seems to be most closely linked to the student's initiation and personal involvement in the school. Accordingly, it is directly related to the student's self-esteem, school satisfaction, and absence of social problems.

Social exploration is of particular interest, because it appears to be so significant for adaptation. People who use this as part of their coping repertoire will tend to have a better grasp of their social environment. They will know where their social resources are and how to make use of them. This mapping of resources is closely related to *anticipation*, which is a significant coping method used by adolescents. The development in adolescence of the cognitive capacity for formal operations allows the adolescent to engage in thoughts of hypothetical situations (Flavell, 1963).

Social exploration thus has important adaptive consequences. Its exercise provides information about the student's environment useful for both immediate coping efforts and anticipatory cognitive coping (rehearsing). By its nature, social exploration provides an active, initiating style to coping. This will be most adaptive where the person has to contend with change. In static environments, social exploration will be less adaptive or perhaps even maladaptive — leading others to view the explorer as a maverick or troublemaker. This is the thesis of Kelly (1966, 1967, 1969, 1970; Kelly et al., 1971) — that environments differentially reinforce exploration and that socialization factors can strongly facilitate or discourage social exploration. The two schools of the present study do provide some environmental differences that could influence the manifestation of a preference for social exploration.

A *group problem-solving* situation was chosen for the present research. With representative school problems assigned, the task amounted to anticipatory coping. Actual group problem solving and anticipatory problem solving of school-related problems are common adolescent events and significant adaptive efforts. Social exploration came into play in two ways: (a) in social engagement of the dyad partner and use of him as a resource in the problem-solving situation; (b) in students' verbal behavior (such as presenting information) as reflected in the solution of the problem.

The literature of problem solving and decision making offers little that is directly relevant to the present research. In particular, nothing exists concerning adolescent, dyadic, problem solving. However, some findings do bear on the present research problem. Collins and Guetzkow (1964), in their general review of group problem solving, make the summary statement that a person who has been successful in the past and who has a reputation for competence will have power and influence over other group members. The work of Bales et al. (1951) also suggests that well-liked, dominant persons who are perceived as competent will tend to influence others and probably to be less influenced themselves by others.

Kelley and Thibaut (1969), in their review of the group problem-solving literature, focus on the exchange of *information*. They indicate that there is good and sufficient evidence for predecision information-seeking. They posit that when one's outcome (solution or cognitive mastery of the problem) falls below one's comparison level for outcomes (aspiration), one will engage in information seeking. Persons with higher comparison levels, likely to engage in information seeking, tend to be outgoing, confident, and with high power. Information seeking is related, Kelley and Thibaut (1969) go on to say, to internal locus of control, which involves an information orientation to tasks, responsiveness to task cues, and frequent information-seeking behavior. Social exploration preference, it should be noted, has a low but positive correlation with internal locus of control (Kelly et al., 1971).

Kelly and Thibaut (1969) go on to point out an apparent interaction between ability level and problem difficulty in their effects on information exchange. Goldman (1965), using a relatively easy task, found in the group problem-solving condition that the bright subjects were able to reach the solution on their own and did not contribute to each other. The dull subjects did contribute to each other. Laughlin and Johnson (1966), using a more difficult task, obtained opposite results. The bright subjects interacted significantly more than the dull ones did.

There is some available evidence that bears on the effect of *homogeneity* vs. *heterogeneity* of attitudes and personality characteristics on group problem solving. Hoffman (1959) found that college student groups heterogeneous in terms of personality did better on a difficult, objective problem than did homogeneous groups. He found no difference between the two types of groups in the time taken to reach a solution. There was a nonsignificant tendency for the heterogeneous groups to develop more inventive solutions. Triandis, Hall, and Ewen (1965) investigated heterogeneity for attitudes and ability in problem-vsolving groups. They found that dyads with heterogeneous attitudes and homogeneous ability levels were more creative than dyads heterogeneous or homogeneous on both regards.

Collins and Guetzkow (1964) summarized the literature regarding personality and attitude heterogeneity and their relation to group problem solving. They concluded that group heterogeneity can lead to difficulty in building interpersonal relationships, conflict, less effective division of labor, lower social rewards, and lower group cohesiveness. These effects are most likely when: (a) the dimensions of the differences are directly relevant to the interpersonal relationships of the group; and (b) when the task requires elaborate interpersonal relationships.

Collins and Guetzkow (1964) state that under some conditions, heterogeneity can lead to greater group problem-solving potential; that is, more alternatives are provided, biases cancel out, wider critical bases exist. These beneficial effects are most likely to occur when the dimensions of difference are relevant to the task and when the task is difficult.

Familiarity of problem-solving group members with each other has been demonstrated to affect problem-solving performance. Hall and Williams (1966), using managers as subjects in a social judgment task, found established groups to be more effective and creative than ad hoc groups. Goldberg and Maccoby (1965) compared problem solving of second-grade children on a tower-building task. They found that problem-solving experience with the same individuals led to more efficient problem-solving behavior than experience with a variety of individuals.

The above review described the group problem-solving literature relevant to the present research effort. There is some difficulty in integrating this literature, because of the diverse characteristics of the subjects, especially age; the differing perceptual, motor, cognitive, and social tasks; and the differing instructional sets. In spite of these problems, the results in regard to social influence, information exchange, group homogeneity, and familiarity are fairly consistent or can be ordered sensibly. Unfortunately, there is a dearth of group problem-solving research using adolescents as subjects, and thus we cannot be as sure as we might of the relevance of these results to the present research problem. The tendency to use quality of solution rather than indices of group processes as dependent variables likewise limits the relevance of this literature to the present problem.

There is a last, nagging reservation about the group problem-solving literature, and that is the comparability of problem solving in the laboratory to problem solving in the real world. As Brown (1965) noted, the existence of the risky shift is certainly news to anyone who has sat through many board (bored?) meetings. It is impossible to evaluate the seriousness of this reservation, because few studies have been of actual, nonhypothetical, problem-solving behavior in its natural settings.

SOME COMMENTS ON RESEARCH METHODS

The research on coping and adaptation tends to use survey methods (such as Silber, Coelho, et al., 1961) or natural observation (such as Murphy, 1962). Survey methods are economical and tidy but present the biases of self-report data. Natural observation provides valid and representative results, but this method is usually difficult, unwieldy, and time consuming. In addition, there are problems in isolating and manipulating variables. A further problem with research employing natural observation in the area of coping is that the findings tend to be idiosyncratic, difficult to compare to other findings, and noncumulative. Weick (1968) suggests modifying settings in ways to help the observer utilize explicit behavioral measures and ease the difficulty of deciding which category a behavior belongs to. By these subtle modifications of the setting, the advantages of natural observation are preserved, and some of the disadvantages are removed.

Research on the cognitive aspects of coping, including problem solving, tends to use laboratory methods. These provide the obvious advantages of isolation and manipulation of independent variables and the possibility of experimental controls. Because this type of research also tends to be concept oriented rather than purely inductive, the results tend to add up and build on each other. Unfortunately, the laboratory can have an unrealistic and unrepresentative climate. The naturally occurring and powerfully influential person–setting and individual–group units are often unavoidably disrupted.

The main study here, (Kelly, 1967, 1969, 1970; Kelly et al., 1971) has used the multitrait–multimethod approach of Campbell and Fiske (1959) to achieve convergent and discriminant validation. Initial guiding concepts were used, but these were revised and given new empirically derived meanings as the research results accrued. The present study is experimental in terms of variable control and use of standardized setting and tasks. On the other hand, the tasks and setting are realistic for the subjects, and they are allowed a considerable range of behavior within the setting. The study is exploratory, involving new ground with little previous relevant research to guide hypotheses. At the same time, the study is rationally designed with concepts leading to measures. Weick (1968) states that the rational method is more appropriate and safer when it has been preceded by more inductive steps, as indeed occurred with the main study. The problem with rationally derived studies that is alleviated by preceding inductive, empirical work is that when they do not pan out, it is difficult to know why. It may be because of imprecise concepts or problems in their translation to measures.

My first preference was for a completely naturalistic study. Looking at social exploration in its natural habitat as an approach seemed to hold the most validity. I began to wonder about such things as how an adolescent high explorer would go about getting a school parking sticker from a limited supply. Would a low explorer tend to handle it differently? Would they already, before the problem presented itself, have assimilated different kinds and amounts of parking-sticker-relevant information? Would they already have perceptual and cognitive sets relevant to social exploration that would influence how they sought to get that sticker or whether they would even try?

Clearly there is much stress and even some opportunities in a high school. As a corollary, there must be a lot of coping going on, including that in a social exploration style. The problem was how to get at it. I began to sour on the naturalistic approach. Considerations deterred me that would not have deterred Robert Coles or the early Margaret Mead. In a high school, there is the outside-observer-as-sore-thumb phenomenon to contend with. Especially in trying to observe social exploration, there are problems getting observations that allow one to make comparisons across subjects. Simulation as an approach seemed the next best thing.

Gradually, the research design evolved to the present one, and the variables were selected. The present design is a compromise, providing the controls and statistical possibilities of a truly experimental design. At the same time, a simulated and somewhat realistic problem-solving setting was developed in which the natural styles of adolescent interaction might be expected to emerge.

Variables

Social exploration preference (EP) was retained as an independent variable. This variable is, of course, a personality variable. Because social exploration manifests itself predominantly in social situations, some attention was required for the characteristics of those situations. Of particular interest were the EPs of other persons in the setting. The type of dyad was selected as an independent variable on the situational—interpersonal level. Dyads consisted of homogenous high EP, homogenous medium EP, homogenous low EP, or mixed high and low EP. Would high EP boys deal with the situations differently, depending on whether their partner was similar or dissimilar in this regard, etc.? School, a variable on the organization—cultural level, was also used as an independent variable, as the school's organizational characteristics might be expected to influence student interaction as well as the students' perceptions and knowledge of the school.

The study remains an exploratory one that attempts to find out the differential effects of these independent variables on the verbal interaction and problem-solving processes of high school boys. The dependent variables, ratings of aspects of their verbal interaction, were chosen without the benefit of much previous empirical research. The solution variables measure the amount and diversity of problem solutions and solution components. They presumably tap something close to the heart of the cognitive structuring of effective coping. The input variables (information, opinion, suggestion) include the substantive contributions of the subjects to the task. They reflect knowledge and cognitive structuring of the environment, probably the cumulative results of the use of social exploration as a coping style. The input request variables tap the subject's overt use of his partner as a resource, perhaps the essence of social exploration. The other dependent variables had no strongly persuasive conceptual links to the independent variables but were included because they measure quite salient phenomena in the interaction. The grouping of the dependent variables presented here is thus conceptual. A list of dependent and independent variables is found in Table 1.

In most cases, the variable names clearly describe the phenomena they represent. Three are not so clear. "Suggestion" refers to nontask-oriented suggestions only, excluding solutions. "Interaction control" occurs when a student attemps to control the direction of the discussion. This phenomenon has a tendency to

TABLE 9.1
Principle Variables

Independent variables:	1. Exploration preference — low, medium, high
	2. Dyad Type — LL, MM, HH, Mixed (HL)
	3. School (2)
Dependent variables:	
Solution variables	4. Initial solution proposed
	5. Alternate solution proposed
	6. Solution elaboration
Input variables	7. Opinion given
	8. Information given
	9. Suggestion given
Input request variables	10. Opinion requested
	11. Information requested
	12. Suggestion requested
Reaction-to-other variables	13. Agreement
	14. Disagreement
Interaction direction variables	15. Discussion initiated
	16. Interaction control
	17. Attempts to close discussion
	18. Attempts to control relation of solution
Involvement variables	19. Words
	20. Time

close off or limit by fiat the ohter directions the discussion can go in. Examples are: "Let's get back on the track." "Wait a second, how about. . ." Attempts to control relation of solution occurs when a dyad member tries to determine which of the partners will relate their problem solution to the experimenter.

Solution variables (initial solution, alternate solution, solution elaboration). Exploration — that is, indicated preference for diversity, change, and innovation and perception of self as change-agent — should relate to the range of problem solutions. EP should be related to knowledge of the details and dynamics of the social environment as a cumulative result of the use of this coping style. This environmental knowledge should make solution formation easier and therefore be directly related to number of solutions proposed.

Input variables (opinion, information, suggestion).   These variables, like the following input request variables, are taken from Bales (1970). The behavior measured by these input variables tends strongly here to be task oriented. Together with the solution variables, they comprise the task-relevant and substantive content of the interpersonal style of the subject such as assertiveness, productivity, task directedness, and ascendancy.

The *input request* variables (opinion request, information request, suggestion request) will to some extent tap exploratory behavior. In these instances, the input requests would be explorations of the social environment, gathering relevant data from the dyad partner to facilitate coping with the presented task. Sometimes these input requests reflect behavior that is task directed but passive, compliant, dependent, and deferent.

Reaction to other variables (agreement and disagreement) will probably tap passive—compliant or counterdependent interpersonal behavior. People who score high here will tend not to be active participators in terms of showing high involvement, high solution input, or other task input.

Interaction direction variables (discussion initiated, interaction control, attempts to close discussion, attempts to control relation of solution) are a heterogeneous bunch. They have to do with exerting control over the direction of the interaction. Initiating the discussion and interaction control will tend to be characteristic of assertive, ascendant, dominant subjects high in initiative. Attempts to close the discussion and attempts to control who relates the solution, on the other hand, are probably similar to reaction-to-other variables. They are characteristic of subjects who respond in passive or counterdependent ways. These variables reflect the control and competition that seem so marked in peer relations for early male adolescents.

The *involvement* variables (number of words, time) would mirror the subject's (a) situation involvement; (b) verbal facility; and (c) the upward and forward interpersonal style, in the sense of Bales (1970). The involvement variable does not necessarily reflect the subject's knowledge of the school environment.

Table 1 and the foregoing show the conceptual grouping of the dependent variables. In addition, a factor analysis was performed, following the suggested procedure of Nunnally (1967). The analysis produced five factors, which together accounted for 78.8% of the variance. The initial factor accounted for 39.0% of the variance. The orthogonal factors were rotated by the varimax method and are described as new variables as follows:

Heavyweight problem solving.   This factor by its loading shows task orientation (alternate solution, opinion), ascendancy and dominance (alternate solution, interaction control), and positive involvement of the partner (opinion request).

Information–verbality.   This factor shows involvement with information (giving and requesting information). It might be called preparatory problem solving. It shows attention to detail (information, information request, words, and time). It is task oriented (opinion) but not necessarily in a direct, solution-oriented way.

Suggestion.   This factor is loaded highest for suggestion and suggestion request. The factor probably reflects off-the-target problem-solving efforts. Keep in mind that the variable suggestion does not include task-oriented "suggestions" (alternate solution, solution elaboration). A suggestion request can amount to effectively utilizing one's partner, but it often reflects passivity and submission. So this factor probably reflects less effective problem solving than the first two.

Lightweight contributions.   This factor is heavily loaded for solution elaboration, which is task oriented, but in a less crucial way than is alternate solution. Solution elaboration is sometimes valuable as an elaboration of the solution. At other times, it is more like jumping on the bandwagon. This factor is loaded for agreement, which shows a positive, supportive regard for the partner. Agreement tends to be indirectly task oriented in varying degrees. There is a substantial loading also for attempts to control relation of solution, which is probably a compensatory behavior. These three variables in this factor are all probably more or less constructive things to say when you do not know something better to say.

Disagreement.   The last factor loads heavily only on one dependent variable, disagreement.

Predictions

School effects.   Because of the perceived greater influence of students at Wayne Memorial High School, the school's clearer norms and options, and its greater flexibility, the students at Wayne should be able to bring more information and ideas from their past school experiences to the problems and should be able to deal with those problems with less of a sense of futility, hence greater involvement. These factors will outweigh the probable counteracting effects of verbal skills; students at Lee M. Thurston High School could be assumed to have greater verbal skills related to the higher socioeconomic levels of their parents. Therefore, Wayne should be higher than Thurston for solution, input, and involvement variables and should also be higher for the factor variables, heavyweight problem solving, information–verbality, and suggestion (see Table 2).

Exploration effects.   High exploration-preference (EP) subjects, because of their histories, will bring a larger fund of relevant experiences to the problem-solving task. Because of these past experiences and because of the behavioral predisposition of the high EP to seek change and diversity, the high EP could be expected to deal with the problem-solving situation with greater involvement, thoroughness, and competence.

Therefore, a direct relationship is posited between EP and the solution, input, and involvement variables, as well as for the factor variables — heavyweight

TABLE 9.2
Predictions

School effects		
Hypothesis	1:	School 1 $>$ School 2 for solution variables
	2:	School 1 $>$ School 2 for input variables
	3:	School 1 $>$ School 2 for involvement variables
	4:	School 1 $>$ School 2 for heavyweight problem solving
	5:	School 1 $>$ School 2 for information–verbality
	6:	School 1 $>$ School 2 for combined suggestion
Exploration effects	7:	H $>$ M $>$ L for solution variables
	8:	H $>$ M $>$ L for input variables
	9:	H $>$ M $>$ L for involvement variables
	10:	H $>$ M $>$ L for heavyweight problem solving
	11:	H $>$ M $>$ L for information–verbality
	12:	H $>$ M $>$ L for combined suggestion
	13:	H $>$ M $>$ L for input request variables
	14:	H $<$ M $<$ L for reaction-to-other variables
	15:	H $>$ M $>$ L for initiative variables
	16:	H $>$ M $>$ L for interaction-control
	17:	H $<$ M $<$ L for attempts to close discussion and attempts to control relation of solution
School–exploration interaction effects		
	18:	Interaction effects for solution variables and input variables
Dyad effects	19:	Mixed $>$ LL, MM, HH for variance on dependent variables
	20:	Mixed intermediate between HH and LL for dependent variables
	21:	H and L in Mixed will converge for dependent variables compared to HH and LL

problem solving, information—verbality, and suggestion (high EP > medium EP > low EP).

The high EP could be expected to maximally utilize his opportunities for exploration in a setting. In a problem-solving situation, he could be expected to bring his predilection for exploratory behavior to bear. He would engage his social environment so as to gather relevant data and ideas for plans to meet the problem. So, a direct relationship should exist between EP and the input request variables.

Agreement and disagreement in the problem-solving situation will tend to be expressed by those who are contributing relatively little in terms of solution efforts. The pilot study suggested that agreement tends to be used as filler by those who do not otherwise have much to say relevant to the problem solving, but who want to say something. Disagreement will probably tend to be obstructive, being used as a way to influence the problem-solving interaction and salvage self-esteem without having to contribute anything substantive. EP will be inversely related to the reaction-to-other variables.

In regard to the interaction direction variables, high EPs would be expected to score high on those reflecting initiative and task involvement. Low EPs would be more likely to focus their interaction direction efforts in more picayune directions where less mastery of the problem-solving task was required. Therefore, a direct relationship should exist between EP and initiate discussion, initial solution, and interaction control. However, an inverse relationship should exist for attempts to close discussion and attempts to control relation of solution.

School—exploration interaction effects.   The descriptions of the two schools suggest that a high EP student would fit better at Wayne. The flexibility, clearer norms and options, and perceived greater influence of students at Wayne would appear to provide more opportunities for adaptation for high EPs. The rigidity, ambiguity, and lack of influence at Thurston would perhaps leave high EPs demoralized; it would be difficult for them to express their exploration in a sanctioned manner within their school. The converse could be expected for low EPs. They would be expected to fare better at Thurston than at Wayne. It would be reasonable, then, to expect that school and exploration preference would affect in an interacting way the problem-solving dyad interaction. In particular, this interaction effect should be expected in the solution and in the input variables, as these two sets of variables are probably most directly relevant to the problem solving.

Dyad composition effects.   In the study there are four different types of dyads: homogeneous high EP, medium EP, low EP, and mixed high—low EP. In the homogeneous groups, similarities exist for interaction style and cognitive style. These similarities between the dyad members will lead to mutual reinforcement of behavioral predispositions. For the mixed dyads, differences will exist for interaction style and cognitive style. These differences, on one hand, could lead to protracted and possibly conflictful interactions. On the other hand, these dissimilarities might be perceived as too great to handle in a short time span, and the interaction might be abbreviated and muted. A prediction is thus rather hazardous, although it might be safe to hypothesize that variances would be higher for mixed dyads on the dependent variables than for the various homogeneous dyad types.

Perhaps a more intriguing question is: If the high EP and the low EP affect each other's performance in the mixed dyad, which way is the effect? Dyad sum scores for the mixed dyads would be expected to be intermediate between the homogeneous high EP and low EP dyad, even if the members of the mixed dyad did not affect each other. Probably there is mutual influence, because of behavioral expectations, social reinforcement, modeling, cohesion building, etc. A convergence of some sort should be expected. For example, low EPs in the mixed dyad would act more like high EPs than their counterparts in the homogeneous low EP dyads. So mixed dyads should be at intermediate levels on the dependent variables between the homogeneous high and low dyads. And with the mixed dyad, the high and low members should converge.

Method

Sample.   The two *schools* have been described. They are fairly similar, suburban high schools with differences in terms of SES and organizational climate.

The *subjects* were 100 10th-grade boys, 50 each from the two schools. These students were selected from the larger, representative main study sample, which was based on the exploration preference scale (Edwards, 1970). For each school, 10 medium EP, 20 high EP, and 20 low EP subjects were randomly chosen as subjects for the present study. For each school, the subjects were arranged into 5 pairs each of homogeneous high, medium, and low EP subjects and 10 pairs of mixed high–low EP subjects.

Procedure.   The subject pair was brought to the research setting by a student volunteer and seated. The experimenter introduced himself and briefly explained the aims of study and what would be asked of them. Then they were asked to participate; all agreed.

The instructions were then given. The dyads were given three typical school problem situations, one at a time, and were asked to discuss them and come to a joint solution. While the dyads were discussing the problem, the experimenter left the area. He remained out of earshot of the subjects but near enough to be easily signaled. When the dyad indicated that they were through with their strategy session, the experimenter returned. He wrote down the solution as the dyad related it. This procedure was repeated for each of the three problems. The entire interaction was recorded by a visible but unobtrusively placed recorder.

Following the problem solving, the dyad members were separated and were individually asked several questions about their perceptions of and their reactions to the experiment.

At Thurston, the *setting* was a small, informal room used as a sort of student lounge; at certain hours it also served as a sanctioned gripe forum. The experimenter waited in an adjacent antechamber while the subject pair interacted.

At Wayne, the student lounge was used as the experimental setting. This is a large room furnished with comfortable, overstuffed chairs and couches. The pair interaction took place on one side of the room, and the experimenter waited at the opposite end, well out of earshot for normal conversations.

The *problem situations* that the student pairs jointly resolved were developed and chosen with the consultation of research staff members, field coordinators, teachers, and students. They were tested in a pilot study and later modified. They were intended to be realistic and representative of the dilemmas that students occasionally find themselves in at these two schools. The problem situations are: (a) what to do when one cannot get into a drivers' education class because of a lost application and resulting snafu; (b) how to help a friend who has been evicted from school as a result of an unwilling involvement in a fight; (c) how to start a scuba diving club in the school.

Coding. The problem-solving interactions of the dyads were transcribed from the tape recordings. The mean number of estimated missing words per subject was 10.59, 3.43% of the total identified words. There was relatively little trouble in identifying and distinguishing between the dyad's voices; thus, transcription was accomplished without much difficulty.

The transcripts were scored for all 16 dependent variables. A category was coded each time the corresponding phenomenon occurred. A communication unit could only be scored in one way. Scoring was by phenomenon units rather than by time units. For example, if a solution were proposed, whether by 5 or 50 words, it was only scored once. Repeats and redundancies were not scored.

Three coders were used who were experienced in similar tasks. They were trained in several sessions. The coding was done blindly, without the coder being aware of the standing of the subjects in the independent variables. After the transcripts were all coded, about 25% (14 of the total 50) were selected randomly and coded again by a different coder in order to measure reliability of the coding procedures.

Data analysis. The basic plan was to use a two-way analysis of variance, with schools and exploration as independent variables. If the subjects within dyads turned out to be strongly correlated on the dependent variables, then the analysis would have to be on dyad sum scores with dyad type rather than exploration as the second independent variable. Comparison of variances (hypothesis 13) involves an F test. Comparisons with the mixed group (H vs. L) and the comparisons mixed H vs. HH and mixed L vs. LL (hypothesis 15) require t tests.

Results

The intercoder correlations indicate satisfactorily high *coding reliability* coefficients for many of the dependent variables. Initial solution, solution elaborations,
opinion given, suggestion given, opinion request, suggestion request, agreement,
discussion initiated, and words all have reliability coefficients in the .80s and
.90s. This is certainly satisfactory, given the nature of the coding task. Moderately
high reliability coefficients, in the .60s and .70s, were found for information
given, interaction control, and attempts to close. Disappointingly low coefficients, in the .40s, were found for alternate solutions, information request,
disagreement, and attempts to control who relates the solution. Some confusion
for coders is indicated between solution elaborations and alternate solutions and
also between the input variables.

Many of the phenomena measured by these variables occur infrequently in
the interactions. Several of the variables have a median of zero, indicating that
the respective behaviors occurred with less than half the subjects. This is the case
for suggestion given, opinion requested, information requested, suggestion requested, disagreement, interaction control, and attempts to control relation of
solution. In addition, the variables tend to be skewed to the right. This skewness
is particularly characteristic of variables 5 through 12, 14, 16, and 18.

Concurrence within the dyad.   Subjects within the dyad were randomly
assigned to category 1 or category 2. These categories were tested for correlations between dyad members on the dependent variables. The correlations were
generally positive, and many attained statistical significance.

Since there is substantial concurrence within the dyads, it follows that the
individual scores have not been independently measured. This violates a basic
rule for the analysis of variance. For this reason, it was decided to use the dyad
sum score for the main analysis. The distributions of the sum scores have greater
ranges and tend to be more normally distributed. For these reasons, also, they
are superior to the individual scores for statistical analysis.

The matter of verbal facility.   Most of the dependent variables, as it turned
out, correlated positively and significantly with number of words. The question
presented itself, do these verbal interaction measures reflect only verbal intelligence? There is probably a necessary relationship between the number of words
used in the interaction and the other dependent variables. If a subject presents
many solutions, opinions, information, etc., he will need to use a certain number
of words to convey these elements. If he presented no solutions, opinions, information, etc. in the interaction, he would need to use fewer words and probably
would use fewer words.

To assess the effects of verbal intelligence, correlations were examined between the dependent variables and several measures that might bear on verbal

intelligence. These measures, which were fortunately available, included Hennon–Nelson I.Q. (Thurston), Lorge–Thorndike I.Q. (Wayne), Raven's Progressive Matrices (IQ), G.P.A., Duncan SES for the head of the student's household. The number of words in the interaction correlates significantly only with the Lorge–Thorndike I.Q. ($r = -.240$) and with SES ($r = .222$). It appears, then, that the number of words is not directly related to these accepted measures of verbal ability. A small portion of the correlations between these auxiliary measures and the dependent variables were significant, but they were all quite low. The largest was $r = .380$, thus accounting for less than 16% of the variance between the two variables. Some of the significant correlations may have been spurious, as they tended not to hold up across schools.

Control variables.   It turned out that the relationships between the dependent variables and partner knowledge were curvilinear. For example, it was found that those who did not know each other talked least, good friends talked more, and acquaintances talked most. Partner knowledge as a variable held little intrinsic interest, considering the goals of the study. However, if unaccounted for, it threatened to obscure or confuse the results of the study.

It was decided that the optimum solution was to use partner knowledge as an independent variable. Since there were only five dyads who regarded themselves as good friends, use of this as a category led to empty cells in the analysis of variance design. Unfortunately, computer programs at my disposal were unequipped to handle empty cells. The best solution appeared to be combining the good friends and acquaintances categories. Thus, partner knowledge as an independent variable had two categories:

1. Neither partner knew each other.
2. The partners were either acquaintances or good friends.

This preserved most of the variance that partner knowledge accounted for in the dependent variables.

The two other control variables, perceived situation reality and perceived story reality, are really not control variables, because they are likely to be the results of treatment effects. At any rate, these two variables do not correlate significantly with any of the dependent variables. There are no indications of nonlinear relationships, either.

The main analysis.   The main analysis was a three-way analysis of variance, the independent variables being dyad type, school, and partner knowledge. Skewness for some of the variables led to significant differences between cell variances, as measured by the Box test. To satisfy the equal variance assumption for the analysis of variance, a log transformation was used where necessary, following the advice of Dixon and Massey (1969), Snedecor and Cochran (1967), and Blalock (1960). For several of the variables, the ranges were quite restricted; and the corresponding behavior did not occur at all for many of the dyads. For these variables, the data were recoded into two categories, occurrence and non-occurrence of the measured phenomena. X^2 was used for these variables rather than the analysis of variance. Results of the main analysis are shown in Table 3.

School effects.   The obtained school differences were predominantly in the direction opposite that predicted. Two of these differences were statistically significant, for opinions and for the factor variable, heavyweight problem solving. Only for the variable solution elaboration was the obtained difference in the predicted direction.

Exploration (dyad type) effects.   Significant differences were obtained for opinion, words, and combined input. In each case, there was a direct relation-ship between EP and these dependent variables, with the mixed dyad type per-forming in a manner similar to the L—L dyads. A direct relationship (HH > MM > LL) with insignificant differences was found for interaction control, combined input, combined input request, combined interaction direction, heavyweight problem solving, and information—verbality. With the exception of alternate solution, the other hypothesized relationships stood up (albeit nonsignifi-cantly) in respect to the order of the HH and LL dyads but not in respect to the order of the MM dyads. The mixed dyads generally performed similarly to the LL dyads. None of the hypothesized inverse relationships was found. Few of the findings here were significant, but most were in the hypothesized direction, at least for L—L and H—H dyads.

School-interaction effects.   None of the findings here was significant. This was also the case for partner-knowledge effects.

Dyad composition effects.   The mixed H—L dyads did not show greater variance than the homogeneous dyads, contrary to what was hypothesized. Again contrary to hypotheses, the mixed dyad was usually not intermediate be-tween the H—H and L—L dyads on the dependent variables. The average order was in fact H—H > M—M > L—L > Mixed.

There is some evidence of a conversion effect. Hs and Ls within the mixed dyad were compared, using the paired t test. For variables with very limited ranges, McNemar's Test for Correlated Proportions (Siegel, 1956) was used. In no case were significant differences found. Thus Hs and Ls tend to perform similarly in the mixed dyad. High EP subjects did give more alternate solutions and more total solutions (initial solutions and alternate solutions [$p < .145$]), more information requests ($p < .09$), more interaction control, and more initia-tion of discussion ($p < .072$). These differences are in the directions that we would hypothesize, but they are all statistically insignificant.

TABLE 9.3
Main Analysis

Variable	Dyad Effects F	Dyad Effects X²	School Effects F	School Effects X²	Partner Knowledge Effects F	Dyad X School Effects F	Log transformation Used
5. alternate solution	1.510		1.216		3.235	.206	
6. solution elaboration	.714		1.552		1.375	2.566	
7. opinion	4.229*		5.461*		3.599	.555	x *p < .05
8. information	2.089		.712		–	.724	x
9. suggestion	–	.559	–	1.299	–	–	
10. opinion request	.960		2.886		.097	.373	x
11. information request	1.123		2.642		.741	.573	x
12. suggestion request	.832		.064		.002	1.647	x
13. agreement	1.569		.046		.017	.733	
14 disagreement	–	.440	–	0	–	–	
16. interaction control	–	2.871	–	2.000	–	–	
17. attempts to close	1.504		1.301		1.994	1.331	
18. attempts to control relation	–	1.850	–	.095	–	–	
19. words	3.076*		2.249		3.435	1.564	
20. time	2.047		1.051		.724	1.449	x
24. combined solution	1.010		.384		2.416	1.574	
25. combined input	3.208*		2.935		3.713	.580	x
26. combined input request	.697		3.778		.324	1.893	x
27. combined interaction direction	.790		3.384		1.767	1.032	
28. heavyweight problem solving	1.714		4.424*		1.902	.193	x
29. information–verbality	2.038		3.143		.636	.877	x
30. suggestion	.388		.019		.161	.785	x
31. lightweight contributions	1.003		1.155		.532	2.151	
df =	3 & 34	3	1 & 34	1	1 & 34	3 & 34	
level necessary for p < .05	2.89	7.82	4.13	3.84	4.13	2.89	

167

To complete the analysis of the dyad effects, tests were made to determine whether low EPs in the mixed groups performed differently than low EPs in the L−L dyads and whether high EPs in the mixed groups were different from those in the H−H groups. Student t tests were used for this analysis. For variables that had a median of zero, the scale was changed to 0−1, occurrence−nonoccurrence, and the chi-square test was used. There were three significant differences for the comparison L (mixed) vs. L−L. Those in L−L dyad type had more alternate solutions, total solutions, and information requests.

For the comparison H (mixed) vs. H−H, there were five significant differences. High EPs in the mixed dyad type gave more suggestion requests, whereas those in the H−H type gave more opinions, more combined input, more words, and more information−verbality.

It appears that the mixed dyad type has a muting effect on its members, both high EP and low EP. When significant differences occur, Hs or Ls in the mixed dyads are likely to score lower on the dependent variables than Hs or Ls, respectively, in the homogeneous groups.

Discussion

The results show consistent trends, but the relationships are weak, as demonstrated by the relative lack of statistically significant findings. Some of the error is probably due to methodological factors. One source of error is coding unreliability. A second source may be that the sampled verbal interaction segments are too small. There is also the possibility of error due to a possible lack of correspondence between the experimental situation and real-life problem solving.

Developmental differences between subjects provide another important source of error. These 10th-grade boys are in a period where there are great differences in developmental level. Some are childlike and small, others are full-grown. There are correspondingly wide differences in social and interpersonal behavior and skills. This maximum developmental variability of this age could also obscure the hypothesized relationships.

In this research, I have predicted from a paper−and−pencil measurement of a variable that has to do mainly with personality (EP) to behavior in an interpersonal situation. Between the two, there is invariably lots of slippage, variance that may obscure bona fide relationships.

There is a similar difficulty with the school variable. School as a variable refers to a large environmental unit. Here, the school is assumed to provide socialization experiences and to constrain and facilitate behaviors relevant to exploration and problem solving. In terms of cause and effect, it is a long way from school to behavior in the experimental situation. There is room for many intermediary and confounding factors. In sum, the independent variables, school and EP, may be too far removed from the experimental situation for their effects to be salient.

The last issue has to do with the fact that I have worked only with overt verbal behavior. Other undetected cognitive events may have occurred that were important to the problem-solving interaction. Cognitive screening of verbal responses might have been in operation. A high EP subject might internally consider several alternative solutions but reject most of them as unfeasible. He might mention only one in the verbal interaction with his partner.

Exploration (dyad) effects. Three significant differences between dyad types were found for the dependent variables. These were for words, opinions, and combined input. When the results, including trends, are taken *in toto*, there seems to be a direct relationship between effective problem solving and interpersonal behavior on one hand and the three levels of EP (L—L, M—M, H—H) on the other. Among the four types, the L—L dyad type is ranked highest only for disagreement. These subjects rank lowest for many variables that suggest low involvement (words), low substantive contributions (information, opinion, total input), limited use of partner as resource (opinion, request, combined input request), and few attempts to influence the course of the interaction (agreement, interaction control, combined interaction direction). They are least verbal and articulate, provide fewer ideas, and have the least demonstrated interpersonal effectiveness. This description is especially true for Thurston L—L dyad members.

The M—M dyad type is hardest to characterize. These students' performance seems uneven and inconsistent. They are highest on variables that indicate problem-solving competence (alternate solution), use of their partner as a resource (opinion request), and social responsiveness (agreement, attempts to determine relation of solution). They rank lowest on variables indicating knowledge of the environment (information), passive use of the partner as resource (suggestion request), and decisive efforts to influence the interaction (attempts to close, disagreement). In general, they demonstrate some problem-solving competence and interpersonal involvement; this is particularly true at Thurston.

The H—H dyad members are ranked lowest on none of the dependent variables. They are highest for many variables indicating problem-solving competence with attention to detail (solution elaboration, combined solution), input preparatory to problem solving (information, opinion, combined input), use of partner as a resource (information request, combined input request), task involvement (time, words), and directing and channeling interaction (interaction control, attempts to close, combined interaction direction). For this task, these boys demonstrate the most cognitive structuring, problem-solving competence, and effective interpersonal behavior, particularly at Thurston.

A case could be made that these behavior differences for the dyad types are due only to their differential attitudes toward adults and peers. The idea would be that H—H types perform better than L—L types, because they are more comfortable with their partners and the adult researchers and not necessarily because of any intrinsic problem-solving superiority. Weigl (1973) and unpublished project data indicate that high explorers do have more interactions and more satisfying interactions with adults and peers than do low explorers. The transcripts and the actual data suggest that the H—H dyads are more comfortable in the experimental situation than L—L dyads.

My impression from the transcripts, however, is that those who are more effective in this dyad problem solving bring more to the situation than comfortableness. The H—H dyads seem to already have at hand cognitive maps of the school and to have already reached well-thought-out conclusions about such things as whether the vice-principal would bend a rule. The transcripts show that most of those students, like other adolescents, engage in preparatory and hypothetical problem solving. Most of them, for example, had previously thought about how to obtain driver's education as soon as possible (one of the problem stories) and had discussed it with friends. They appeared, especially the H—H dyads, to come equipped with at least elementary notions of problem solving: identifying a solution, evaluating and elaborating it, and selecting alternatives if the initial solution seemed inadequate. The least effective dyads, particularly the L—L types, displayed more primitive approaches. Some saw the notions of planning a strategy before acting or even acting at all as completely alien. So, clinical impressions of the interaction transcripts support the idea that there are differences between dyad types that are not accounted for by social ease.

The school switcheroo.   There is the puzzling matter of the data tending to support the opposite of my school hypotheses. The rationale was that Wayne would facilitate the expression of exploratory behavior because of its clearer norms and greater flexibility.

Wayne subjects appeared by their behavior to be enthusiastic and highly motivated. They seemed to be more identified with the students in the problem stories. They appeared generally to be more spontaneous and exuberant in their behavior, more at ease with their partners and the experimenters. However, Wayne subjects give less major problem-solving efforts, less input, less input requests, etc. The picture is one of less effective and less thorough problem solving and of less focused communication. Interestingly, Wayne subjects are high for solution elaboration, which suggests knowledge of some of the fine points of adaptation in their environment.

Thurston subjects appear more effective in terms of dyad problem solving and communication. They give more substantive problem-solving efforts (alternate solution), give more relevant input (information, opinion), make better use of partner as resource (input requests), use more structured and assertive communication (interaction control, attempts to close), and their involvement and verbality are greater (time, words). The factor variables similarly underline superiority in general problem solving (heavyweight problem solving), greater verbality and informational focus (information—verbality). My general impression, based on observations of their behavior in the experimental situation, was that Thurston subjects interacted with each other and with the experimenters in a task-oriented, businesslike, somewhat reserved, and more generally mature manner.

The reasons why the school hypotheses did not hold up are not clear. It is possible that the two schools shape behavior in the posited ways but that insufficient time has elapsed for these effects to show up. The results show that SES differences between the two schools do not provide a good foundation on which to build a good explanation of dependent variable differences. It is certainly possible, however, that there are important social and cultural differences between the two populations that are not tapped by an SES measure that could explain the school differences on the dependent variables.

One possible explanation for the surprising school results has to do with psychosocial maturity. Project data reveal that Wayne boys are 3/4 of an inch shorter than boys at Thurston. Wayne boys also have more involvement with parents and more often obtain help and advice from them. These differences suggest that boys at Wayne are more dependent on and less differentiated from significant adults in their environment and therefore are less psychosocially mature. Developmental level would partly determine the student's ability to stay on the track and to make his statement more relevant to previous statements. Less mature boys would be more likely to be sidetracked by irrelevant cognitive and affective associations. They would have more difficulty in maintaining task orientation and in functioning on a hypothetical task.

A second explanation has to do with the effects of anxiety and absence of anxiety on behavior. Because Wayne boys are more relaxed and comfortable with peers and adults, they engage in more expressive behavior, which may interfere with effective problem solving. Thurston boys, relatively more uptight, emphasize the cognitive aspect of their communication. They intellectualize, hence controlling their anxiety about the interaction and in the bargain increasing their effectiveness in the problem-solving situation.

The third explanation concerns socialization of coping styles. In deriving the hypotheses, a case was made for Wayne being more likely to encourage exploratory behavior because of the school's clearer norms and greater flexibility. There is another way of looking at it, though. It may be easier to be a social explorer at Wayne, but it may also be less crucial. For instance, if information about norms is freely available, there is less need to acquire coping styles to help obtain it. Thurston provides a rigid but murky environment. Norms are not clear. Students are not as comfortable with peers or staff. There is tension and ambiguity. Under these conditions, a high explorer may get more mileage out of his coping style, in spite of the lumps he may take. In sum, the noxious environment of Thurston may actually provide greater rewards for exploratory behavior and with it develop greater capabilities for school problem solving.

The person–environment interaction.   There was no statistically significant evidence for this interaction, and so the hypothesis was not confirmed. The data do, however, show some trends relative to person—environment interaction. L—L dyads at Wayne show more involvement, assertiveness, and task direction than their counterparts at Thurston. L—L dyads at Wayne seem more comfortable. M—M dyads at Thurston are more similar to the H—H pattern than M—M dyads at Wayne. H—H dyads at the two schools are similar overall; but at Thurston, they are much more verbal with correspondingly higher input and input requests.

The original hypothesis was that Wayne, with its clarity and opportunities, would favor high EP students, whereas Thurston would brand them as misfits. Low EP students would keep their noses clean at Thurston but would be lost in the shuffle at Wayne. The data suggest something else may be going on. Wayne, with its legible signposts and more frequent social interactions, is apparently a more equalitarian environment as regards adaptation. Low EP students can and are encouraged to cope actively, as the study results suggest. Thurston, with its murkiness, rigidity, and less frequent social interactions, separates the men from the boys. Social exploration becomes more salient as an adaptive style. For example, information is harder to come by and requires a more skilled and motivated seeker. At Thurston, the data have wider ranges, the L—L dyads are lower, and the H—H dyads are much higher for many variables. To be an effective problem solver and social interactor at Thurston seems to require a certain minimum of EP. Differences at the upper levels of EP seem to be more crucial at Thurston. The ecological hypothesis is not disproved by these results, but it does appear in need of revision.

Heterogeneity. The mixed dyad proved to be the least effective dyad type at problem solving. It is similar to the L—L group, only more so. The dyad type as a whole performs poorly, and its individual components perform poorly, too. Both Hs and Ls are at the low end of significant differences compared to their homogeneous dyad counterparts. There is barely a suggestion of the H—L differences within the mixed dyad that show up in comparison of L—L and H—H groups.

What seemed to happen is that the attitudinal and stylistic differences were creating a sense of social unease. The dyad members did not "click." Furthermore, the unease cannot be explained by differences in the degree that the partners know each other. My initial hunch was that the high EP in the mixed dyad would provide a facilitative interpersonal environment in which the low EP could flower, in terms of problem solving and manifest social exploration. However, the principle distilled by Collins and Guetzkow (1964) seemed to apply better. They stated that group heterogeneity for personality attributes and attitudes in a problem-solving situation frequently leads to difficulty in building interpersonal relationships, conflict, lower social rewards, and lower group cohesiveness; and that is pretty much what happened.

Morale. The relationships found in this study are not particularly strong. However, the trends suggest that problem-solving ability in group situations is related to initiative and engagement of the school environment and also to characteristics of the school environments themselves. As the parameters of these relationships become clearer, this information can be used in planning environments and opportunities therein in order to maximize development of group problem-solving and decision-making skills.

REFERENCES

Bales, R. F. *Personality and interpersonal behavior.* New York: Holt, Rinehart, and Winston, 1970.

Bales, R. F., Strodtbeck, F., Milds, T. M., & Roseborough, M. E. Channels of communication in small groups. *American Sociological Review,* 1951, *16,* 461–468.

Blalock, H. M. *Social statistics.* New York: McGraw–Hill, 1960.

Brown, R. *Social psychology.* New York: Free Press, 1965.

Campbell, D. T., & Fiske, D. W. Convergent and discriminant validation by the multitrait–multimethod matrix. *Psychological Bulletin,* 1959, *56,* 81–105.

Collins, B. E., & Guetzkow, H. *A social psychology of group processes for decision-making.* New York: Wiley, 1964.

Dixon, W. J., & Massey, F. J., Jr. *Introduction to statistical analysis* (3rd ed.). New York: McGraw–Hill, 1969.

Edwards, D. W. *A questionnaire method for the assessment of exploration preferences.* Unpublished manuscript, The University of Michigan, 1970.

Edwards, D. W. *Exploration and the high school experience: A study of tenth-grade boys' perceptions of themselves, their peers, and their schools.* Unpublished dissertation, The University of Michigan, 1971.

Flavell, J. H. *The developmental psychology of Jean Piaget.* Princeton, N.J.: Van Nostrand, 1963.

Goldberg, M. H., & Maccoby, E. E. Children's acquisition of skill in performing a group task under two conditions of group formation, *Journal of Personality and Social Psychology,* 1965, *2,* 898–902.

Goldman, M. A comparison of individual and group performance for varying combinations of initial ability. *Journal of Personality and Social Psychology,* 1965, *1,* 210–216.

Hall, E. J., & Williams, M. S. A comparison of decision-making performance in established and ad hoc groups. *Journal of Personality and Social Psychology,* 1966, *3,* 214–222.

Hoffman, L. R. Homogeneity of member personality and its effect on group problem-solving. *Journal of Abnormal and Social Psychology,* 1959, *58,* 27–32.

Kelly, H. H., & Thibaut, J. W. Group problem-solving. In G. Lindzey & E. Aronson (Eds.), *The handbook of social psychology* (2nd ed.), *4,* Reading, Mass.: Addison–Wesley, 1969.

Kelly, J. G. Social adaptation to varied environments. Paper presented at the annual meeting of the American Psychological Association, New York, September, 1966.

Kelly, J. G. *Adaptive behavior in varied high school environments.* Unpublished research proposal, The University of Michigan, 1967.

Kelly, J. G. Naturalistic observations in contrasting high schools. In E. P. Willems & H. L. Raush (Eds.), *Naturalistic viewpoints in psychological research.* New York: Holt, Rinehart, and Winston, 1969.

Kelly, J. G. *Adaptive behavior in varied high school environments.* Unpublished grant renewal application, The University of Michigan, 1970.

Kelly, J. G. *The socialization of competence as an ecological problem.* Paper presented at the American Psychological Association meeting, Washington, D.C., 1971.

Kelly, J. G., with Edwards, D. W., Fatke, R., Gordon, T. A., McClintock, S. K., McGee, D. P., Newman, B. M., Rice, R. R., Roistacher, R. C., & Todd, D. M. The coping process in varied high school environments. In M. J. Feldman (Ed.), *Studies in psychotherapy and behavior change, No. 2.* Buffalo, New York: State University of New York, 1971.

Laughlin, P. R., & Johnson, H. H. Group and individual performance on a complementary task as a function of initial ability level. *Journal of Experimental Social Psychology,* 1966, *2,* 407–414.

Murphy, L. B. *The widening world of childhood.* New York: Basic Books, 1962.

Nunnally, J. *Psychometric theory.* New York: McGraw–Hill, 1967.

Pervin, L. Performance and satisfaction as a function of individual–environment fit. *Psychological Bulletin,* 1968, *69,* 56–68.

Siegel, S. *Nonparametric statistics for the behavioral sciences.* New York: McGraw–Hill, 1956.

Silber, E., Coelho, G. V., Murphy, E. B., Hamburg, D. A., Pearlin, L. I., & Rosenberg, M. Competent adolescents coping with college decisions. *Archives of General Psychiatry,* 1961, *5,* 517–527.

Snedecor, G. W., & Cochran, W. G. *Statistical methods* (6th ed.). Ames, Iowa: Iowa State University Press, 1967.

Triandis, H. C., Hall, E. R., & Ewen, R. B. Member heterogeneity and dynamic creativity. *Human Relations,* 1965, *18,* 33–35.

Trickett, E. J., Kelly, J. G., & Todd, D. M. The social environment of the high school: Guidelines for individual change and organizational redevelopment. In S. Golann & C. Eisdorfer (Eds.), *Handbook of community mental health.* New York: Appleton–Century–Crofts, 1972.

Weick, K. E. Systematic observational methods. In G. Lindzey & E. Aronson (Eds.), *Handbook of social psychology* (2nd ed.), *2.* Reading, Mass.: Addison–Wesley, 1968.

Weigl, R. K. *Family interaction and adolescent social exploration: A community study.* Unpublished doctoral dissertation, The University of Michigan, 1973.

Yinger, J. M. *Towards a field theory of behavior.* New York: McGraw–Hill, 1965.

III TWO APPROACHES TO THE HIGH SCHOOL SOCIAL STRUCTURE

10

Contrasting Adaptations to the Social Environment of a High School: Implications of a Case Study of Helping Behavior in Two Adolescent Subcultures

David M. Todd[1]

Institute for Social Research
The University of Michigan

The importance of informal peer groups for adolescent socialization has been widely noted by Gordon (1957), Coleman (1961), and McClintock, Chapter 3 in this volume. The "adolescent society" provides roles, status rewards, and models in addition to those established by the formal structure of the school. In fact, the peer groups in a high school may be viewed, in part, as alternative adaptations to the formal social structure of the school, i.e., as "subcultures" that may support, transform, buffer, or counteract the direct impact of the formal social system on students.[2]

Helping transactions may provide a sensitive barometer of the nature of social interdependence — both formal and informal — in a particular setting or culture. Feldman (1968), for example, has interpreted varied patterns of help giving with foreigners and compatriots in terms of contrasting cultural ingroups—outgroups. London (1970) presents exploratory data that suggest that marginality in the predominant culture was prerequisite to a willingness to help Jews in Nazi Germany. In both of these situations, the help-giving process reflects the positions of both helper and helped in a sociocultural network.

---

[1] Present address: The University of Massachusetts, Amherst.

[2] It is common in organizational literature to view the informal social system as an adaptation to the formal structure, in response to needs of members that the formal system does not satisfy. Though adolescent peer groups undoubtedly have stronger origins outside the school than do most informal work groups in an organization, it is reasonable to assume that the peer groups also develop in response to the characteristics of the particular school environment. Some empirical support for this view in the context of the work reported here is presented elsewhere (Todd, in preparation).

The value of helping behavior as a sign of relationships between persons and their social environments has been reviewed in the first chapter of this volume. This perspective considers the patterns of interdependence between the elements of a social system (i.e., persons, roles, settings, and policies) as one of several critical points of view for defining appropriate intervention goals and strategies. The specific elaboration of the ecological perspective for helping behavior was initially stated as follows (Trickett, Kelly, & Todd, 1972):

> One of the critical sources of data for defining the form of interdependence [in a high school] is an understanding of how help is given — when it is given, and to whom it is given, under what circumstances, and to what extent individuals will express helpful behavior to others over periods of time . . . Looking at ways in which help is expressed is one source for seeing how help-giving roles are identified with specific individuals. Concurrently, which of many types of help-giving roles are defined in a school, how they are developed, and under what conditions they are expressed provides a diagnostic view of the school that is relevant for understanding the adaptive behavior of the organization [pp. 378–379].

This chapter discusses some findings and implications of a case study of helping in two contrasting peer groups in a predominantly white, middle-class, suburban high school (Thurston High School). This study used a variety of methods to identify groups that represent varied adaptations to the school, with a particular focus on delineating patterns of help giving. The specifics of helping behavior in the two selected groups and the unique functions of help giving in the life of each group are reported separately (Todd, in preparation). The objective of the present discussion is to explore the implications of this study for the broader impact of the high school on the socialization of boys in the two contrasting peer subcultures.

THE DESIGN: A BRIEF OVERVIEW

An objective of this research was to provide more clarity for a school social environment that had appeared, on the basis of earlier contacts, to be especially subtle and elusive (Stillman, 1969). Help giving seemed an especially appropriate variable in the high school, which appeared nonsupportive. The task was to identify, select, and study two contrasting peer groups in a way that could provide information about the broad social environment of the school, as well as a more specific view of helping processes in the two groups.

These objectives were pursued through a "funnel design" in which several methods were combined in succession to focus upon specific aspects of the school social environment, as illustrated in Table 1.

TABLE 10.1

Overview of the Objectives, Methods, and Samples for Each Phase of the Study

Phase	Objective	Method	Sample
I. Exploratory study	Describe the peer structure of the high school	Semistructured interviews, group and individual	Heterogeneous sample of students (N = 18) and staff (N = 11)
II. Questionnaire survey	Extend view of selected subcultures, identify members	Survey questionnaire, group administered	71% sample of senior boys (N = 224)
III. Intensive study	Explore helping behavior in the selected groups	Written log reports and structured interviews	Small samples of senior boys in two contrasting peer groups (n_1 = 7; n_2 = 8)

A broad view of the peer structure of the school was first sought through semistructured interviews with a heterogeneous sample of students (N = 18) and adults (N = 11). These interviews generated a wide variety of peer group descriptions and perspectives on the social structure of the school.

Additional information was gathered through serendipitous spin-offs from these interviews, e.g., a class discussion of peer groups that one student initiated and a mapping of school settings that one of the teachers assigned to a class.

In the second phase, a questionnaire was constructed to evaluate and refine the preliminary descriptions of several key groups that emerged from exploratory interviews. Respondents were asked to rate themselves on each of seven brief, peer group descriptions and to answer a variety of questions about the school environment (involvement with peers, social settings, activities, adults, and rules), sociometric choices, help giving, and demographic characteristics. On the basis of these data, two peer groups were identified — labeled *citizens* and *tribe* — that seemed to represent important and contrasting adaptations to the school.

The third phase of the study involved small samples of boys in these two groups. Seven "citizens" and eight "tribe" boys kept extensive log reports of help-giving incidents for a period of 2 days and participated in from 1- to 2-hour interviews about help giving, as well as about their peer group, school experience, personal lives, and future plans.[3]

_____

[3]Some of these boys were also involved in an earlier, more extended collection of log reports. These earlier reports were too unreliable for systematic analysis, but they did provde additional background for viewing data from the subsequent log reports and interviews.

THE SCHOOL PEER STRUCTURE AND CITIZEN AND TRIBE
SUBCULTURES: SELECTED FINDINGS

The exploratory interviews, survey questionnaire, and intensive study of help giving provide varied and complementary sources of information about the citizens and tribe as subcultural adaptations to the social environment of Thurston. The exploratory interview and survey data describe the citizens and tribe orientations, the status of those groups as subcultures, and their relationship to the broader peer structure and social system of the school. Selected findings about help giving validate, extend, and provide a basis for further speculation about these same issues.

Broad Impressions of the Peer Structure

The exploratory interviews supported the initial perception of a weakly differentiated peer structure. Most informants reported a few highly visible groups; but there was less agreement about other groups, and there seemed to be few shared labels even for the most visible "cliques." It was often suggested that many students in this school were not identified with any particular orientation but rather seemed to have a few close friends and moved through the school quite unobtrusively. Instead of a passive collection of data, many of these interviews became collaborative efforts to delineate and define the contours of the peer society. Through these exchanges, as well as reports of other discussions they stimulated, it was possible to describe at least seven different group orientations that varied widely in their apparent strength, cohesiveness, deviance from predominant norms, and visibility and in the consistency with which they were identified by the informants.

The Validation of Central and Contrasting Subcultures: Citizens and Tribe

Of the various descriptions generated in the exploratory interviews, two seemed to represent important but contrasting modes of engaging the social milieu of Thurston High.

The group we have labeled the "citizens" was actively involved in school activities and was generally satisfied with the formal rules, functions, and academic process of the school. These students seemed to use the formal system to channel their interests, structure peer interaction, and develop competence. This group was distinguished by many informants from students exclusively involved in athletics, as well as those who participated actively in only one "specialty" activity such as drama or journalism.

The contrasting group was not involved in school activities and was frequently at odds with school rules and authorities. These students did, however, use school settings to originate and carry on extensive informal interaction. Because it was an identifiable subgroup that departed from the predominant norms of the school, this group was called the "tribe." These students were differentiated from the "hard guys" or "greasers" who tended toward more destructive and disruptive behavior, as well as from other "deviant" groups such as those heavily involved with drugs or the political activists.

The validation of the citizen and tribe orientations was pursued in three steps prior to the intensive study of helping transactions. It was first necessary to see if self-ratings on descriptions of the two groups would yield groups that were mutually exclusive and large enough to allow for statistical comparison and further sampling. It was, in fact, possible to select samples of 42 citizens and 64 tribe members on the basis of these self-ratings.[4]

A second step in the validation of these groups was to assess the cohesiveness of the "members." Although the notion of "subculture" implies mutual patterns of involvement in the school, it was expected that interpersonal attraction within each of the groups should at least exceed that expected by random distribution. An analysis of friendship choices confirmed a degree of cohesiveness exceeding chance for both citizens ($p = .05$) and tribe ($p < .01$), although choices across group lines were more frequent than might be expected.

As suggested above, the critical issue in defining these groups as subcultures was whether they had contrasting orientations to the activities, settings, rules, and norms of the school. Survey items designed to tap these "orientations" yielded strong differences in the expected directions in a wide variety of areas. They confirmed that the citizen group was more positively oriented to the formal activities, settings, rules, and school adults than was the tribe. Moreover, the tribe group placed a stronger emphasis on interaction with friends, informal settings, and out-of-school activities. The citizens also reported more actual participation in school activities and higher academic aspirations than did the tribe.

These survey data create a picture of considerable permeability in group boundaries with respect to friendship choices, but they do allow a definition of discrete samples of boys who ascribe to the respective characteristics of citizen and tribe and who differ in their stated orientations to critical aspects of the school social environment.

Help Giving for Citizens and Tribe: Selected Survey, Log, and Interview Findings

The survey data already presented provide strong indications that the citizens and tribe represent distinct and contrasting orientations to the school environment. The intensive study of helping transactions in these two groups provides

---

[4]The specific criteria included a rating of 4 or higher (on a 7-point scale) on one of the two descriptions and a rating of less than 4 (and at least 2 points lower than the dominant rating) on the contrasting description. A total of 18 boys, many of whom seemed involved in athletic teams, rated themselves 4 or higher on *both* descriptions.

data that is richer in detail — and in the case of log reports, more directly behavioral — to explore, extend, and speculate on the nature of these orientations and the social environment of the school.

An interest in differences between citizens and tribe should not obscure how boys in these two groups relate to the school environment in some rather similar ways. The help-giving data reflect such similarities. It is true of both groups, for example, that log reports of help giving more often involve peers than adults, that a majority of helping incidents are *not* related to school activities, and that transportation is the most frequent form of peer assistance provided. Contrary to expectation, the tribe respondents did not report a greater use of informal school settings for help giving than did citizens; most school-based help for both groups, even among peers, occurred in classrooms. In this and other important respects (e.g., the incidence of dramatic or exceptional helping acts), the brief time period sampled (2 days) is probably insufficient to explore expected differences.

Given these broad areas of similarity, other findings on help giving confirm the central differences expected for citizens and tribe in orientation to the school. Both survey and log data indicate that citizen help giving is more often school related (academic and extracurricular) than is tribe help giving. Though the attempt to express tribe priorities in questionnaire items was less successful, log responses indicate that these boys place a greater emphasis than do citizens on nonschool-related helping such as providing transportation and loaning such commodities as money, food, and cigarettes. Similarly, citizen logs report more frequent incidents of peer helping in school settings, whereas tribe-peer help giving occurs more often in settings out of school. Also, in comparison with the tribe, citizens report a greater likelihood of receiving help from adults (survey) as well as a greater incidence of actually doing so (logs).

Data concerning helping behavior and the nature of peer relationships offer some support to a view of the tribe as more cohesive than the citizens, but these findings are less conclusive than those just reported. Members of a strongly cohesive peer subculture might be expected to provide more ready help to a "comrade" who is in the same group than to an "acquaintance" who is not in the group, whereas this distinction might be less important to a member of a less cohesive group in determining his willingness to help. Questionnaire data do indicate that the tribe are more likely to make such a distinction between comrades and acquaintances than are citizens. Questionnaire data also support the related expectation that tribe helping will involve a stronger norm of reciprocity than will citizen help giving. Although both of these qualities indicate a stronger ingroup orientation to the male peer group for the tribe, supporting results are not found in the log report data. Of a more speculative and unanticipated nature are indications in the log reports and interviews that relationships with girls are quite different for boys in the two groups. The possibility is raised that citizen boys are more likely to engage in exclusive dating relationships at the expense of male peer interaction, whereas these relationships remain more peripheral, though often important, for tribe boys.

The data on help giving clearly support the existence of contrasting orientations to major features of the school environment for citizens and tribe. Citizen help giving, to a much greater extent than for the tribe, supports involvement in the academic and extracurricular activities of the school. In contrast, tribe help giving has relatively little relationship to school activities and revolves more around an active, informal pattern of interaction. These data have less clear implications for the nature of peer group relationships, but they do lend tentative support to a stronger ingroup orientation on the part of the tribe.

CITIZEN AND TRIBE ADAPTATIONS AND THE OPPORTUNITY STRUCTURE OF THE SCHOOL

What are the adaptive consequences of membership in the citizen and tribe subcultures in this school environment? If future roles are accepted as criteria for adaptive functioning in the school, it might be argued that all is well. Most citizens are well prepared for the mix of academic and extracurricular activities that are the marks of good college citizenship. In contrast, the high school "tours of duty" of tribe boys have probably prepared them well for the military or semiskilled jobs where the greatest rewards are in interacting with peers on the job and during leisure time.

If the satisfactions of the boys and the development of their skills and potentials are included in the equation, the picture is less encouraging, especially for the tribe. Few of these boys were pleased with their futures or the high school experience, for that matter, although most were resigned to both. Their successes were those of survival in the psychological sense and an acceptance of limited opportunities. It is quite clear that the tribe do not, for the most part, look for satisfaction or success in those very activities and settings that are most valued in the formal culture. More discouraging from a socialization point of view is that they seem to have very few alternative modes for positive experience. School for the tribe member seems to be a series of "irrelevant" activities against which the tribe member structures a supportive peer system, but even this informal network defines few opportunities for experiencing competence and self-worth.

Within the citizen group as well, of course, are individuals whose lives seem unsatisfying. These boys seemed to have only limited success in academics and school activities and appeared isolated in peer relationships, low in self-esteem, and often withdrawn and sullen. These boys have bought citizen values but do not measure up as well as they would like, and they seem to take it personally.

The impact of membership in the citizen or tribe subculture is conditioned by the weakly differentiated nature of the social environment of the school. A "tolerant" system has positive benefits for some of its members: Active citizens can find faculty support for creating new activities, and a few teachers try to recognize and cope with the importance to tribe boys of talking with friends, ducking out for a smoke, or meeting at a restaurant for late breakfast. However, the fluidity of this environment also has negative effects to which the school seems less responsive. Members of both groups can easily fall through the loose weave of the social network. If the citizen-oriented student can neither achieve status in an ongoing activity nor muster the personal and social resources for creating a new setting, he has little recourse. The tribe boy who cannot maintain the support of a group of peers may also have little to fall back upon except perhaps a more extreme means of gaining visibility.

In the areas just noted, Thurston High School may simply highlight problems that are quite common to American high schools. The most visible and readily available status is accessible only to those who can demonstrate scholastic competence and extracurricular leadership. Students who aspire to this status do risk failure in a highly competitive system. Competence that is specific may be untapped and unrewarded in a given school.[5]

Students who do *not* aspire to this status system must cope with an array of activities that they are required to attend but in which they cannot expect to experience success or satisfaction. Those competences that a student may value — e.g., mechanical skill, athletic ability, or persuasive manipulation — are viewed as nonlegitimate or irrelevant within the school. Carlson (1964) has correctly noted that mandatory attendance leads schools to respond to students like these by developing "holding patterns" such as vocational programs, whereas attention is concentrated on "serious" students. Such a boy must hope for a visible peer system in which his areas of strength will gain the praise and respect of his friends.

IMPLICATIONS FOR RENEWAL

The findings and speculations of this study are not sufficient to design preventive interventions for the social milieu of Thurston High School, but they do suggest some thinking about citizens and tribe. For the citizens, there is a need to reach beyond the most visible and active members and to expand the activities in the school that merit status. One approach would be to create more settings that Barker and Gump (1964) would call "undermanned" in order to increase the demand for individual resources in the school. This also means increasing the

---

[5]Barker and Gump (1964) note that large schools are more likely to provide appropriate outlets for specific areas of competence than are smaller schools, where broader and more diverse competence is likely to be valued.

ease with which a citizen-oriented student can identify or create opportunities to make use of his interests and abilities. Continued and even increased emphasis on intramural sports would provide a "niche" for the many boys who stake their self-esteem on proven athletic ability in junior high, only to find that they are not able to play varsity sports in high school. Faculty and students alike could provide crucial help in the form of energy and resources for identifying and developing new activities and encouraging the school "culture" to assign value to them.

The negative fallout of the tribe adaptation is more difficult to counteract within the existing structure of the school. These boys do seem responsive to a strong expression of self-confidence, concern, patience, and above all straightforwardness on the part of adults. In contrast, the teacher who is tolerant without expecting anything is taken advantage of, and the adult who makes demands arbitrarily is rebelled against or, if possible, avoided. Under these conditions, it is the rare adult who is effective, and trying is more often stigmatized than it is encouraged and rewarded.

The problems of the tribe strike at some of the most basic formal traditions and assumptions of the school. Moreover, as may be inherent in school organization (Miles, 1967), Thurston High has not developed a faculty culture that adequately supports the collective assessment and solution of problems concerning the impact of the school on students. The discrete, individualistic, and nonincremental efforts that result do not do justice to the "whole cloth" of the tribe subculture. This implies creative approaches to many aspects of school experience, for example, the redefinition of appropriate "learning environments" and a recognition of the potential value of peer relationships for student interest and learning. Prerequisite to any valid change, however, is the development among school adults of a spirit of receptive and respectful inquiry into the interests, orientations, and prejudices of the tribe boys. Most of the people who counsel and teach (and do research!) in schools are not prepared to make sense of a culture that is organized around events that seem to them insignificant.

This study is limited to two peer groups within one high school, with a particular focus on help giving as an expression of social interdependence. Studies of much broader scope — including a direct focus on social structure, as well as varied aspects of the socialization process — are needed to move beyond the speculative nature of these comments. The data reported here do suggest the value of viewing peer groups as subcultural adaptations to the school environment. Extending this kind of analysis is obviously a demanding task that requires the investigator to derive many concepts and hypotheses from the nature of the particular social environment. If this approach can provide a basis for supplementing natural forms of help giving with preventive interventions that are cognizant of group subcultures and congruent with the ecology of the school, it will be worth the effort.

REFERENCES

Barker, R., & Gump, P. *Big school, small school.* Stanford, Calif.: Stanford University Press, 1964.

Carlson, R. O. Environmental constraints and organizational consequences: The public school and its clients. *National Society for the Study of Education Yearbook,* 1964, *63,* (Pt. 2), 262–639.

Coleman, J. S. *The adolescent society.* Glencoe: The Free Press, 1961.

Feldman, R. E. Response to compatriot and foreigner who seek assistance. *Journal of Personality and Social Psychology,* 1968, *10,* 202–214.

Gordon, C. W. *The social system of the high school.* Glencoe: The Free Press, 1957.

London, P. The rescuers: Motivational hypotheses about Christians who saved Jews from the Nazis. In J. Macaulay & L. Berkowitz (Eds.) *Altruism and helping behavior.* New York: Academic Press, 1970.

Miles, M. Some properties of schools as social systems. In G. Watson (Ed.), *Change in school systems.* Washington, D.C.: National Training Laboratories – National Education Association, 1967.

Stillman, H. *An exploratory study of two high school environments.* Unpublished manuscript, The University of Michigan, 1969.

Trickett, E. J., Kelly, J. G., & Todd, D. M. The social environment of the high school: Guidelines for individual change and organizational redevelopment. In S. E. Golann & C. Eisdorfer (Eds.), *Handbook of community psychology.* New York: Appleton–Century–Crofts, 1972.

Todd, D. M. The social context of help-giving: A case study of two male adolescent subcultures in a high school. In preparation.

11 Persons and Settings: A Comparative Analysis of the Quality and Range of Social Interaction in Two High Schools

Philip R. Newman
Institute for Social Research
The University of Michigan

Current concepts and research in the behavioral sciences affirm that the social settings individuals confront on a day-to-day basis serve as important determinants of the patterns of their psychological growth and development, adaptation, or maladaptation (Bachman, Kahn, & Mednick, 1968; Brim, 1966, 1968; Mechanic, 1962; Orth, 1963; Parsons & Bales, 1955). At heart, this is an ecological statement. It specifies that there are important relationships between an individual and his or her social environments. The biologist studying flora and fauna has come to realize that it is the biological system itself that is the important unit for analysis. There is a particular kind of harmony within each system, e.g., animal and plant life exist in relation to each other and are in a very real sense interdependent upon one another for growth and survival. A particular kind of animal or plant adjusts to the interdependencies and resources of its particular habitat and thus becomes somewhat different from the same kind of animal or plant in another habitat. A psychologist studying individuals and organizations can realize as the biologist that it is the system that is an important unit for analysis, particularly the social system and its effects on individuals.

But why refer to a psychosocial system as an ecosystem? Because such a point of view helps us get closer to a statement of actual social conditions. The ecological perspective maintains that it is the total system that must be studied in order to understand the similarities and differences in persons and environments. An intelligent person in a "culturally rich" environment will behave quite differently from the intelligent person in a "culturally poor" environment; that individual will do different things, choose different paths for survival, and develop a different set of strategies for attaining his or her goals.

The bright student in a "culturally rich" high school may be able to take advantage of the variety of opportunities present in the culture to channel his or her talents and interests in socially acceptable and valued ways. He or she may become a school leader, a respected citizen of that culture. The bright student in a "culturally poor" high school may feel bored and frustrated by the climate of the school and may find his or her own talents undeveloped there. He or she may turn to leadership roles in the peer culture in an attempt to change the school or to destroy it. Such a student may turn to the role of hustler on the streets and in the school, trying to drum up "business" for personal gain.

The "bright" student in a high school where interaction with adults is plentiful may be expected to define adults as resources and models for behavior. Such students may learn to seek favor from adults in gaining status, college or job recommendations, high grades, etc. They may learn to develop a variety of skills and abilities in learning to relate to people in positions of authority. The "bright" student in a high school where interaction with adults is scarce and not encouraged may turn more to peers as models for behavior. Such individuals may learn to manipulate adults on the basis of image. They may have difficulty learning to relate to people in positions of authority in a variety of ways.

The ways in which each of these persons is similar are important for study. But the ways in which each differs are also important. The similarities and differences in response to social environments reflect how persons seek to adapt to local conditions.

Kelly (1968) and Trickett, Kelly, and Todd (1972) have applied the principles of interdependence, cycling of resources, adaptation, and succession to functioning social systems. The theoretical approach postulates a series of interrelationships between the individual person and his or her social environment, much as the biologist postulates that the ecosystem is a series of interrelationships between the living and nonliving organisms in a setting. The task for research in each case is to accurately describe the interrelationships between organisms and environments rather than simply to describe the organisms. The work reported in this monograph has applied this theoretical strategy in the study of adolescent boys and their high schools.

The present chapter reports a method for assessing school environmental differences and for understanding how these differences may influence the adaptive histories of individuals with different coping preferences. Drawing from preliminary studies and from the author's own observations of the two schools over a period of several years, the environmental assessment work reported in this chapter focused upon comparisons between: (a) the *quantity* of interaction between students and school adults and between students at each school; and (b) the *quality* of interaction between students and school adults at each school; (c) the effectiveness of socialization at each school; and (d) the social functions of a variety of social settings at each school.

The theoretical rationale for the present study is derived from an ecological analogy that is represented by the principle of interdependence. Persons, it is assumed, are dependent on one another for information and affectional supplies, but the process by which these are transmitted varies from place to place. The quantity of social interaction between people and the quality of this interaction are assumed to affect individual adaptation, because adequate psychosocial supplies are essential for adequate personal adaptation (Caplan, 1969). Because teachers constitute a special set of resources in the school situation and because adolescents are in the process of dissolving infantile dependencies and reintegrating new and mature ways of relating to authority (Douvan & Adelson, 1966), the quantity and quality of social interaction between students and adults in the school setting are assumed to affect individual and group styles for relating to persons in positions of authority. In addition, there is the premise that an environment that generates interaction between students and faculty is a more active setting for student socialization than is an environment that does not. In reality, the question asks whether "high" levels of social interaction between students and adults communicate shared expectations for behavior more clearly than "low" amounts of interaction of an impersonal nature. The question may be extended further to ask whether higher amounts of social interaction produce a social setting where students wish to relate to adults.

HYPOTHESES

The central question to be explored is how the cultural and institutional characteristics of two school environments are translated into psychological consequences for the student populations. The hypotheses tested in this study are generated from a number of sources.

1. *The ecological perspective.*   This affirms that "organisms" in an ecosystem are interdependent and that the nature of the interdependencies as reflected in social interaction may differ from one system to another. The preceding discussion has pointed out the ways in which social interaction may be viewed as a systemic variable. The discussion has also indicated ways in which differences in the quantity and quality of social interaction may differentiate social systems that might otherwise be thought of as the same. The point to be made here is that two schools are not necessarily the same social environments because they appear to have similar functions and goals. Differences in the quantity and quality of social interaction may mean that two schools are very different environments.

2. *Previous studies in this research project.*   Stillman (1969) suggests that the two schools differ in the nature of role relationships between students and

teachers. She finds role relationships more formal at Thurston, with role bound-aries more permeable at Wayne. There is also an implication in Stillman's work that there is more student—teacher interaction at Wayne than at Thurston. Stillman also comments upon differences between the two schools in the way behavioral settings are used for interaction. Fatke (1971), in a study of new students at each of the two schools, notes that "new students" have a greater amount of interaction with teachers at Wayne during their 1st year of school attendance than do new students at Thurston. Both of these preliminary studies converge on the variable of social interaction between students and teachers as one that differentiates the two schools.

3. *Direct observation and impressions of the social climate.* During 2 years of observing at the two schools and interviewing students, teachers, counselors, and administrators, the investigator formed certain clear impressions of the social climates at each school. At Wayne, there appears to be a great deal of con-tact between students and faculty and between students and other students in the hallways and other public places in the school. In contrast, at Thurston there does not appear to be much contact between students and school adults in public settings. The interactions between students and adults at Wayne are characterized by joking and bantering, whereas at Thurston, when interactions have been observed, they are generally serious and problem oriented. Students at Wayne seem to know about faculty members beyond their role as teachers, and teachers seem to know at least some students personally. At Thurston, there appear to be two parallel social structures — one for teachers and one for stu-dents — with little overlap between them.

Previous research by Fatke and Stillman and the author's own direct obser-vations offer some specific suggestions about differences in social interaction at Wayne and Thurston. The specific hypotheses to be tested in this study concern-ing the quantity and quality of interaction are generated from the sources mentioned earlier. They are as follows.

QUANTITY OF INTERACTION

1. There will be a greater amount of interaction between students and school adults at Wayne Memorial High School than at Thurston High School.

2. The quality of social interaction between students and school adults will be perceived as warmer and more personal at Wayne High School than at Thurs-ton High School.

The remaining hypotheses of the study are to some extent contingent upon the observation of differences in social interaction at the two schools. Earlier, the author mentioned premises that were seen as logical psychological outcomes of differences in the nature of interdependence in two social settings. It was suggested that a school environment that generates a great deal of interaction between students and faculty is a more active setting for socialization than a school that generates little interaction. This global hypothesis will be tested by examining differences in the perceived norm structures at each school and by examining differences in the ways in which students relate to adults at each school.

Direct observation in the two schools leads to the conclusion that the expectations for student behavior that emanate from school policy and personnel are different in content. At Wayne, expectations for students seem to have a great deal to do with social behavior, including interpersonal style, social participation, and appearance. Although there are also demands generated by the academic structure, these seem to be less a part of the school atmosphere. At Thurston, expectations for student behavior have a great deal to do with task performance, including academics, future aspirations/college attendance, and work. Differences in interaction levels at the two schools lead us to predict not only content differences in the normative structure, however. It is hypothesized that Wayne will in fact transmit its expectations more clearly and that these expectations will have a greater socialization impact upon students than will be true at Thurston. The specific hypotheses concerning the effectiveness of socialization at the two schools follow.

EFFECTIVENESS OF SOCIALIZATION

3. There is a greater clarity of normative expectations at Wayne High School than at Thurston High School.

4. There is a greater expectation of negative consequences for norm violation at Wayne High School than at Thurston High School.

5. Students will exhibit a greater preference for task orientation across settings at Thurston High School than at Wayne High School.

6. More students will perceive normative expectations for social behavior at Wayne High School than at Thurston High School.

7. More students will perceive normative expectations for task-oriented behavior at Thurston than at Wayne.

In addition to an assessment of student behavior, attitudes, and opinions, an assessment of faculty behavior, attitudes, and opinions was conducted. Earlier, Edwards, in Chapter 6, found that students at Wayne were more satisfied with their school as a whole than were students at Thurston. The assessment of faculty conducted by this author was designed to explore differences in teacher satisfaction at the two schools. The hypotheses to be tested are consistent with findings about student satisfaction. They are as follows:

FACULTY SATISFACTION

8. Faculty members at Wayne will be more satisfied with their jobs than will faculty members at Thurston.

9. Faculty members at Wayne will be more satisfied with how others in their school do their jobs than will faculty members at Thurston.

TABLE 11.1
The Two High School Environments

Characteristics	Wayne	Thurston
Demographic characteristics		
1. Sociocultural	Suburban-industrial Middle class	Suburban-residential Upper middle class
2. Student enrollment and exchange rates[a]	1,963 18.7%	2,126 8.0%
3. School adults	Adults live in school district	Adults live outside school district
Architectural Design	Multiple Story	Single story
Organization of curriculum	Heterogeneous design Ability grouping 10th-graders take English with upperclassmen Comprehensive curriculum	Homogeneous design No ability grouping 10th-graders take English with 10th-graders College preparatory curriculum
Extracurricular Activities	Socially Oriented	Task Oriented
Formal organization		
1. Principal	Autonomous Leader Long tenure in position	School-board directed Facilitator Short tenure in position
2. Assistant	Clear division of labor	Similar responsibilities
3. Counselors	Division of students by grade and ability	Division of students by sex
4. Faculty	Departmental organization Faculty Council	Interdepartmental organization Implementation committee

[a]These are the average rates of population exchange (number of students entering and leaving the school/total school population) for 3 years (1968–1971).

Finally, much staff observation at the two schools indicates that there are different patterns of influence and decision making at the two schools. At Wayne, the principal is seen as having a great deal of influence administering a rather democratic decision-making structure. At Thurston, the board of education is seen as having a great deal of influence in administering a rather authoritarian decision-making structure.

METHOD

Sample

The schools.   The social and demographic background of the school environments has been described in Chapter 4 by Rice and Marsh. On the basis of anecdotal evidence and descriptive data available, there are indications that although the schools are similar in many respects, there are also some differences between them. Table 11.1 summarizes these differences.

Student sample.   The major requirement of the sample selected at each school was that it be representative of the student population at that school. In order to insure a representative sample, a large, randomly selected sample, stratified by sex and grade level, was used via cluster sampling. The characteristics of the final representative sample at each school are summarized in Table 11.2.

Adult sample.   An attempt was made to sample 100% of all school faculty at the two schools. This included administrators and counselors as well as teachers. This assessment was required in order to provide an accurate reflection of the total social environment — to include reports from faculty as well as students. The final sample includes 89 adults at each school (total N = 178) or a 75% response rate from the faculty at each school.

TABLE 11.2
The Random, Stratified Sample
of Students at Wayne and Thurston

School		Grade Level	Male	Female	Total
Wayne		10	67	68	135
		11	58	58	116
		12	42	41	83
	Total		167	167	334
Thurston		10	66	66	132
		11	64	64	128
		12	52	51	103
	Total		182	181	363

The Instrument

The environmental assessment inventory. Assessing the similarities and differences between the social structures of the two study schools required an instrument that could accomplish many goals. It was important to provide a description of the environmental life space of the students in the sample. The instrument was designed to gather data regarding the collective behavior and views of all members of the two schools. A decision was made to organize the instrument around various school social settings that would be relevant places for people to spend time and then to assess who spoke to whom in these settings. Students and faculty, within the constraints imposed by the instrument, were asked to report about their social interaction in these global settings. Barker and Gump (1964), in their research on high schools, utilize the concept of specific behavior settings in order to compare participative opportunities in a variety of schools. For their purposes, for example, a single class, one basketball game, and one club meeting are considered as behavior setting units. This study makes use of the notion of global behavior settings as the behavior setting units. Classrooms, hallways, offices, etc. are considered to be the places in which behavior occurs. Table 11.3 presents a list of the various settings in which students were asked to report about their social interaction. In addition to Barker and Gump, other researchers (Astin, 1968; Pace, 1963) concerned with environmental assessment in educational settings have concluded that when a survey research instrument is used, it is most effective when respondents are asked to report about their actual behavior in these environments rather than about their perception and opinions of settings.

The present writer concluded that the collective report of social interactions by students in a variety of settings would be a viable method for assessing the organization of the social environments under study. Thus, the instrument was designed to provide a descriptive map of the social environment in terms of social interactions within a variety of global settings. This technique would allow

TABLE 11.3
Settings for Social Interaction

1. Study hall	12. Gym or pool
2. Band, orchestra, or music room	13. Athletic field
	14. Locker room
3. Art room	15. Rest-room
4. Shop room	16. Principal's office
5. Computer center	17. Counselor's office
6. Science lab	18. School office
7. Drama or speech room	19. Halls or on the stairs
8. Classroom	20. School parking lot
9. Auditorium	21. Student lounge
10. Library	22. Newspaper/year-book office
11. Cafeteria	

comparison of the two schools in terms of student–adult interaction and would allow comparison of how different places in the school served as settings for interaction.

In addition to investigating the nature of social interaction at the two schools, several of the hypotheses of this study concern the nature of the normative structure and the effectiveness of socialization at the schools. A series of items was developed that asked students to rate their perceptions of faculty and peer expectations for behavior. These items employ a 7-point Likert-type rating scale. Subjects are asked to rate the strength of expectations for obedience, social involvement, and task performance in the school setting. A rating of 1 represents the lowest rating ("not at all"), and a rating of 7 represents the highest rating ("very much") for "how much teachers/other students expect S to act a certain way." The author is attempting, therefore, to adapt traditional survey research methodology in order to ask for self-reports of behavior from subjects.

A self-report inventory, called the Environmental Assessment Questionnaire (EAQ), was designed to provide comparable data at the two schools. Parallel instruments were developed for students and school adults who were asked to report: (a) specific interactions with members of different role groups in a wide range of behavioral settings; (b) perceptions of the quality of interaction between students and school adults; and (c) perceptions of the normative social structure of the school. Data about quantity of interaction are based upon respondents' recollections of behavior during the previous day or previous week. It was felt that this type of data could serve as a bridge between observation and attitude and as a preassessment for actual observations within the two school social environments, indicating settings where interaction might be fruitfully observed in later studies. Data concerning quality of interaction and normative expectations for obedience, social involvement, and task performance are based on respondents' perceptions of the nature of their interactions and of the nature of expectations that others have for their behavior in the school setting.

Procedure.   The classroom administrations were supervised by a group of nine graduate and advanced undergraduate students at The University of Michigan as well as a member of the project staff. The procedure and schedule were discussed carefully with these administrators, and a set of written instructions was reviewed by each. The administrators were asked not to deviate from the written instructions except for answering questions.

The test administrator arrived at the classroom at an allotted time and introduced himself to the teacher. Teachers left the room. The administrator introduced himself to the class and told them that he was going to ask them to fill out a questionnaire as part of a research project that had been going on at their school over the past 3 years. The administrator passed out the research instruments to the class and then read aloud to the students the instructions on the cover sheet. The instructions reiterated the remarks about the research project, emphasized the fact that the students' answers were confidential, and thanked the students for their help. Then the administrator read questions about grade, sex, and age, that appeared on the cover sheet and asked the students to fill them in. After this, the students were allowed to proceed at their own pace.

Administration of the Faculty Questionnaire

The present writer attended a meeting of the faculty of each school and explained the purpose of the study in general terms. The procedure for distribution of the instrument and for its return was also explained at this meeting. The faculty were asked to respond to the instrument on their own time during the subsequent 2-week period. The research instrument was placed in the teachers' mail boxes after the conclusion of this meeting, and a labeled box was placed in the school office at each school in which completed questionnaires were to be placed. In order to guarantee anonymity and yet know who had and had not returned questionnaires, faculty members were asked to cross their names off a list attached to the box upon returning the form. After 2 weeks, the field coordinator at each school personally contacted individuals who had not returned the instrument. This procedure was repeated after one more 2-week period.

RESULTS OF THE STUDENT QUESTIONNAIRE

Hypothesis 1: There will be a greater amount of interaction between students and school adults at Wayne High School than at Thurston High School.

The hypothesis is confirmed. Table 11.4 presents a comparative analysis of the mean number of interactions reported between students and school adults at Wayne and Thurston. The totals of the reports of interaction for all settings indicate that, in general, more interaction between students and adults occur at Wayne than at Thurston ($p < .001$). Looking at this table more closely, one can observe that more interactions with the assistant principals ($p < .001$), the counselors ($p < .001$), teachers ($p < .001$), coaches ($p < .05$), and other school workers ($p < .05$) are reported at Wayne than at Thurston. Thus, for every adult role group but the principal, more interactions are reported at Wayne High School than at Thurston High School.

Hypothesis 2: The quality of social interaction between students and school adults will be perceived as warmer and more personal at Wayne High School than at Thurston High School.

Table 11.5 presents results of a comparative analysis of two summary variables that were constructed to assess important aspects of quality of interaction.

The first summary variable is an index of the amount of personal interest that students perceive as expressed by the various school adults. This variable was

TABLE 11.4

Comparative Analysis of Mean Number of Interactions
Reported Between Students and Adults at Wayne and Thurston

School Adult	Mean Number of Interactions		Standard Deviations		t^a	Significance Level
	Wayne	Thurston	Wayne	Thurston		
1. Principal	0.51	0.42	1.200	0.835	1.089	N.S.
2. Asst. principals	0.63	0.34	1.460	0.795	3.321	$p < .001$
3. Counselors	0.93	0.48	1.449	0.839	5.055	$p < .001$
4. Teachers	4.00	3.38	2.851	1.941	3.377	$p < .001$
5. Coach	0.96	0.69	1.929	1.337	2.134	$p < .05$
6. Other school workers	2.21	1.53	3.121	2.471	3.165	$p < .05$
Sum 1–6	9.24	6.84	3.989	3.053	3.851	$p < .001$

[a]Critical values of t for various levels of significance for one-tailed test ($df = 120$) are: $p < .05 = 1.645$; $p < .01 = 2.326$; $p < .001 = 3.291$.

constructed by summing Ss ratings of the personal interest that teachers, counselors, assistant principals, and principal show for students at the school. The second summary variable, which was constructed in the same way at the first, is an index of the degree of comfort and warmth that Ss feel when engaged in informal interaction with school adults.

The results indicate that students at Wayne feel that school adults exhibit more personal interest in them than do students at Thurston ($p < .001$). There is some evidence to suggest that students at Wayne also feel somewhat more comfortable in informal interaction with school adults ($p < .07$). The hypothesis is partially confirmed.

TABLE 11.5

Comparative Analysis of Selected Summary Variables for Quality of Interaction

Summary Variable	Mean		Standard Deviations		t^a	Significance Level
	Wayne	Thurston	Wayne	Thurston		
Perceived personal interest shown by faculty	13.06	11.99	4.091	4.022	3.400	$p < .001$
Comfort in interaction with faculty	10.94	10.43	4.233	3.780	1.639	N.S. ($p < .07$)

[a]Critical values of t for various levels of significance for one-tailed test ($df = 120$) are: $p < .05 = 1.645$; $p < .01 = 2.326$; $p < .001 = 3.291$.

EFFECTIVENESS OF SOCIALIZATION

Hypothesis 3: There is a greater clarity of normative expectations at Wayne High School than at Thurston High School.

Subjects were asked to rate the clarity of normative expectations at their school. Figure 11.1 is a histogram that summarizes the percentages of subjects responding to each scale point at Wayne and Thurston.

A much higher percentage of subjects at Wayne (30.7) feel that teachers' expectations for behavior are *very clear*. Higher percentages of subjects at Thurston indicate that teachers' expectations for behavior are not very clear. The raw data were used to compare the two distributions of responses. The distributions were found to be significantly different statistically (X^2 = 21.851; $p < .01$). This finding offers confirmation to the hypothesis that there is greater clarity of normative expectations at Wayne than at Thurston. This is reflected in the very high percentage of students at Wayne who feel that how teachers expect them to act is very clear and in the relatively high percentage of subjects at Thurston who feel that how teachers expect students to act is not very clear.

Hypothesis 4: There is a greater expectation of negative consequences for norm violation at Wayne High School than at Thurston High School.

Subjects were asked what happens to an individual who does not do the things that teachers expect him to do. The possible responses included "nothing

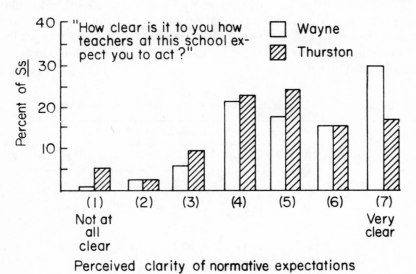

FIG. 11.1   Perceived clarity of normative expectations at Wayne and Thurston.

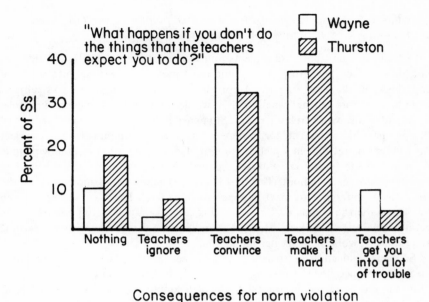

FIG. 11.2   Perceived consequences for norm violation at Wayne and Thurston.

happens," "teachers ignore you," "teachers try to convince you to do what they expect," "teachers make it hard on you," and "you get into a lot of trouble." These responses were selected, because they represented a wide range of possible responses of the two schools on this question.

At both schools, a high percentage of subjects report that teachers make it hard on the norm violator. The next consequence that high percentages of subjects at both schools perceive is that teachers try to persuade the violator to do what they (the teachers) expect them to do. The differences between the schools appear at the extremities of the consequences continuum. At Wayne, 10% of the subjects report that you get into a lot of trouble for not doing what teachers expect. At Thurston, on the other hand, 25% of the subjects report either that nothing happens or that teachers ignore the violator. At Wayne, 13% of the subjects report this kind of consequence. The frequency distributions of responses were used to test for differences in patterns of consequence for norm violation at the two schools. The distributions were found to differ statistically (X^2 = 19.90; $p < .01$). This result offers confirmation to the hypothesis that there is a greater expectation of negative consequences for norm violation at Wayne than at Thurston. In addition, it may be said that there is a greater expectation at Thurston than there is at Wayne that nothing will happen to the norm violator.

Hypothesis 5: Students will exhibit a greater preference for task orientation at Thurston High School than at Wayne High School.

A series of questions asks subjects to indicate across settings (both inside and outside of school) whether they would most prefer to meet new people, learn and think, work, relax, or play. A corresponding set of questions asks subjects to indicate across settings whether they would least prefer to meet new people, learn and think, work, relax, or play. Summary indices of preference for each of the five possible rating categories were constructed by summing for each subject the number of settings in which he preferred, for example, to meet new people. A mean of the individual summary scores for each rating category was then calculated for each school. The mean rating is taken as an indication of the strength of preference to meet new people in general. The mean scores for each school can then be compared for each rating category. Table 11.6 presents a comparative analysis of subjects' strength of preference for meeting people, learning and thinking, working, relaxing, and playing.

Subjects indicate the strongest preferences at both schools for relaxing, meeting new people, and playing in settings both inside and outside of school. This is noted by observing the relatively high summary preference scores (relaxing, 3.18 and 2.90; meeting new people, 2.84 and 3.19; playing, 2.25 and 2.45) for preferring most to engage in these activities and the relatively low summary preference scores (relaxing, 1.18 and 1.15; meeting new people, 0.96 and 0.65; playing, 1.18 and 1.15) for preferring least to engage in these activities. These scores are taken as an indication by subjects of strong preferences for relaxing, meeting new people, and playing.

Subjects at both schools exhibit relatively weak preferences for learning and thinking and working in settings both inside and outside of school. This is indicated by observing the relatively low summary preference scores for most preferring to engage in these activities (learning and thinking, 1.30 and 1.35; working, 1.09 and 0.89) and relatively high summary preference scores (learning and thinking, 2.03 and 2.07; and working, 5.68 and 5.98) for least preferring to engage in these activities. It should be noted that "working" is the least preferred activity of them all. It seems evident from these data that subjects from both schools, if given their choice, would most prefer to be relaxing, meeting new people, and/or playing. The hypothesis predicts that subjects at Thurston will exhibit a greater preference for task orientation than subjects at Wayne. A comparative analysis of summary preference scores between the two schools does not confirm this hypothesis. Table 11.6 presents the comparative analysis of mean summary preference scores. The analysis indicates that subjects at Wayne have a significantly higher summary preference score for most preferences to work than subjects at Thurston ($p < .05$). There are no signficianct differences between the summary preference scores at the two schools for least preferences to work or for most or least preference to learn and think. This would indicate that the preference for a task orientation, though low at both schools, is some-

TABLE 11.6

Comparative Analysis of Mean Summary Preference Scores
for Each Rating Category at Wayne and Thurston

Rating Category	Summary Preference Scores		Standard Deviations		t^a	Significance Level
	Wayne	Thurston	Wayne	Thurston		
Prefer most to:						
Meet new people	2.84	3.19	2.725	2.721	1.660	.05
Learn and think	1.30	1.35	1.165	1.297	0.500	N.S.
Work	1.09	0.89	1.424	0.945	2.221	$p < .05$
Relax	3.18	2.90	2.576	2.088	1.576	N.S.
Play	2.25	2.45	2.111	2.209	1.192	N.S.
Prefer least to:						
Meet new people	0.96	0.65	2.030	1.517	2.302	$p < .05$
Learn and think	2.03	2.07	2.382	2.496	0.226	N.S.
Work	5.68	5.98	3.630	3.624	1.079	N.S.
Relax	1.18	1.15	1.691	1.669	0.265	N.S.
Play	1.16	1.21	1.549	1.743	0.430	N.S.

[a]Critical value of t for one-tailed test ($df = 120$) are: $p < .05 = 1.645$; $p < .01 = 2.326$; $p < .001 = 3.291$.

what greater among subjects at Wayne than among subjects at Thurston. This finding tends not to confirm the hypothesis.

In summary, it may be stated that subjects at Thurston do not have a stronger preference for a task orientation than students at Wayne, disconfirming the hypothesis about the effectiveness of socialization. Task-related aims do not seem to be more strongly inculcated at Thurston than at Wayne. In general, subjects at both schools have strong preferences for relaxation, meeting new people, and playing and weak preferences for learning and thinking and for working. Subjects at Wayne exhibit a somewhat greater task orientation than subjects at Thurston.

Hypothesis 6: More students will perceive normative expectations for social behavior at Wayne High School than at Thurston High School.

Hypothesis 7: More students will perceive normative expectations for task-oriented behavior at Thurston High School than at Wayne High School.

The nature of the comparisons performed on data relevant to these hypotheses makes it expeditious to discuss them together. A comparative analysis at Wayne and Thurston of student perceptions of task-oriented and socially oriented teacher expectations for student behavior is presented in Table 11.7.

There are no significant differences between the schools in subjects' perceptions of task-oriented teacher expectations for student behavior. At both

TABLE 11.7

Comparative Analysis at Wayne and Thurston of Perceptions of Task-Oriented and Socially Oriented Teacher Expectations for Student Behavior

Normative Statements How much teachers expect me to . . .	*School*	*Frequency Distribution by Scale Points* 1 (*not at all*)	2	3	4	5	6	7 (*very much*) 6 d.f.	X^2	*Significance Level*
Task-Oriented Expectations										
1. To think out work clearly and carefully	Wayne	1.8	1.5	3.9	18.7	17.2	18.7	38.3	6.717	N.S.
	Thurston	.6	1.7	5.8	14.9	17.7	22.1	37.3		
2. To plan to attend college	Wayne	10.1	8.5	10.1	22.3	14.9	10.1	24.1	2.453	N.S.
	Thurston	8.4	8.4	10.1	20.5	14.6	13.5	24.4		
Socially Oriented Expectations										
3. To be involved in school activities	Wayne	9.4	10.9	13.4	18.2	12.5	13.1	22.5	18.060	$p < .01$
	Thurston	13.0	15.7	13.8	19.1	13.0	14.1	11.3		
4. To be friendly and outgoing	Wayne	8.9	5.5	8.6	16.5	15.0	19.6	26.0	12.732	$p < .05$
	Thurston	5.6	9.8	10.1	13.5	17.4	23.6	19.9		

schools, large proportions of subjects feel that teachers very much expect them to "think out work clearly and carefully." Relatively small proportions feel that this behavior is not expected of them. There is no difference between the schools on the distributions of perceptions about teacher expectations for college attendance. In the case of this expectation, there is less of a tendency for large numbers of subjects to perceive this as an important teacher expectation. In general, subjects perceive that teachers rather strongly expect them to think out work clearly and carefully. There is less of a consensus about teacher expectations for college attendance. There are no differences between the schools in their perceptions of these task-oriented norms. The hypothesis that predicted that more students at Thurston would perceive normative expectations for task-oriented behavior than subjects at Wayne is not confirmed.

There are differences between the schools in subjects' perceptions of socially oriented teacher expectations for student behavior. In comparing Wayne and Thurston, it may be observed that at Wayne more subjects perceive that teachers very much expect them to be involved in school activities, and fewer subjects perceive that this is not important than is true at Thurston ($p < .01$). At both schools there is diversity across the range of expectations, but the above difference still occurs. At Wayne, once again, more subjects perceive that it is very much expected that students be friendly and outgoing, and fewer students feel that this is not important ($p < .05$). It should be noted also that at both schools, increasing proportions of subjects perceive this as an important norm for behavior. The schools still differ in the relative strength of this norm. Thus, the hypothesis that predicted that more subjects at Wayne would perceive normative expectations for socially oriented behavior than subjects at Thurston is confirmed.

In summary, the schools do not differ as predicted on the number of subjects perceiving the importance of task-oriented norms. They do differ in the predicted direction, however, on the number of subjects who perceive the importance of socially oriented norms. At both schools, students perceive that teachers expect them to "think out work clearly and carefully" and to "be friendly and outgoing."

SUPPLEMENTAL ANALYSES

The data as collected allowed for the post hoc investigation of questions related to: (a) ways in which the social settings at each school play similar or different functions; and (b) the patterns of interaction between school adults and students in different grades and sex groups.

Differences Between Settings

The data allow a comparison of specific settings at both schools in terms of the quantity of interaction between students and school adults. This type of analysis gives further information about the quantity of interaction and provides a detailed description of differences for the functions of social settings at the two study schools.

Table 11.8 presents a comparative analysis of the 22 common settings at the study schools in terms of social interaction between students and school adults. The results summarized in this table suggest that there are 7 settings at the two schools that appear to be considerably different in terms of social interaction between students and school adults. These settings are the cafeteria, the school office, the counselor's office, study halls, the auditorium, the athletic fields, and the rest-rooms. The nature of this difference is that more students at Wayne report social interactions with the various kinds of school adults than do students at Thurston.

There are 8 settings at the two schools that are somewhat different. The differences between these settings are once again in the direction of more social interaction reported at Wayne. There are 7 other settings where there are no cell differences between the schools. These settings, then, function quite similarly at each school.

This descriptive analysis highlights the general finding that adults are to be found in a greater number of settings at Wayne than at Thurston. Seven settings at the schools are considerably different; 8 are somewhat different; 7 are similar. The pervasive finding is that a greater number of subjects report social interaction with school adults consistently at Wayne.

A similar analysis has been performed for differences between settings at the schools for social interaction between students. Table 11.9 presents a comparative analysis of the 22 common settings at the study schools in terms of interaction between respondents and their peers.

The results summarized in this table suggest that there are 6 settings that appear to be considerably different at the schools in terms of social interactions between respondents and their peers. These settings are the counselor's office, the school office, study halls, the principal's office, science labs, and the halls or stairs. It appears that at Wayne, the various school offices and the study halls are definite places where greater amounts of peer interaction take place; whereas at Thurston, the hallways and the science labs are the settings for greater amounts of peer interaction. There are 6 settings at the two schools that are somewhat, although not consistently, different; and there are 10 settings where there are no differences between the schools.

Differences in Quantity of Interaction that are Related to the Sex and Grade Level of the Respondents

Supplemental analyses were performed within each school in order to compare sex and grade level groups in terms of social interaction with adults. These results indicate that there are significant differences at both schools between grade level groups and between males and females in the amount of interaction

TABLE 11.8

Comparative Analysis of Differences Between Settings for Interaction
with School Adults at Wayne and Thurston[a]

| | | Settings Where a Significantly Greater Number of Ss Report Interaction | | | | | | | | | | | |
| | | Wayne | | | | | | Thurston | | | | | |
Setting	Degree of Difference[b]	P	AP	Coun	T	C	OSW[c]	P	AP	Coun	T	C	OSW[c]
Cafeteria	5	x		x	x	x	x	x					
School Office	5	x	x		x	x	x						
Counselors' Office	4		x	x	x	x	x						
Study Hall	3	x	x	x	x	x							
Auditorium	3	x	x	x	x								
Athletic Field	3	x	x				x						
Rest-room	3				x	x		x					
Computer Center	2				x		x						
Hall or stairs	2			x		x							
Other Places	2				x	x							
Music Rooms	1	x											
Science Lab	1			x									
Classroom	1							x					
Gym or Pool	1		x										
Principal's Office	1		x										

[a]Other settings that were included in this analysis but where no differences were found between the two schools include: art room, shop room, drama room, library, locker rooms, parking lot, newspaper/yearbook office.

[b]Based upon number of cell differences (six possible).

[c]Abbreviations: P – Principal; AP – Assistant principals; Coun – Counselors; T – Teachers; C – Coaches; OSW – Other School Workers.

TABLE 11.9

Comparative Analysis of Differences Between Settings for Interaction with Peers at Wayne and Thurston[a]

Setting	Degree of Difference[b]	Settings Where a Significantly Greater Number of Ss Report Interaction											
		Wayne						Thurston					
		CF	B	G	10	11	12[c]	CF	B	G	10	11	12[c]
Counselors' Office	6	x	x	x	x	x	x						
School Office	6	x	x	x	x	x	x						
Study Hall	6	x	x	x	x	x	x						
Principal's Office	4		x		x	x	x						
Science Lab	3				x		x					x	
Halls or Stairs	3							x		x	x		
Art Room	1												x
Computer Center	1					x							
Classroom	1				x								
Library	1									x			
Athletic Field	1						x						
Rest-room	1				x								

[a]Other settings that were included in this analysis but where no differences were found between the two schools include: music room, shop room, drama or speech room, auditorium, cafeteria, gym or pool, locker rooms, parking lot, newspaper/yearbook office.

[b]Based upon number of cell differences (six possible).

[c]Abbreviations: CF – Close Friends; B – Boys; G – Girls; 10 – Tenth Graders; 11 – Eleventh Graders; 12 – Twelf Graders.

TABLE 11.10
Mean Number of Interactions Between Students and Adults
Reported by Sex and Grade Level
at Wayne and Thurston

		Mean Number of Interactions	
School	Grade Level	Male	Female
Wayne	10	7.4545	6.2174
	11	6.2167	5.1250
	12	6.200	5.5349
Thurston	10	5.5077	4.5152
	11	6.4516	5.0140
	12	4.7273	4.5833

that they have with school adults. Tables 11.10 and 11.11 summarize the analyses of variance that were carried out to test school differences.

There are statistically significant differences between the grade levels in quantity of student—adult interaction at each school. It is interesting to note that the patterns are different at the two schools. At Wayne, the 10th-grade students report the greatest amount of social interaction; and at Thurston, the 11th-grade students report the greatest amount of interaction. These patterns may be indicative of a different socialization sequence at the schools.

Each school also shows significant differences between males and females in the amount of interaction they have with school adults. At both schools, the direction of the difference is the same. At every grade level, male students report more interaction with school adults than females.

In addition to differences between Wayne and Thurston in quantity of interaction with school adults, there are also differences within each school in the quantity of social interaction with school adults between students in different grades and between male and female students.

TABLE 11.11
Analyses of Variance of Mean Interactions
Between Students and Adults
by Grade and Sex

School	F	df	P
Wayne			
Grade	3.0599	2.328	$p < .05$
Sex	5.6429	1.328	$p < .01$
Thurston			
Grade	4.0455	2.357	$p < .025$
Sex	7.7359	1.357	$p < .01$

RESULTS OF THE FACULTY QUESTIONNAIRE

Hypothesis 8: Faculty members at Wayne will be more satisfied with their jobs than will faculty members at Thurston.

The analysis of the staff questionnaire indicates differences in the level of satisfaction of the staffs at the two schools. Of the faculty at Thurston, 19% are unsatisfied with teaching as a profession, and 22% are unsatisfied with their present job. At Wayne, only 5% of the staff are unsatisfied with their profession and with their present jobs. The differences between the distributions on both of these items are statistically significant (satisfaction with profession $- X^2 = 14.051; p < .01$; satisfaction with job $- X^2 = 20.467; p < .001$).

Correlates of Satisfaction

A correlational analysis was performed in order to determine if degree of satisfaction with one's current job was related to age, tenure, teaching technique, or satisfaction with the performance of others. Table 11.12 summarizes the relationships between these variables and current satisfaction level. As can be observed from Table 11.12, there is little relationship between age, length of tenure, teach-

TABLE 11.12
Relationship Between Faculty Satisfaction with
Present Job and Selected Variables
(N = 89 at each School)

Variable	Correlation with Job Satisfaction[a]	
	Wayne	Thurston
Age	−0.1153	0.139
Years on staff	−0.1725	0.073
Years in present position	−0.0684	0.141
Current step level	−0.3074	0.070
Classroom technique		
A. Amount of structure	0.0657	−0.185
B. Amount of teacher−student discussion	−0.1976	0.131
C. Amount of student−student discussion	−0.1865	0.132
Satisfaction with others		
A. Principal	0.3065	0.206
B. Assistant principals	0.1889	0.205
C. Faculty	0.2947	0.175
D. Counselors	0.2488	0.204
E. Other school workers	0.2796	−0.074

[a]Pearson Product−Moment Correlation Coefficient.

ing technique, or satisfaction with the performance of others at either school. The strongest relationships are with satisfaction with the performance of others, but even these are slight correlations. The people at Thurston who are dissatisfied are distributed across age groups, tenure levels, and faculty using different teaching techniques.

Hypothesis 9: Faculty members at Wayne High School will be more satisfied with how others do their jobs than will faculty members at Thurston High School.

Staff members at Thurston are less pleased with how the principal, the assistant principals, the faculty, and the counselors are doing their jobs than are members of the staff at Wayne. Table 11.13 presents the comparative analysis of staff assessments of how well various people and groups of people are doing their jobs at the two schools.

Perceptions of Influence

In general, the faculty at Wayne indicate that the principal, the assistant principals, the department heads, the counselors, the student body, the student government, and the individual faculty have significantly more influence in how their school is run than do the same groups at Thurston. On the other hand, faculty at Thurston indicate that parents of students have more influence. Table 11.14 presents the comparative analysis of staff perceptions of the amount of influence that various groups or individuals have in how the school is run.

SUMMARY

The findings indicate confirmation for the hypothesis concerning differences in quantity of interaction between students and counselors and students and assistant principals at Wayne and Thurston. Support is indicated for the hypothesis concerning differences in quantity of interaction between students and teachers, coaches, and other school workers at Wayne and Thurston. The hypothesis concerning differences in quality of interaction betweenthe study schools is confirmed for perceptions of personal interest expressed by school adults, supported for expression of comfort in informal interaction, and not confirmed for perceptionsof the typical student—faculty interaction. The hypothesis comparing the effectiveness of socialization at the two schools is confirmed in general. Specifically, students at Wayne perceive greater clarity of normative expectations for behavior and greater expectations of negative consequences for norm violation. Students at Wayne demonstrate greater preference for the company of adults than students at Thurston, and as predicted, subjects at Wayne perceive

TABLE 11.13
Comparative Analysis of Staff Assessments on How Well Various Persons Are Doing Their Jobs at Wayne and Thurston

People and Groups of People	School	How happy are you with the way these people are doing their jobs in your school? (percentages)							X^2 (6 df)	Significance Level
		Very Happy 1	2	3	4	5	6	Very Unhappy 7		
Principal	Wayne	0	0	1	6	16	34	43	41.089	.001
Principal	Thurston	7	9	16	9	21	28	10		
Asst. Principals	Wayne	0	1	4	13	26	34	22	13.890	.05
Asst. Principals	Thurston	2	6	7	17	29	33	6		
Faculty	Wayne	0	1	3	15	31	26	15	48.322	.001
Faculty	Thurston	5	6	19	37	23	9	1		
Counselors	Wayne	1	6	9	21	28	26	10	24.706	.001
Counselors	Thurston	3	13	22	35	12	15	1		
Other School Workers	Wayne	1	0	11	14	29	29	16	11.174	N.S.
	Thurston	1	2	10	23	25	35	4		

TABLE 11.14

Comparative Analysis of Staff Perceptions of Amount of Influence
That Various Groups or Individuals Have in
How the School Is Run at Wayne and Thurston

Group or Individual How much influence . . .	School	Perceived Amount of Influence (%)					X^2 (4 df)	Significance Level
		None at all	Very little	Some	Quite a bit	A lot		
The School Board	Wayne	5	7	29	39	21	8.149	N.S.
The School Board	Thurston	2	5	18	37	38	7.858	N.S.
Central Administration	Wayne	2	5	22	55	16		
Central Administration	Thurston	3	5	24	37	32		
Principal	Wayne	0	1	1	31	67	45.521	$p < .001$
Principal	Thurston	0	8	28	42	23		
Assistant Principals	Wayne	2	7	30	48	12	14.830	$p < .01$
Assistant Principals	Thurston	0	14	52	26	0		
Department Heads	Wayne	4	23	35	37	1	54.637	$p < .001$
Department Heads	Thurston	44	34	23	0	0		
Teachers	Wayne	4	28	42	19	7	5.876	N.S.
Teachers	Thurston	1	26	51	21	1		
Counselors	Wayne	4	18	48	28	2	24.486	$p < .001$
Counselors	Thurston	6	41	48	4	0		
Student Body	Wayne	2	36	41	17	4	11.346	$p < .05$
Student Body	Thurston	10	47	36	6	1		
Student Government	Wayne	6	42	41	11	0	13.301	$p < .01$
Student Government	Thurston	16	51	32	1	1		
Parents of Students	Wayne	2	42	42	12	1	10.864	$p < .05$
Parents of Students	Thurston	1	23	51	19	7		
Yourself	Wayne	7	43	31	15	4	12.685	$p < .02$
Yourself	Thurston	10	47	40	2	0		
Educational Association	Wayne	6	16	54	21	3	5.500	N.S.
Educational Association	Thurston	2	21	64	12	1		
PTA or PTO	Wayne	33	47	18	2	0	7.831	N.S.
PTA or PTO	Thurston	46	30	18	0	5		

normative expectations for social behavior. The hypotheses that were not confirmed indicate that students at Thurston do not exhibit a greater preference for task preference than those at Wayne; in fact, this hypothesis appears to be reversed. In addition, students at Thurston do not perceive normative expectations for task-related activities, as had been expected. Finally, there is no conformation for the hypothesis that there will be fewer identifiable social groups at Wayne than at Thurston.

Additional supplementary analyses focus on the use of social settings at the two schools. The results indicate that there are some differences in terms of the number of settings used by student role groups Tenth- and 11th-graders report more settings for interaction at Wayne than at Thurston; female students also report more settings for interaction at Wayne. Several settings at each of the schools have been shown to differ in terms of the interaction that occurs there.

The results indicate that the method has successfully demonstrated that differences between the schools do exist in terms of quantity of interaction, quality of interaction, and effectiveness of socialization. In characterizing the differences, it appears that school adults play a more important role in the life of students at Wayne than they do at Thurston, and this results in a more consistent pattern of socialization.

Thurston is characterized by a relatively large number of staff members who are unsatisfied with teaching as a profession, with their own jobs, and with how other staff members are doing their jobs. The overall findings, therefore, suggest greater dissatisfaction among both student and faculty groups at Thurston. In addition, Thurston faculty feel that they personally, as well as most other groups in the school, have relatively little influence in how their school is run. Staff members at Wayne, on the other hand, appear to be more satisfied with teaching, their own jobs, and their colleagues.

IMPLICATIONS

There are many implications of these findings that deserve discussion. The literature on adolescence indicates that there have been few studies of high schools and adolescents that focus on relationships between adolescents and adults (Trickett, Kelly, & Todd, 1972). The literature also indicates that at least from a theoretical point of view, one of the important developmental task of adolescence involves dissolving "infantile" dependencies and establishing effective patterns of relating to people in authority (Douvan & Adelson, 1966). The current study has demonstrated that at a school such as Wayne where there are active, diverse, and plentiful interactions between students and adults, the students perceive themselves as having an involved role in the school. In addition, one could infer from the findings that schools with different patterns of social interaction between students and school adults provide very different environments for the tasks of adolescence.

The theoretical rationale for the present study is derived from ecological theory. The amount of social interaction that occurs between persons and the quality of this interaction was assumed to affect individual adaptation. Information, affectional supplies, expectations, and rules are all transmitted through social interaction.

The differences in patterns of interaction between the schools can be linked to effectiveness of socialization. At Wayne, where conditions for greater amounts of social interaction across a variety of settings are observed, there is a clearer perception on the part of students about normative expectations for behavior. Students exhibit a greater identification with social goals, as had been expected; but in addition, students exhibit greater identification with work goals as well. There is a focus in this setting on consequences for norm violation and greater perceptions of harsh punishment. There seems to be a sense of constantly being in an adult-centered environment. Foci for behavior in many instances revolve around adult demands. One has a sense of a group of students who, among other things, must be very tuned to the adults around them and to the multiple demands that these adults are making.

Where the conditions of lower amounts of interaction in a more restricted number of settings are observed, normative expectations for behavior are perceived to be less clear. Students identify less strongly with work-oriented goals and less strongly with a general social orientation. It does not seem to be true, as had been expected, that students exhibit a strong orientation for task-related activities.

In many ways, it appears that Thurston relies on the students' own social mechanisms to maintain order. Students who have a need for adult contact and supervision are likely to feel somewhat adrift in this school. Students wrestling with problems of internal control are not likely to find easily identifiable guidelines for behavior in their dealings with school adults. As long as these students remain invisible, this will be a personal problem. As soon as they become visible, they are likely to become disturbing to the school, which has few mechanisms for dealing with student behaviors that do not fall inside the boundaries of "proper" behavior.

At Wayne, some students may be able to develop some relationships with adults and with persons in positions of authority, because of their high degree of contact with a variety of role models in a variety of settings during the course of their high school experience. However, students who are very rebellious or who do not easily meet adult standards may encounter difficulty at this school. At Thurston, some students may have difficulty developing mature relationships with adults in positions of authority, because of their relatively low degree of contact with school role models during their high school experience. For the Thurston students may be more dependent on the adult resources that are available outside of school. Some students in Thurston, however, may be forced to become more independent of adults. There are also implications that a wide variety of deviant behaviors can be tolerated in this school as long as the individual does not come to the attention of school officials. The preceding discussion raises some possibilities about different patterns of adaptation that may occur in each of the two schools.

The findings that Wayne students exhibit strong preferences for work activities disconfirmed a hypothesis of the study. This finding raises some important questions about the work atmosphere in each of the two study schools. Relative lack of interaction between students and adults may interfere with students' developing a positive and interested attitude toward work. It is possible that low interaction may generate an atmosphere of mutual mistrust between students and faculty that impairs the school's ability to meet its academic goals. On the other hand, students may feel that the faculty trust them because they are not around. This condition may facilitate academic perfromance, and students may feel freer to express their true feelings about work. Where there is a high degree of social interaction between students and school adults, students may feel pressured and watched by adults. The work orientation may be a form of compliance with adult demands, and quality of academic performance may suffer.

The findings of the present study imply that the development of social relationships with role models and persons in authority is an important topic for future investigation. It is particularly noted that schools that differ in the quantity and quality of interaction between students and school adults may provide quite different paths for adaptation and development in these areas. This provides an empirical baseline for the longitudinal work to follow with these two schools.

The current study has demonstrated that the two high schools, though similar in some external respects, do differ in social atmosphere. For the students at Wayne, the faculty constitute an active part of the social context. There appears to be interaction with various kinds of adults across many settings in this school. In addition, student socialization encourages involvement in the life and activities of the school. There are also indications that work-related issues are involved in the socializatio process. Further research with these schools could be developed to clarify the students' familial and adult relationships, including styles of relating to authorities and the utilization of adults as resources. In addition, the congruence between faculty and peer demands might also focus more intensively upon the quality of social interaction with adults in various settings in the school. The effect of relatively numerous contacts with adults who are perceived as personally interested in students upon students' work-related objectives should also be studied. For Wayne, there appear to be relatively clear implications for action. This school, with appropriate planning, may be able to benefit from its socioemotional atmosphere to enhance work-related activities among students. For example, students could be motivated to develop reading skills by watching some of their teachers debate about current novels on closed-circuit television.

At Thurston, it appears that further research should be directed toward the peer culture. In addition, the nature of classroom interaction deserves attention. The classroom is the primary setting for student—adult interaction at Thurston. Future work there should also investigate the sources of teacher dissatisfaction with their jobs, their professions, and their colleagues. It may be that these morale issues inhibit social interaction between students and faculty. Improving the morale of the teachers, then, may enhance the social atmosphere of the school by promoting more student—teacher interaction, which in turn might serve to increase student as well as teacher involvement in the life of the school. A program of this type could help the Thurston faculty gain an accurate overview of the functioning of their school. A committee constituted to facilitate such an effort and to search out sources of staff dissatisfaction, low evaluation of colleagues, etc. could be a helpful step. The findings from the present study, for example, could be a source of initial data for such a group.

There is a very important point to be emphasized in concluding this chapter. The social environments of the two schools have been shown to differ along a number of dimensions affecting student growth and development. These differences should be useful to the faculty in helping to understand patterns of student adaptation at each school. As has been suggested, efforts to improve the environment at both schools would be different because of the differences in the local culture. In the case of Wayne, the design for change can rely upon the social atmosphere that already exists to facilitiate the attainment of new educational goals. In the case of Thurston, its design would be first to create an educational program to help the faculty effect a more benign social atmosphere.

IMPLICATIONS OF THE METHOD

The Environmental Assessment Questionnaire has been successful in providing a comparative analysis of the two study schools. The EAQ has provided data that allowed us to distinguish between schools on a number of dimensions. Another contribution of the EAQ is that it provides a systematic data base about the quality and quantity of social interaction and about social settings where social interaction occurs. In addition, the instrument has provided perceptual data concerning the effectiveness of socialization in the two schools.

The EAQ was designed to provide data about social interaction that would help to test whether or not a survey technique could be used to bridge the gap between behavioral observation and perceptions of environments. There are some shortcomings to the instrument that should receive comment at this point. The instrument is somewhat long. This is true from the point of view of the students (some of whom had difficulty completing the instrument when it was administered) as well as from the point of view of data analysis. Behavioral observations may provide valuable information about the validity of the reports of interaction obtained in the EAQ. At this point, it is assumed that this type of data provides the most accurate information possible about patterns of social interaction in each school. The EAQ does provide data that has allowed us to distinguish between schools on the dimension of quantity of interaction.

The instrument does not allow for the differentiation of a particular setting. For example, the hallways may house many different settings. This is particularly true at Thurston. Nowhere does the instrument provide any clues as to which groups congregate in which subsettings. The instrument does, however, indicate to us that we could expect to find groups of 10th-graders or groups of boys in these subsettings. The instrument also does not provide data about some settings that may be used at certain times of the day or during certain seasons of the year. Data about these types of places may be available only by direct question about the relative importance of such settings, but this would require further work.

Information about the quality and range of interaction in a wider number of schools would help to determine the importance of these variables for school functioning and for student socialization. If the finding that the quantity and quality of interaction between students and school adults related to student socialization continues to be upheld in further work, there are many implications for the organization and development of high schools.

REFERENCES

Astin, A. W. *The college environment*. Washington, D.C.: American Council on Education, 1968.

Bachman, J. G., Kahn, R. L., & Mednick, M. T. *Working paper II: Univariate statistics describing a nationwide sample of tenth grade*. Ann Arbor, Mich.: Institute for Social Research, July 1968.

Barker, R. G., & Gump, P. *Big school, little school*. Stanford, Calif.: Stanford University Press, 1964.

Brim, O. G., Jr. Socialization through the life cycle. In O. G. Brim, Jr., & S. Wheeler (Eds.), *Socialization after childhood: Two essays*. New York: Wiley, 1966.

Brim, O. G., Jr. Adult socialization. In J. A. Clausen (Ed.), *Socialization and society*. Boston: Little, Brown and Company, 1968.

Caplan, G. Opportunities for school psychologists in the primary prevention of mental disorders in children. In A. J. Bindman & A. D. Spiegel (Eds.), *Perspectives in community mental health*. Chicago: Aldine, 1969.

Douvan, E., & Adelson, J. *The adolescent experience*. New York: Wiley, 1966.

Fatke, R. The adaptation process of new students in two suburban high schools. In M. J. Feldman (Ed.), *Studies in psychotherapy and behavioral change, No. 2, Theory and research in community mental health*. Buffalo: State University of New York at Buffalo, 1971.

Kelly, J. G. Towards an ecological conception of preventive interventions. In J. W. Carter, Jr. (Ed.), *Research contributions from psychology to community mental health*. New York: Behavioral Publications, 1968.

Mechanic, D. *Students under stress.* Glencoe, Ill.: The Free Press, 1962.

Orth, C. D. *Social structure and learning climate: The first year at the Harvard Business School.* Boston: Harvard University Press, 1963.

Pace, C. R. *College and university scales.* Princeton, N.J.: Educational Testing Service, 1963.

Parsons, T., & Bales, R. F. Family structure and the socialization of the child. In T. Parsons & R. F. Bales (Eds.), *Family, socialization and interaction process.* New York: Macmillan, 1955.

Stillman, H. *An exploratory study of two high school environments.* Unpublished manuscript, The University of Michigan, 1969.

Trickett, E. J., Kelly, J. G., & Todd, D. M. The social environment of the high school: Guidelines for individual change and organizational redevelopment. In S. Golann & C. Eisdorfer (Eds.), *Handbook of community psychology.* New York: Appleton—Century—Crofts, 1972.

IV

FEEDBACK, CRITIQUE AND COMMENTARY

12 Observations on the Opinions of Youth Study from the Participating High Schools

George Bell, Norm Boyea
Wayne Memorial High School

Jan W. Jacobs
South Redford School District

Jack R. Harms, Jack Knox
Lee M. Thurston High School

GEORGE BELL, PRINCIPAL, WAYNE MEMORIAL HIGH SCHOOL

As I look back upon the research of the Opinions of Youth Study at Wayne Memorial High School, I am very much impressed with the professional level of the staff. They have conducted themselves so that the activities, the wishes, and the concerns of the faculty and students have been listened to. In fact, the project staff often reminds us that we are not getting as much from the study as we could. It is rare to find academic researchers asking how they can help and then finding out that they really mean it! Though it is difficult to evaluate any one study in terms of the practical significance of the findings, it is interesting to note that major contributions in educational research seldom, if ever, result from a single study but rather are the result of a series of interconnected studies by a number of investigators. From this perspective, I would be premature in making any conclusive statements about the interrelationship of the studies that have been done and are presently going on at our school. But from the data collected, the faculty at Wayne are optimistic that the findings will be very useful to us.

One of the primary gains we have made from our association with this study is that our views of youth have changed. It is very easy for those of us who work with high school students daily to become cynical in how we see them develop. We can easily take credit for those youths who do become responsive and informed citizens and also easily disclaim those who do not perform up to our standards. What we have learned already is that many of those students who do well in our school may do so in spite of our social environment, whereas some of those who do not participate in our school are not involved as a result of our shortcomings. This realization is at least a start toward a more balanced view of the school's role in our community.

In reviewing the project at Wayne, there are two questions that should be asked: First, to what extent has the behavior of the faculty and students in the school been affected or changed; and second, to what extent has this project helped students, teachers, and administrators solve the problems of the school? As principal of a large suburban high school, I have had the opportunity to encounter educational and psychological research that can be called, justifiably, fragmented, overspecialized, or just plain dull, with little concern for the practical and human problems of the school. On the other hand, I have also encountered research projects that have attempted to deal with real issues facing our schools, but the methods were so shoddy and small that the results were equally bad.

This project deserves very high marks in terms of preplanning of the design, methods, and general concern for all of us at Wayne. This study is one of the few efforts that has seriously tried to understand the natural setting of the school before designing treatment programs and curriculum reforms. Using a wide range of research techniques, the researchers have expressed a great deal of flexibility in studying what I am increasingly finding is a complex social institution. I must admit that my duties as principal have not allotted me sufficient time to contribute as actively to the project as I would like. I also feel that there is much we can do to improve schools for most students that does not require research or knowledge beyond what we now possess. However, I am pleased that we have been able to take advantage of our relationship with this research program. It is also my prediction that research in years ahead will refer to this work as a primary example of how field research should be done.

Ideally, every teacher should be concerned with research and evaluation, but because teachers have a history of being "used" by outside researchers who burden them with tests and procedures and leave them ignorant of what was learned or how to use the information, teachers are suspicious of the value of most research. It has been a pleasure to see many teachers take a spontaneous and active interest in this project. Much of the credit goes to Norm Boyea, our coordinator for the study, who has made it easy for our faculty to be involved in this research.

When I say the educational research of the future will follow this study as an example, I am referring to two important ingredients this relationship has validated. First, the academic research staff cares about how they do their work; and second, the collaborating school is able to appoint a member of the faculty to work with the staff. We have been able to have Norm Boyea serve as an integral liaison between our school and the university. The research coordinator can facilitate the research efforts and identify how the school can benefit from the study. The research coordinator knows his school system, the staff, and the community. By earning the respect and trust of faculty and students, he can maintain the standards of both the school system and the university. Even more important, he has to protect the school system from unwanted demands, educate the researchers to the needs of the school, and reassure teachers whose classes are being observed that "research" does not mean espionage.

Every administrator will tell you that one of his or her most difficult tasks is keeping in touch with faculty and students in the school. Teachers must also be aware of the attitudes and values of their students. Students, teachers, or administrators rarely have an accurate view of each other. It is my opinion that this project has enabled me to find out how students perceive me as an administrator, how they view each other, and most important, how the students view all of us. This study has opened lines of communication that were not previously opened and on occasion has helped us collectively to feel good about ourselves. When we know how other people feel and think, we can do something about it. The project findings have been presented to the faculty, students, and the administration at least once every year. This study also has supplied us with data to present several reports to the Wayne—Westland Community District Board of Education and the District Curriculum Council, and the staff has been willing to meet with the Board of Education.

I would like to emphasize that this project has been successful, because the staff at the university have maintained a close relationship with all of us — the staff, the students, and the faculty — during the past 5 years. Secondly, the relationship has been sustained and cohesive. Because educational problems do not lend themselves to "one-shot" research, the coordinated nature of the longitudinal research has been a key to its success. The essential ingredient of our collaboration with the university from the beginning has been the shared value of equality in planning and designing the research, and making the findings available to the school.

NORM BOYEA, SOCIAL SCIENCE FACULTY, FIELD COORDINATOR, WAYNE MEMORIAL HIGH SCHOOL

Someone once said that the best scientific scholarship consists of subjecting to minute inspection objects that are taken for granted just because they are under our noses. This is exactly what this research program has tried to do — submit the social environment of the school to minute inspection.

The project, from onset, has attempted to look at the high school as a complex and dynamic social system. The studies have not fallen into a fixed pattern that is often demanded of contemporary social science research; but through the use of multidimensional methods and techniques, the school has been studied at a level and in directions never before attempted.

Historically, the university has looked upon the school as an available laboratory to train its graduate students in educational and psychological research. However, the school has been a reluctant "guinea pig" and often has felt used and unjustly criticized by naive researchers who knew little about the difficulties and problems associated with public education. It is indeed fortunate that the research staff has been cognizant of these past inadequacies and successfully geared this project toward serving the community and the school rather than using it. A great deal of time, effort, and money has been expended in this direction.

The basic philosophy of this project has been to increase the effectiveness of the school by providing a better understanding of the school environment. In order to accomplish this objective, the researchers had to become sensitive to the problems of the school. Part of my job as research coordinator has entailed: (a) helping the researchers become sensitive to Wayne Memorial High School; and (b) presenting new research proposals to the administration and staff of each school. This often involved matching priorities in terms of value to the school or to the larger project. It was not unusual to meet with the research staff several times before acceptance, rejection, or the necessary changes could be made. The needed cooperation and trust, however, did not come overnight. Four years ago, the staff at Wayne was very skeptical and reluctant about participating — partly due to feelings of inadequacy and fear of the worst. This attitude is perhaps typical of any group that sees "outsiders" looking in as a threat. There are many reasons why these fears eventually diminished. One critical factor seemed to be the attitude of the staff doing the research. They did not consider their role as that of outside authority but rather as a role that has been without special status or privilege. They never rendered criticism or gave unsought advice, yet they always were available to help when called upon.

Because many of the individual studies required that a great deal of time be spent at the school, the Wayne faculty began to look at the staff from the university not as "outsiders," but as members of the staff. Friendships grew, and acceptance increased. The researchers became part of the school in the sense that they were aware of the attitudes and values of the individual staff members whom they met in teachers' lounges and lunchrooms. Once the teachers and administrators recognized that these people were not only interested but also understood our problems, the reluctance gave way.

The most important aspect of this project is its ability to look at the total school environment: the interplay among people, processes, and events in the life of the school. The importance of teachers and administrators knowing how students and other teachers feel about themselves, their values, expectations, satisfactions, and dissatisfactions over a period of time cannot be overstated. Often all three groups were surprised to find how different groups in the school perceived a policy. Administrators learned something about themselves, the background, and the plans of their students and teachers. Sometimes the reality of the responses was denied. The feeling that "it can't be true because I don't perceive myself or my policy as repressive or threatening" was heard. Now the administration finds it easier to make changes in curriculum, student rules, extracurricular activities, etc., because they have a better understanding of the attitudes and feelings of the staff and students.

Questionnaires and individual interviews completed by Dan Edwards and George Gilmore, reported in Chapters 5, 6, and 7, helped define the objectives of the school and assess the extent to which they are being met. Phil Newman's study of teacher attitudes, reported in Chapter 11, opened up communications between teachers, counselors, and administrators that had been closed because of misunderstandings for a number of years. Another study revealed that the policies on orientation of new students into the school were totally inadequate and that a few simple changes by teachers and counselors could remedy the problem (Fatke, 1971). Barbara Newman's study, reported in Chapter 8, attempted to observe and report interpersonal behavior. Some of her findings are most interesting and have been instrumental in bringing about curricular changes. She found that 10th-grade boys at both schools had difficulty in discussing and conceptualizing their ideas. This held true no matter what the context was. Her observations coincide with George Gilmore's data that most 10th-grade boys perceive their chief competences as athletic in nature and that the school offers little opportunity for actual participation except for a very few with special talents.

In many ways, the work completed during 1971–1972, when the students were in the 11th grade, holds even greater promise and should prove more valuable. The groundwork has been completed, and some earlier problems have been eliminated. The process of building upon previous findings implies that our results should have more meaning and in some cases will be more precise.

At Wayne, the next 2 or 3 years are going to be a time of tremendous change. I see the value of the project as a useful resource that will keep us in tune with each other. Teachers can use this information to evaluate their own performances as seen by students and to locate areas of difficulty. Hopefully, this will open channels of communication with students, other teachers, and administrators. It should also lead to evaluation of new teaching methods and curricular changes as they are made. Individual teachers and administrators can now compare and will continue to compare responses to those of other teachers and administrators. I am indeed optimistic that the future results will continue to be as beneficial to the school as those of the past.

JAN W. JACOBS, ASSISTANT SUPERINTENDENT, CURRICULUM AND INSTRUCTION, SOUTH REDFORD SCHOOL DISTRICT AND JACK R. HARMS, PRINCIPAL, LEE M. THURSTON HIGH SCHOOL

The Opinions of Youth Study has had considerable benefit for Lee M. Thurston High School and the South Redford School District. First, the project has stimulated our professional staff to become aware, to a greater degree than previously, of students' attitudes about their school environment. Much of the time, research deals with the cognitive domains to the exclusion of the affective areas; this project clearly addressed itself to both. Interestingly, the impact of the student data gathered thus far has been primarily on the attitudes of the professional staff, who are beginning to feel a pressing need to make changes in the social environment of the high school.

Another important benefit of the project is that the professional staff of the high school are beginning to acquire the skills and attitudes needed to conduct research. In this sense, the project has served as a means of in-service training for high school teachers and administrators. A number of staff members who have been associated with the project are currently pursuing advanced degrees. Of greatest value is the fact that members of the faculty have seen the process of research in action and have begun to apply it to solve their own professional problems. The studies have focused attention on topics in specific enough detail so that the curious students, parent groups, and professional staff feel encouraged to maintain a probing inquiry. They have become more accustomed to raising questions about who is doing what, where, when, and why.

In addition, they have gained some basic information that has become a foundation from which they are seeking clarification of specific aspects of the total program. For example, although a large majority of staff members responding to a questionnaire expressed dissatisfaction, the report of the dissatisfaction stimulated inquiry of *why* they were unhappy. Longitudinal analysis on several topics is now under consideration. These topics include new teacher orientation programs, staff interaction related to room assignments, multiple teacher lounge facilities, staff perceptions of counseling and administrative roles, and interpersonal relationships related to length of service at the school.

The project has also provided the impetus for a sweeping renewal of the instructional improvement system of the district. Previously, the instructional system was rather haphazard. Now new components of secondary education have been identified as integral parts of the instructional improvement system in the district, stimulated by the study's findings of student and faculty perceptions of the social environment of the high school: (a) needs assessment; (b) goal formulation; (c) objectives formulation; (d) delivery system development; (e) program implementation, program evaluation, and recycling of the system; and (f) recommendations for change.

The greatest area of benefit has to do with the way in which the staff perceived how the data was gathered, analyzed, and made available to us from the number of interrelated studies. The total study was one that viewed high school youth from a number of perspectives — the degree to which the objectives of the school were being met, the nature of teacher attitudes, the orientation of incoming students, and the interpersonal behaviors within the school, among others.

The staff are becoming more aware of the relationship between the role of the community, parents, and Board of Education and the nature of the social environment within the school. The fact that various groups felt that the high school administration did not completely control the destiny of the high school, so to speak, has important meaning to us. It has become obvious that certain changes need to take place in the way incoming students are oriented to Thurston High School.

Equally obvious is the need to open up other avenues of student participation than presently exist. Since most of the students perceived their competences as athletic in nature, the development of a comprehensive intramural program as well as the fostering of activities that would enable students to feel competent in areas other than athletics is now in order. Another need is to open up experiences that would allow students to exercise more initiation and participation. The reader of the many project reports from the study does receive the feeling that this topic can be greatly enhanced. Social interaction in our high school is not as warm, extensive, or meaningful as we prefer. The project has great potential as an agent of change. The research staff has performed its role in the highest possible fashion, and the task we face is to make use of the data to improve the climate in which we ask youth to be educated.

JACK KNOX, COUNSELOR AND FIELD COORDINATOR, LEE M. THURSTON HIGH SCHOOL

My contribution to this volume is limited to three themes. The first is reactions and comments concerning some of the findings from the research that have been reported in the various chapters. The second is my personal reflections regarding this type of research. And finally, I offer some observations about the evolving role of the field coordinator.

It should be noted that when referring to relevant and significant research findings, especially as related to this research program, there are several traps one can fall into. The tendency is ever present to expect more than can be produced rather than to accept the reality that usually in research, more issues are generated than are settled. Another is to expect too much too soon. This is particularly true of this project in that we are still only in the initial stage of a longitudinal study; and yet there are teachers on the Thurston staff asking for what the "U. of M." has found out — and they are really referring to dramatic results. Perhaps another pitfall is to overlook the fact that this project is somewhat novel and pioneering with a built-in risk factor of error through inexperience. Hence, the payoff will be less, because we are experimenting. With these reservations in mind, I present some comments about what has been reported in previous chapters.

The findings thus far, although not particularly surprising, lend credence to suspicions we at Thurston have had for years but have not had much tangible evidence to support. Also, because of the comparisons with Wayne, we have some basis on which to evaluate our impressions. First, the case of "Harold" should give any school something to ponder. Here is a student who by all apparent indications is "in" as far as being involved in school is concerned. He appears to be a pleasant, well-adjusted student; but as we have heard from the work of Edwards, Gilmore, and B. Newman in Chapters 5, 6, and 7, he actually feels "out of it" rather than "in." If this is actually the case, and if he is typical of all 10th-grade boys, then we at Thurston have a real problem of helping students feel better about themselves and school. "Harold" and others like him evidently need assistance in becoming more satisfied with and involved in school. Other findings that stand out are the need for outlets and learning opportunities in sports and social skills, particularly for 10th-grade boys. The reports of our inability to teach or involve the "tribe" members in school and the apparent unrest or discontent of our staff provide other important data. Each of these is a real problem, and we at Thurston have avoided the temptation to explain or rationalize them and have begun to take steps toward trying to understand more about them.

As a result of feedback from the research program, we have spent some time brainstorming about staff discontent. What we have come up with might be worth mentioning, just as an example, to show the complexities of the problem. We can trace the practice or habit of complaining and criticizing back to the beginning of the school's history. Thurston began as a student-centered school, and the staff disagreed over the issues of structure vs. nonstructure and child-oriented vs. subject matter-oriented approaches to teaching. In effect, the staff has agreed to disagree over the past 15 years. Over a period of years, polarization set in, and power struggles developed. As a result, discussion turned to argumentation and ill feelings, which in turn led to a reluctance to communicate with those not sympathetic to one's viewpoint on education. We have apparently reached the point where we agree not to disagree and remain silent in our respective groups.

Compounding the problem of communication has been the rather flexible manner in which the administration has operated and the way program and policies have been implemented. We have always had a portion of our staff upset by a lack of direction and structure and by the latitude and tolerance of diversity. These factors alone could possibly generate considerable discontent. There are probably more factors (e.g., contract disputes, administration turnovers, board of education and central administration power struggles, etc.). But on the other hand, we have the added challenge of explaining why none of our staff, when given the opportunity, preferred a transfer to the junior high school and why we have a waiting list of teachers within the district wanting to joint the Thurston staff. Also interesting is the fact that we have 10 teachers who are graduates of our own high school. Thus, the issue of staff morale is most perplexing and has presented an additional challenge to the research staff, to us at Thurston, and to me as field coordinator. The challenge is to go beyond the recognition or detection of an apparent problem and get at the dynamics of the "why" and the "how come" of it.

It should be noted that any project such as this will have difficulty finding cooperative host schools and even more difficulty maintaining the arrangement. Any school offering itself and its constituents as social science guinea pigs has much to lose and very little to gain. The risk is great, because not everyone completely trusts social scientists or wishes to subject himself to investigation. And there are those who object to disruption of the educational process. Keep in mind, too, that schools today are usually very sensitive political entities whose financial security can be destroyed by a dose of bad publicity or ill will. In short, being a host to research is a delicate situation loaded with risk. Considering this, much depends on good sense and careful planning that, to date, we have been fortunate to have had. The sincere concern shown by the research program and the professional manner in which they conduct themselves within our schools are especially commendable and, of course, rewarding.

Besides the public relations problem, there is another factor that could be detrimental to the progress of the study; and this has to do with the working relationship between the school and research staff. There always exists, whether we like it or not, the tendency for some to feel that they are being used or exploited in a project such as this (e.g., someone in the school commenting: "We're not making scientific history; we're really making PhD's!"). Akin to this feeling is the general skepticism teachers have about the productivity of research. And similarly, there exists the apparent reluctance of some researchers to discuss or reveal what they are trying to investigate. All these perceptions we have about research investigations serve to frustrate a positive, productive relationship. With respect to this project, these problems have been rather successfully avoided or buffered, mainly because feedback and consultations have been an integral part of the whole project. When the staff are warm, pleasant, and responsive people, a good deal of the possible alienation is averted.

Therefore, the Opinions of Youth Study is doing well at Thurston. I see the good image of the project enhanced if over time the topics to be studied can be adapted to the needs of our school. This brings me to my third theme: the evolving role of the field coordinator.

When I first accepted the assignment, the responsibilities were mainly of a mechanical, facilitative nature; that is, to make sure all arrangements were made so surveys could be administered and interviews conducted with a minimum of disruption to the educational program. Over the last 5 years, additional duties have been added that are discretionary and analytical in nature. I have become, for instance, the person responsible for anticipating adverse reactions by parents, students, or school personnel and for coming up with precautionary measures. I find, too, that I am expected to formulate ways of providing meaningful feedback as a supplement, of course, to ideas generated in Ann Arbor.

Perhaps the most challenging evolving function is to assist the staff at Thurston in judging the adaptability and compatibility of each phase of the project to our school and its program. I am not referring here to the "nuts and bolts" arrangements of providing kids and rooms. This is the way it started 3 years ago. But I now see the possibility and the need to add another dimension to this task — that of facilitating a modification of the study design so that the school as well as the research project can pose the problems to be investigated. In effect, my role as field coordinator could develop toward helping the major study become an investigating service for the school without necessarily detracting from the project's main goal. Cooperative planning could stimulate added interest and increased involvement on the part of the high school faculty and induce even greater compatibility between it and the research project.

Since the research staff has, from the inception of the project, envisioned and encouraged involvement on the part of the faculty within both schools, the problem is not whether this can occur but rather how it is to be implemented. The first steps have already been taken. An advisory committee of Thurston staff members, including me, has been established and has begun to provide input to the study. This committee meets alternately by itself and with representatives from the research program to consider ways of investigating issues derived from the main study and from the concerns of the staff at Thurston.

Presently, we are cooperatively revising Philip Newman's questionnaire, reported in Chapter 11, primarily because his findings suggest that a morale problem exists at Thurston. These revisions are directed toward probing into the effectiveness of a reorganized and more experienced administration, the dynamics of the staff (i.e., who does what and how well), and what degree of compatibility prevails among the teachers and administration regarding educational values. We are also attempting to identify the idiosyncrasies of numerous groups within the staff, e.g., department and lounge cliques, new and experienced teachers, etc. This data might tell us a little more about the "what" and give us some insight into the "why." These initial efforts, hopefully, are just the beginning; and if they are any indication of what is to come, we could indeed make scientific history!

REFERENCES

Fatke, R. The adaptation process of new students in two suburban high schools. In M. J. Feldman (Ed.), *Studies in psychotherapy and behavioral change, No. 2, Theory and research in community mental health.* Buffalo, N.Y.: State University of New York at Buffalo, 1971.

13 Reflections on a Multi-Method Investigation of High Schools and Their Inhabitants

Paul V. Gump
The University of Kansas, Lawrence

As noted in James G. Kelly's introduction, *ecology* is a tricky word now carrying a variety of noncoordinate meanings. As a minimum and beginning statement, we might agree that an ecological study includes a concern with how life goes on for a selected species in its natural (noninvestigator-generated) habitat; also, it appears reasonable to the author that the nature of that habitat, as well as the species behavior, is the target of an ecological investigation. However, the environmental side of many so-called ecological studies is often given only brief attention and fragmentary description; this seems an unreasonable outcome that we consider later on.

The habitats investigated here were two high schools; the species were adolescent males and, to some extent, their school staffs. Our interest in reports of these environments and these people might travel in several directions. For example: How are these people getting along? What are their environments like? How does the quality of the environment relate to how they fare? A different direction is more technical and research oriented: What methods described and employed here show promise? What extensions of approaches begun here appear appropriate?

The simplest outline of the basic research strategy was study of the adaptation, *over time*, of contrasting persons (persons with high, moderate, and low preferences for exploration) to contrasting high school environments. Various "dependent variables" were used to measure adaptation. Hopefully, these variables would show main effects of differences in persons and of differences in environments; also to be tested were interaction effects, effects based on the "person—environment transaction hypotheses" described by Edwards and others.

If the preceding simple outline could have been followed, a more integrated series of investigations could have been presented. However, there were several developments making the outline less feasible. First, this is an interim report; therefore, the longitudinal aspect of the study — one of its very strong points — has not had time to develop. Most measures over time presented here are stability or reliability indices rather than successive pictures of how a cohort of boys develops over the high school years.

Less obvious is the effect of the choice of main variables whose potency turns out to be less than impressive. Selection of exploratory preferences as a major person variable was, as Kelly noted in his introduction, a "risk." It appears to the author to be a risk that did not pay well. The measurement of an exploratory preference variable presented Edwards and his colleagues with a challenge in test construction, and they met that challenge well; parallel forms were developed, and good stability was demonstrated. However, the differences in exploratory preference did not relate tightly to some of the major differences in boys' reactions to their environment. As Edwards summed it up: "The exploration measure at the present time is a tentative predictor at the 10th-grade level" (Edwards, Chapter 5, p. 95). With the weakness of the exploratory preference as a main variable, hopes for clear-cut interaction effects must also diminish. To demonstrate that persons with low exploration preferences would score differently depending on the social environment rests upon the assumption that low exploration is well related to the dependent variables.

The contrasts in the environments also present difficulties. The nature of these schools and the communities they serve is excellently documented. Although it is clear that there are statistically significant differences between the communities, it is also clear that the schools were located in white, home-owning, middle-class, suburban neighborhoods. Differences between the neighborhoods are not great enough to assume that contrasting school environments must result from the contrasting community contexts. Some school and community contrasts became less sharp, even as the study proceeded. For example, the degree of residential mobility, the exchange rate, of one school became markedly closer to that of the other. Such an outcome is perhaps instructive to those of us who hope to capitalize on contrasts in naturally occurring conditions to provide an "experiment." We are accustomed to struggling with possibly contaminating variables — but when the independent variable loses strength even while we are trying to trace its effects, the hazards of "natural experiments" become quite sobering. The investigators themselves say the contrasts between the schools, as operating environments, were not great; obviously, the contrast that later evolved as a result of skillful investigation could not be part of the beginning research scheme.

Though the failure of preselected independent variables to show strong effects is not new or even blameworthy, we can reflect on the influence this failure must have on long-term, complicated, investigative projects. Just an example: One may start with variables around the "social structure" of the student body. Social class or prestige variables are often favorites here. Research may show, however, that there is no "leading crowd;" that there is no truly "in group;" that most students go about as individuals, pairs, or small informal groups, not caring about our favorite "social structure" variables. If such a condition exists, the investigator who depends on the social structure variables not only loses findings; he or she loses rubrics, loses outline. Strong independent variables drive data into a coherent pattern; when the variables are weak, the pattern is absent until other organizing variables can be developed.

In spite of difficulties with the originally selected contrasts, hundreds of boy subjects kept on going to schools that operated day by day, and the research continued. Methods were developed, descriptions of phenomena were established, and intervariable relationships were discovered. We would like to point specifically to some of these products of the research. We also want to consider the possibility that the studies here represent various aspects of a transition between old-line social science investigations and the more fully understood ecological approach, which we will eventually utilize for study of person–environment interaction.

STUDY OF THE SPECIES

What is a 10th- or 11th-grade boy like as a person? Information may be derived from tests or from observation of behavior in particular ecological contexts; in this latter case, the ecology acts as do the questions in the test — it elicits the behavior. Studies of the first kind were performed by Edwards and by Gilmore; Barbara Newman, employing a series of group discussions, used the second. Results of these studies suggest that the self-image of the modal 10th-grade boy is that of a "regular guy." Evidence warns us not to expect from him a high degree of social competence. The heavy use of fantasy and humor in social interaction is perhaps a more surprising species characteristic. Such a quality appears first in Edwards's chapter, in which 25% of these boys saw themselves as "jokers" in their friendship groups (Edwards, Chapter 6, p. 102). Evidence that this self-report data reflected overt social behavior was reported by Barbara Newman. She noted, "An unanticipated characteristic of the interaction in the two groups was the frequent use of the dramatizing category. This quality of joking, mimicking, and fantasizing was a predominant quality of the boys' response to one another and to the group leader" (B. Newman, p. 149). Speculations about the meanings and the function of this "joker" behavior could serve as the basis of a number of adolescent studies; joking behavior would appear to be an excellent example of adaptive behavior.

When we seek to learn more about subjects by observing their actual behavior in a particular environment, it is important to recognize that this, in principle, is hardly ecological; the environment is there, relations to it are noted, but the aim of the question is toward the specie. Although such efforts may provide information useful in subsequent ecological approaches, it seems confusing and inaccurate to label the efforts *ecological*. Psychologists, with a history of interest and success in person measurement, may readily employ a natural situation as a technique of person measurement. However, an ecological approach would involve the quality of the environment as well as the characteristics manifested by the species in their interaction with it.

Case histories of "Dave" and "Harold" reported by Edwards, Gilmore, and B. Newman illustrate an important point. These investigations pick up actions and reactions at the interface of the subject's behavior and its environmental context. It should be noted that information so derived is then pointed at better understanding of the person, his needs, his coping behavior. Valuable as this is for a reality-grounded personality theory, it does not advance our understanding of environmental operation. The moral we draw is that one cannot learn about the high school environment by studying high school students.

SPECIES RELATION TO THE SCHOOL ENVIRONMENT

Moving toward relations between species and environment, there are findings on how the total group of boy subjects reacted to school; a very simple and straightforward issue is whether the boys found satisfaction in school life.

Edwards presents an "adaptive role" measure that he established as a powerful classifier of students' general reaction to their school environments. On this measure, a sizable minority said they were involved in classes and in school activities, but the majority of boys were less enthusiastic. One large group disliked the classes but enjoyed the remainder. Three other school orientations, manifestly receptive, typified 25% of the students at Wayne and 43% at Thurston (Edwards, Chapter 5, p. 92). Rice and Marsh asked for satisfaction with school; they reported scores on a negative to positive scale that were on the positive side — but not by very much. These authors also noted that the amount of positive feelings for principal or teachers in either school was "not very large" (Chapter 4, p. 74).

From his interview with the boys, Gilmore concluded that most of them had difficulties "in engaging the environment . . . in exercising their competences in school" (Chapter 7, p. 129).

The modal reaction of these young people to their school environment appears to be one of blandness rather than enjoyment or rejection. For many, the demands of school seem less a problem than the vacuities. Todd, remarking about the high school environment for "citizens" and "tribe," says, "Members of both groups can easily fall through the loose weave of the social network [p. 184]. Although Todd uses a *social* network, one could read this as an *activity* network. The problem Todd is dealing with is not simply one of having or not having friends; it is of exercising or not exercising a social function. The employment of competence requires action structures, happenings. For many in a large, suburban high school, the school-related happenings in which they can be active participants are few and remote. Todd's description of tribe's reaction to school is particularly discouraging; he says, "School for the tribe member seems to be a series of 'irrelevant' activities against which he structures a supportive peer system, but even this informal network defines few opportunities for experiencing competence and self-worth" (Chapter 10, p. 183).

The direction of Todd's interest was toward the experience of the tribe group (especially in help giving) in the school. He hints that the school may have generated the tribe by noting that peer groups can be informal systems formed in response to needs that the formal system does not satisfy. Although Todd does not present evidence that high schools can make "outsiders" out of their own students, such evidence is available. For example, Willems (1967) interviewed a group very similar to Todd's tribe. The investigator labeled these students "marginal," because their IQs, their academic histories, and their family backgrounds indicated that they were of marginal suitability for high school study. Several interesting facts were established for the marginals: In the large school, they *were not* used in the formal but extracurricular structure; concurrently they expressed almost no obligation to it. A moderate amount of obligation was expressed by regular students in the large school. In small high schools, marginals *were* used in the extracurricular system, and they reported just as much obligation to it as did the regular students. Both groups reported much more obligation than the large-school regulars. Willems' well-replicated study provides the person—environment interaction evidence that was sought in some of the present studies: The same personal qualities resulted in quite different behavior and attitude outcomes, depending on the environment.

In general, the evidence from a variety of measures would indicate that the modal response of these 15-year-old boys to the school arena was not one of pleasure or enthusiasm. Certain student groups thought they fared better than others, but the overall evidence points to very modest satisfaction with school. Interviews and questionnaires about one's satisfaction with his environment certainly point toward an ecological question; we need further studies to show just what does happen in the moment-to-moment lives of youth in school. We need *events* to attach to these statements of satisfaction and dissatisfaction. We must get at the actual interface between our subjects and their environment — at what they did and what was done to them.

In this connection, an especially impressive aspect of Todd's work was his collection of student diaries or logs that kept track of "help-giving events." The use of logs could be expanded in a number of directions. Roemer (1968) used a log-keeping methodology for black youth similar in age to the present subjects; his purpose was to outline the settings, the activities, and the groupings of this population. It might be possible to have daily recording by students of those events at school that were particularly enlivening or deadening. Data from these records might inform us more specifically about what makes school unsatisfactory to so many youth.

CONTRASTING SCHOOL ENVIRONMENTS AND SPECIES BEHAVIOR

When data are compared for Wayne and Thurston, they can refer to differences in: communities around the schools, characteristics of boy students (probably related to social class and home background), school operations and events, and reactions to school — either as a global context or as a presenter of events or elements. The investigators have documented a wide range of differences. Perhaps those of most central interest deal with how students and teachers are reacting to their school environments. For example, there is repeated evidence that teacher and student satisfaction is better at Wayne than at Thurston.

Barbara Newman found that boys in the discussion group at Wayne expressed less hostility to the leader than did boys at Thurston. Wayne teachers perceived the principal's office and the students as having more influence on school affairs than did Thurston teachers. The latter group perceived more power outside the school, in parents, and in the school board. Another intriguing difference is that Wayne students, relative to Thurston's, liked their teachers better and perceived that these teachers took more personal interest in them (Rice & Marsh, Chapter 4, p. 74; P. Newman, Chapter 11, p. 197).

The investigators identified an impressive list of school differences. The samples show that it is possible to discover distinction in environments, even though they are superficially quite similar. The next obvious question is: How do environmental differences influence the behavior and experience of the target populations? When we get to these questions, there are alternative hypotheses. The greater hostility toward the discussion leader at Thurston could be a transfer of the intrusion defense these youth employ against parents; or, it could be a transfer from their reactions to teachers. Teacher satisfaction at Wayne can be influenced by a sense that power is "inside" their school; it could relate to the fact that many more of them live in the school community. We need to know the way the variables relate in the two environmental realities. And one could go on; what are the links through which "liking of teachers" or sense of teachers' "personal interest" develop?

Paths of influence are always a problem in nonexperimental studies, and there are statistical techniques to help us out. However, I would like to propose a more primitive beginning for the problem. It seems, at least on an intuitive level, that one can better infer direction of influence if the events in question are measured directly. In an ecological study, this means measurement around the specific environments inhabited by the subjects and the behaviors and inputs occurring in these environments.

SETTINGS OF THE SCHOOL ENVIRONMENTS — PRESENT RESEARCH

At least three different investigations used naturally occurring school environmental units, or settings. Edwards looked into "free-time places," Rice and Marsh questioned faculty about their attendance at school-related events, and Philip Newman sought information concerning social interaction in 22 settings common to both high schools.

There are several aspects to Edwards's work that are provocative. First, there is the probability, not proven, that the use of a specific place to obtain a report from informants leads to more useful information. It would seem that when boys are asked: "What do you usually talk about in place X?" they can be more specific and revealing of interests than when we just say, "What do you and the guys like to talk about?"

The "free-time place" might also be employed to assess the hospitality of the environment that the group inhabits. If a boy seeks relaxation and sociality, what places are available? In cases of extreme institutional inhospitality, all such places might be beyond the institution; examples include "a friend's house" or "McDonald's." A more common and less extreme form of inhospitality is operative when only back areas may be used (the boiler room, for example). Somewhat related to back areas are places and times during which the official program for the place is suspended: the band room when there is no longer a band playing, cafeteria when there is no serving and dining. A more hospitable institution would be indicated when places are provided where socializing is the official program; examples would be lounges with Coke machines, or coffee corners for off-times in the cafeteria.

A very important aspect of a "free-time place" is who is present. A fact of possible significance, if we try to understand the roots of the differences in student—staff relationship, is that at Wayne, school adults were reported customarily present at the "free-time place" in 26% of the cases, whereas only 8% at Thurston reported that adults were customarily present (Edwards, Chapter 6, p. 106). A parallel finding by Rice and Marsh shows that Wayne teachers report more attendance at school athletic events than do the staff at Thurston (Chapter 4, p. 67).

The adult presence appears again in Phil Newman's research. Twenty-two settings were employed to create a descriptive map of the social environment. Newman was successful in creating a setting-by-staff-position matrix that did indeed "map" important contrasts between student—staff interaction at the two schools. At Wayne, as compared to Thurston, school adults were more frequently present at these settings and more frequently interacted with students (P. Newman, Chapter 11, p. 196).

The settings data by P. Newman give us a better understanding of why the Wayne student might say that he likes his teachers, that they take a personal interest in him. The Wayne student and the Wayne teacher have more to do with one another in a variety of environments; we presume that this may *reflect* better relationships, but we also assume that it *sustains* and *generates* better relationships. We infer that when people share a variety of settings, they become less alien to one another.

Another aspect of the work on settings by P. Newman helps explain how settings generate interaction qualities. It was not only true that Wayne teachers were more frequently present in a number of nonclassroom settings; Newman suggests that the function of these settings (although they had the same names as those at Thurston) was different. The study hall at Wayne seemed to have only a modest study emphasis; informal peer—peer and even adult—student interaction seemed customary. Differences similar to this were said to be operative in other settings — in the offices, cafeterias, athletic fields, and auditoriums of the two schools (Chapter 11, p. 204).

The specific phrasing of these setting differences can have a subtle but crucial effect on how these ecological contexts are fitted into the environment and inhabitant problem. One might say that when settings of the same name operate differently, they serve different functions. An alternative conception is that when settings operate differently, they are a dissimilar setting regardless of name. The sameness or difference of settings rests upon their milieus and their programs. If one study hall customarily has much student—student and student—staff interaction and the other has only incidental socializing and otherwise study, these two settings exhibit different programs; they are different settings. Similarly, if one cafeteria serves students and staff together and the other serves them separately, this is not just a difference in function; it is a part of the program, the standing pattern of behavior of the two settings (Barker, 1968).

When settings differ, settings differ; this is a more direct and economical conception than to picture the settings retaining the same label but functioning differently. Some habitats of the same name at Wayne and Thurston are different entities.

The program of a setting can put discrete population classes into a particular activity relationship. Traditionally, the classroom puts the teacher in a leadership position over students; when students and teachers share auditoriums, athletic events, lounges, or caefeterias, the activity relationships — as defined by the programs — are likely to be more equalitarian. It is reasonable to suppose that the social activity and the social feeling ("liking") that is stimulated by an equalitarian activity relationship is different from that elicited by a leader—follower pattern. Implied in Newman's data, then, are explanations that the way students at each school feel about staff has to do with two highly related environmental qualities: the number of different settings that student and staff share and the particular programs that operate in the shared settings.

SETTINGS OF THE SCHOOL ENVIRONMENTS — FUTURE RESEARCH

We would suppose that subsequent ecological studies would go even further with the identification and description of the settings of target environments. Future studies would start the search for explanation at the level of "what's happening" in the environment. This seems a reasonable approach; surely, in ecological research, there ought to be much contact with the place—thing—behavior reality. Studies of species characteristics, of species feelings and attitudes, are not the basic ecological reality.

Manifestly, it is not possible to record and analyze all that happens in a high school. The appeal to put matters on a "what's happening" level must be accompanied by some method of handling this level without being swamped with the millions of behavior and environment events that could be identified.

Proper description of settings does tell us, in a molar fashion, what is happening on the environmental side. For example, if we know that there were 10 2-hour operations of the setting *Home Basketball*, we know that there were 20 hours of watching or playing that game, many hours of cheering and yelling, numerous opportunities to eat and drink, much invitation to feel and express aggressive impulses. The more detailed the setting description, the more the available input to a target population is known. Further, we know a minimum about what a subject did if we know he entered or did not enter a described setting; if we also know his *position* in the setting (leader, member, onlooker), we have more specific information about what he was called upon to do. Still needed for a "what's happening" approach are the behaviors and experiences of subjects in settings over and beyond those that are implied by setting occupation and setting position. Such information can come from direct observation or from using students as describers of their own behavior and reaction. The point of a setting focus is that it puts relationships upon a reality basis. With settings, one obtains a grip on what influences from the environment, what events in the environment, contribute to inhabitant reaction.

Regrettably, some "environmental research" avoids the event level on both the environment and the inhabitant sides. Perception or judgment of a complex environmental quality is related to a nonhappening inhabitant one. Rice and Marsh (Chapter 4, p. 71) described the environment in terms of the influence that students can have on school affairs (as this was perceived by teachers). The dependent variable was student satisfaction with school. These investigators found that student influence was judged to be less at Thurston than at Wayne; this condition was said to be responsible for less student satisfaction at Thurston (p. 72). Although this conclusion fits a popular idea that persons become dissatisfied when they lack power, its data base here is quite ephemeral. We don't know from this given statement whether lack of influence even existed; if it did exist, we don't know how students behaved when events showed they had little power. Events in the real environment can be related to the development of feelings or attitudes; how feelings might shape environments and behavior in them could also be inferred. But future ecological research will not have the environment—inhabitant relationship described only with cognitive or attitudinal variables; an event-level anchoring will be required.

SETTINGS AND INTERVENTION

The pertinence of settings for ecological work is also underlined when the issue of intervention comes to our attention. When Todd considered intervention, he spoke of the necessity to expand activities in school in which students could "merit status" (Chapter 10, p. 184). Barbara Newman, from her experience in the discussion groups, suggests that various activity settings could bring warmth and social cohesion to Thurston students; for example, work groups could cooperate in leveling fields, painting houses, or surviving wilderness camping (Chapter 8, p. 148). These suggestions go far beyond the common-sense idea that young people should have interesting things to do; they recognize the principle that setting programs put inhabitants into various kinds of action relationships and that these action relationships in turn can yield certain social relationships.

Potent, durable intervention in environments probably requires changes in the programs and milieus of existing settings or the elimination of some settings and the establishment of new ones. This view is in contrast to attempts to change the quality of inhabitant life by changing attitudes, by raising motivational levels, by personnel selection, or other psychological moves. Changed settings have the capacity to "lock in" other changes; again, the example from Philip Newman's research comes to mind. If settings exist that are shared by different groups and if the action relationships defined by the programs are favorable, good human relationships are perpetuated.

Speaking of intervention in a more general fashion, we can recall a terse but meaningful statement from Todd's work. In speaking of problems in helping the tribe, he notes that staff efforts for change are generally "discrete, individualistic, and nonincremental" (Chapter 10, p. 185). Intervention at the settings level might be able to reverse this trend; it might provide continuous and cumulative benefit. Such strategy cannot depend upon one "good setting" being attached to an unchanged structure. An array of settings must be involved such that the events in each setting support desired events in the others. For example, a school group might decide that a student work project in the community could provide zest and status to otherwise noninvolved students. To have a significant and durable effect, this effort would include creation of new settings and changes in established ones. One can foresee postwork Coke parties, in-school planning sessions, money-raising and recruitment drives. Already existing settings would be connected: Award ceremonies would highlight community service as well as intellectual, artistic, and athletic activity; academic classes would provide relevant information to the work group on some occasions; on others, they would use members of the work group to educate other students on "how it is out there."

The fit of athletics into the environment of the average American high school can illustrate the point we are making. The game setting is fed by, and feeds, many other settings: the game practices, the marching band rehearsals, all-school cheerleader selection assembly, pep club meetings, homecoming celebrations, class meetings for planning the operation of concessions at the game, and so on. For many high school inhabitants, athletics has continuous and incremental impact; a necessary condition for this impact is the network of reciprocally acting settings in which athletics is embedded.

We predict the direction of school reform will eventually be toward setting engineering, not toward better diagnosis and counseling of youth, not toward better teacher training and selection. Education is an *environmental* science.

ECOLOGICAL RESEARCH AND THE HOST INSTITUTIONS

Ecological research takes time. There are a number of reasons for this; Kelly has mentioned the value of a longitudinal approach. The environment is a set of operations with hourly, daily, and yearly rhythms; these changes in the environment are hardly apparent, certainly not meaningful, if a cross-sectional approach is employed. There is also the unfortunate fact that our methodology for measuring environments is underdeveloped as compared to our techniques for measurement of persons. All of this means that the host institution will be asked to endure prolonged examination; the research group is no longer satisfied to have numbers of subjects provided for several hours of testing.

This research project asked for, and received, opportunity for such prolonged examination. The project personnel invested large amounts of time and energy into developing a decent working relationship with host institutions. The remarks of school staff (Bell, Boyea, Knox, Jacobs, and Harms, Chapter 12) testify to the concern, good sense, and professionalism of the research staff. One of the specific moves in developing effective school relations was the appointment of "research coordinators." Since the coordinators worked closely with the researchers but viewed matters from the school's position, their ideas might be quite enlightening. The grim reality that can face would-be researchers in schools was expressed by Knox: "Any school offering itself and its constituents as social guinea pigs has much to lose and very little to gain . . . Schools today are usually very sensitive political entities whose financial security can be destroyed by a dose of bad publicity or ill will" (Chapter 12, p. 229).

Part of the threat of researchers comes from a long history of performing evaluative research in the schools. The usual questions were: Which institution, which administration, which teachers, or which students were doing well? Which were doing otherwise? Too often a research effort meant that an aspect of the school was "exposed." With this as background, it is difficult to convince school people that a research effort does not have to be evaluative, that it may seek to learn "how things are" or "how things work." If researchers in an institution were able to come up with findings that were of help to that institution, the statement by Knox would become less true. The schools would have something to gain; and, if they were not targets for evaluation, they would have less to lose.

To know just what findings would help the school is not easy. However, the experience of Knox is pertinent here. As a research coordinator, his position evidently underwent some job enlargement. He describes a beginning phase as an arranger of times, places, and pupils and then a later period as diplomat and interpreter of research goals. He came to see a third phase, one described so unobtrusively that one can easily read over its revolutionary implications. "But I now see the possibility and the need to add another dimension to this task — that of facilitating a modification of the study design so that *the school* as well as the research project *can pose the problems to be investigated*" (Chapter 12, p. 230, italics mine).

If researchers began to investigate issues proposed by the host school, a number of changes in the ecology of school research would follow. The parasitic relation of the investigators to the school would cease; the action relationship between researchers and school people would change from that of examiners—examinees to one of collaborators in examination. Further, the problems that became investigative targets would less likely be old-time favorites of academic social science; problems would relate more closely to the realities of the institution and its inhabitants.

James G. Kelly and his colleagues deserve much credit for providing useful feedback to the host schools. Every school staff person contributing to this report has expressed real appreciation of this input.

We are all indebted to the research group for a multimethod look at how schools and their inhabitants might be studied over time. We look forward to the analysis of the impact of 4 full high school years upon the boy subjects. Finally, we expect many of the variables and techniques being developed to have considerable value in future ecological studies of our educational institutions and their inhabitants.

REFERENCES

Barker, R. G. *Ecological psychology: Concepts and methods for studying the environment of human behavior.* Stanford, Calif.: Stanford University Press, 1968.

Roemer, Derek. *Adolescent peer group formation in two Negro neighborhoods.* Unpublished doctoral dissertation, Harvard University, 1968.

Willems, E. P. Sense of obligation to high school activities as related to school size and marginality of student. *Child Development,* December 1967, *38*(No. 4), 1247–1260.

14 Exploratory Behavior, Socialization, and the High School Environment

James G. Kelly[1]
Institute for Social Research
The University of Michigan

This volume has been concerned with an ecological analysis of the socialization of male high school students. Since young people spend a major portion of their time in school, the public school system is a critical setting for assessing how skills, beliefs, and dispositions to act are acquired (Brim & Wheeler, 1966; Clausen, 1968; Inkeles, 1968; Smith, 1968). Yet, despite the significance of the topic of socialization for the high school, there are few research examples that dig deeply and intensively into the social processes that determine how students acquire competences in a particular school setting (Inkeles, 1968; Smith, 1968).

At the 1965 Social Science Research Council's Conference on Socialization for Competence, Barbara Biber introduced her remarks with the following comments (Biber & Minuchin, 1965):

> Societies have long regarded their schools as primary institutions for the socialization of competence, created and sustained for the expressed purpose of inducting the child into his culture as a competent and skillful human being. As a crucial socializing force, the school shares its function with the family, the peer group, sometimes other institutions such as the church, but even more than the others its function is described directly in the realm of "competence"; to educate means, at the very least, to make competent.
>
> Within the consensus that the school's function lies in this realm, however, there is a range of viewpoint among educators and in the environments and methods they have created. If we approach education with a research stance, we need to begin with the understanding that schools vary

---

[1]Present address: School of Community Service and Public Affairs, University of Oregon, Eugene.

245

in their vision of what they are trying to accomplish for the child — the scope of what they wish to undertake, the hierarchy of their goals, their cognizance of psychological development as it affects functioning, and the extent of their concern for the propensities, heritage and equipment the child brings with him into the learning situation [p. 1].

The challenge of grasping the organizational life of a school system and defining how students learn to be competent in various roles is gigantic. The topic requires a focus upon multiple levels of the organizational life of the school and how topics such as decision making, communication patterns, and peer group structures affect the expression of individual coping preferences. To succeed in reflecting the organizational life of the school requires that the research develop a variety of methods and improvise approaches. Getting into the life of the school, then, involves defining research so that the methods reflect the life force of the environment. This particular research was initiated to reflect the varied relationships of how persons adapt to the school environment. In focusing upon the functions of the high school environment, we have taken into account such issues as differences in the administration of the two high schools, the variability within the school faculties, and variations in the economic and cultural values of the parents. Though such contextual factors were considered, still, our primary attention was to reflect the attitudes of students and faculty in the school setting.

Although the research has not been strictly ecological, an ecological perspective was present. The research reported here assumed that if we spend enough time in one place, we will acquire, not always with awareness, specific and unique ways of doing our work consistent with the setting. The ecological perspective has generated research to understand the interactions of high school students with the social environment.

In Chapter 13, Paul Gump presented a theoretical perspective that asserts that a change in the behavior of persons affects the environment, just as changes in the social environment may affect the life of individuals. This means simultaneously examining the reciprocal effects of persons and social settings, trying to locate those processes that affect social participation and the regulation of the environment. The spirit of the preceding chapters has been to grapple with these issues.

THE TWO HIGH SCHOOLS AND THEIR IMPACT
UPON THE SOCIALIZATION OF STUDENTS

The two high school environments were similar in many respects; yet they were also different, especially in their informal social structure. Gilmore, in Chapter 7, was interested in identifying the social competences of students with different levels of exploratory preferences. From Gilmore's data, the structured interview revealed that boys with high exploration preferences expressed their competences within the school and were more confident of their ability to influence their friends and parents. These findings offer partial validation of the self-report questionnaire measure of exploration preferences as a predictor of engaging and self-confident behavior. The fact that a large number of boys at Wayne reported more competences than did the boys at Thurston suggests that the Wayne community and Wayne High School foster a positive self-image, *or* that the greater number of reported competences may be an expression of feigned self-importance and bravado. Additional comments on this point are made later.

The relationships between exploration preferences and participation in school affairs found by Gilmore are strengthened by the results reported and summarized by Edwards in Chapter 5. The finding that high-explorer boys express more identification with the school, express more initiative, have higher self-esteem and self-satisfaction, and report that they know the school principal better than moderate- or low-explorer boys is a consistent pattern. The boys with high exploration preferences also report that they have fewer social problems, are less unhappy at school, chat with a fewer number of students at informal settings in the school, and feel less watched and less uncomfortable in group situations. The omega statistic (ω^2) employed by Edwards, however, keeps our vanity low. The foregoing relationships account for between 4% and 15% of the variance between exploratory preferences and the dependent variables.

A few qualitative comments can be made about the types of competences reported by students in Gilmore's sample. In response to Gilmore's question, "What are some of the things you are good at and like to do?", recreation and sports were reported by 61% to 71% of the boys. The relationships of exploration preferences and recreational competences for these boys was positive and linear (45%, low; 75%, mod; 92%, hi), whereas the relationship was more curvilinear at Thurston (83%, lo; 33%, mod; 67%, hi). These findings suggest that competences in sports at Wayne are much more pervasive and define the social conditions for being involved in the culture of school. The boys at Thurston, on the other hand, are involved in acquiring alternative competences via academic work, jobs, or hobbies. Of the first two competences mentioned at either school, only 6% at Wayne and 3% at Thurston were categorized as social competences. A question for future research is whether the more active social environment of Wayne will nurture social competences as the boys continue their high school careers.

The research of William Jones provides insights into questions about developmental levels, competences, and the implication of being a student at each of the high schools. Jones found in his experiment that pairs of boys with high preferences for exploration expressed more of the following behaviors than did matched pairs of boys with moderate or low exploration preferences: elaboration of solutions, giving information, using their partner as a resource, task involvement, and directing the interaction related to the solution. Additional validation data for the Edwards self-report measure of exploration preferences is again obtained. In addition, Jones offered the following testimony based upon an analysis of the transcripts:

> The High—High Exploration dyads seem to already have at hand cognitive maps of the school and to have already reached well-thought-out conclusions about such things as whether the vice-principal would bend a rule. The transcripts show that most of these students, like other adolescents, engage in preparatory and hypothetical problem solving. Most of them, for example, had previously thought about how to obtain driver's education as soon as possible (one of the problem stories) and had discussed it with friends. They appeared, especially the H—H dyads, to come equipped with at least elementary notions of problem solving: identifying a solution, evaluating and elaborating it, and selecting alternatives if the initial solution seemed inadequate (Jones, p. 170).

Jones also provides an excellent discussion (pages 170–171) of possible reasons for the different results obtained for boys attending Wayne and Thurston High Schools. Originally, it was predicted that the students attending Wayne, because of more opportunities for informal social interaction, would perform better than the students at Thurston, where there was some confusion about social norms. Jones found that the Wayne students were more enthusiastic participants but not better problem solvers.

Jones presents an interesting interpretation for what he refers to as the *school switcheroo*. He considers the following possibilities: not enough time in the experimental procedure to allow for the expression of school differences, latent cultural differences in the school populations, varied levels of psychosocial maturity of the boys at the two schools, the role of anxiety in reducing or enhancing problem-solving behavior, and the different socialization of coping styles. In commenting on this last hypothesis related to socialization, Jones suggests a useful clarification that relates to knowledge about the socialization processes at the two schools.

> In deriving the hypotheses, a case was made for Wayne being more likely to encourage exploratory behavior because of the school's clearer norms and greater flexibility. There is another way of looking at it, though. It may be easier to be a social explorer at Wayne, but it may also be less crucial. For instance, if information about norms is freely available, there is less need to acquire coping styles to help obtain it. Thurston provides a rigid but murky environment. Norms are not clear. Students are not as comfortable with peers or staff. There is tension and ambiguity. Under these conditions, a high explorer may get more mileage out of his coping style, in spite of the lumps he may take. In sum, the noxious environment of Thurston may actually provide greater rewards for exploratory behavior and with it develop greater capabilities for school problem solving (Jones, p. 171).

Jones put these ideas about coping styles and environmental qualities into his experimental design, and he confirmed the construct of exploratory behavior while providing a new empirical basis for viewing the socialization media of the two high schools. Our view of the interdependence of personal preferences and social context is expanded and differentiated as a result of Jones's work.

What about the social structure of the high school environment and its functions for socialization? What settings for socialization are these schools providing? In a carefully selected representative sample of the faculty and students at both schools, Philip Newman, in Chapter 11, describes consistent differences in the quantity and quality of social interactions mentioned earlier. Not only was the quantity of social interaction greater at Wayne than at Thurston, but the interactions between students and faculty also took place in more social settings, both informal and formal, at Wayne than at Thurston. With regard to differences in the quality of these interactions, students at Wayne perceived more personal interest from faculty and felt more comfortable in informal interaction with school adults than did the students at Thurston. Wayne also encouraged more active student involvement; norms were perceived as being clearer and consequences for norm violation harsher at Wayne than at Thurston. Students at Wayne demonstrated a greater preference for the company of adults, whereas students at Thurston displayed a greater preference for the company of their peers.

These findings are also consistent with the work of Edwards, reported in Chapter 6, who drew his data from a stratified sample in the longitudinal study. In his high-, moderate-, and low-explorer boys, Edwards found that the students at Wayne expressed more positiveness about the principal, believed they had greater influence over fellow students and student government, and felt that their school was better than did the students at Thurston.

Barbara Newman's work provides independent, complementary evidence of the differences in the cultures of the two high schools. As reported in Chapter 8, she created an informal group setting in which nine boys at each school from Gilmore's sample — three high, three moderate, and three low explorers — met for eight discussion sessions. Her interest was in assessing the verbal and non-verbal behavior of boys within the group. Consistent with the findings of Edwards (Chapters 5 and 6), Philip Newman (Chapter 11), and Gilmore (Chapter 7), Barbara Newman found that there was more diversity in the responses of the boys at Wayne. The boys at Wayne were also more expressive in their participation than the boys at Thurston. The one statistically significant finding, which differentiated between the behavior of the boys at the two schools, was that the Wayne boys asked the leader for information and sought her opinions more than did the boys at Thurston, who were more cautious in their approach to the group and the group leader. From the findings in this unstructured group setting, it was apparent that the cultures of the two schools *were* different. Wayne served as a more active and supportive environment for the socialization of students than Thurston.

One additional insight obtained from Barbara Newman's work regarding differences in the expression of exploratory behavior at the two schools was that high-explorer boys at Wayne were more expressive and involved in the group, whereas the low-explorer boys at Thurston were more expressive. The findings of relatively less expressive behavior on the part of the high-explorer boys at Thurston suggests that the assessment of emotional behavior at Thurston will be more difficult in the future; e.g., the school environment at Thurston does not encourage the expression of emotional behavior. If the boys with high exploration preferences at Wayne continue to be expressive, it will be a relatively easier task to learn about their adaptation.

One of the most striking findings in the work of Barbara Newman was the vast range of individual differences she observed in the boys. At both schools, the boys were different in physical size, interests, and verbal skills. From the wide range of responses in the discussion groups, it seems appropriate in the future to subdivide the exploration groups according to developmental levels in the future. Exploration at a lower developmental level can be expressed via body movements. At more advanced developmental levels, exploration is more likely to be channeled into conceptual activities. If such distinctions can be made, the interaction of social forces and developmental levels can be further illuminated.

Todd, in Chapter 10, reports an intensive study of the help-giving process in the two subcultures, which clarified the nebulous quality of the social structure of Thurston High School. Todd found that the nonschool affiliative group, whom he called the "tribe," reported more reciprocal help-giving acts than the group he referred to as "citizens" in responses to sample surveys. In these log reports of their helping behavior, the "citizens" engaged in more reciprocal helping transactions and were more often involved in receiving and giving help with girls than were the tribe members.

The differences in response to the two research methods were encouraging rather than disconfirming. A marginal subgroup such as the tribe could be expected to present an image of solidarity to an outside research investigator, whereas the opposite would be true for members of the citizen culture who took the "tests" more casually, yet were more dedicated when contributing autobiographical log reports for the "diary" of help-giving behavior. The increased appearance of girls in the lives of the citizens, as reflected in their log reports, was interpreted as reflecting the real significance of girls as friends by the citizens when they were forced to look closely at their personal accounts. The tribe members, on the other hand, seemed to live a more marginal life with girls as well. Girls are a commodity to be dealt with infrequently, but on their own terms. Todd's work provides a provocative approach of "funneling" down into the social structure of the school, without losing the authentic complexities of the environment. Through this approach, we have learned that the socialization of help-giving competences varies within subgroupings at one school.

IMPLICATIONS FOR THE ECOLOGY OF
SOCIALIZATION AND COMPETENCE

On the basis of the data reported in the preceding chapters, it is possible to discuss the social environment of the schools. At Wayne Memorial High School, there is a variety of informal settings in which students may actively express their ideas and participate in school affairs. Students can vary in their mode of accommodating to the school *if* they have the principal's approval, and *if* the extracurricular activities absorb the students. There is a definite social organization at Wayne that creates a forum that involves the school's resources. The social environment functions to provide intact social settings for informal and formal interactions and clear social norms that contribute to socializing new members. At the same time, it is not clear how tolerant the setting is, how rapidly organizational problems can be dealt with, how new extracurricular opportunities can be created, or how cognitive skills are learned.

At Thurston, there are diverse viewpoints within the school and the community, but this variety is not articulated for faculty and students. The social norms generated by the faculty operate to reduce the opportunity for outside resources to influence the school. Although the specific sources for this norm are unclear, one possibility is that the school policies reflect the concerns of the local school board and community leaders and that the school administration works to limit the influence of forces and demands that the faculty and administration cannot meet. One consequence of this condition is that the competences needed by the school, and that are present at the school and in the larger community, often go unnoticed. In the Thurston environment, it appears that the resources that are available are not fully utilized. Instead, the social norms of the larger community operate to reduce the degree to which external influences affect the school.

With regard to implications for the ecology of competence, our findings suggest that one school (Wayne) behaves as if it were a "scout camp," whereas the other school (Thurston) generates ambiguity. What are the consequences of students attending the two different schools? At Wayne, a future question is, what happens to students who are not congruent with the modal social norms of the "scout camp?" At Thurston, the concern is for students who care about their school but cannot locate the social supports for their development. These two requirements for adaptation will have divergent effects upon the students' participation in school activities and in the development of preferences for adult help-giving roles. The results of the study affirm that the quality and diversity of the social environment has a definite impact on the way in which the student learns to cope with environmental demands. To the extent that such effects are empirically demonstrated, this research can provide concepts for designing preventive interventions for varied social environments.

The ecological thesis affirms that the socialization of competences can succeed if the following criteria are met:

1. A diversity of formal and informal social settings encourages social interaction.

2. A variety of informal roles in the social environment allows for spontaneous help giving and for personal interactions across divergent roles.

3. Varied competences are valued, and persons contribute these competences to the larger community.

4. There are clearly recognized social norms for relating to the surrounding external environments.

5. There is a commitment to examine the impact of the social environment upon its members.

6. There exists the design of a social environment where the dominant activities take into account the diverse cultural values of the members.

On the basis of the research findings, our thinking about the ecology of competence suggests the following tentative conclusions:

1. Students at Wayne are expected to learn how to interact with adults in authority roles, initiate social interactions with strangers, and feel optimistic about their ability to influence the events of the school.

2. Students at Wayne are expected to participate in hierarchical relationships and to influence persons with power who are above them in social status.

3. Students at Wayne are expected to learn how to deal with and engage those with social influence.

4. Students at Thurston, on the other hand, are expected to move toward their individual life goals without deviating from their objectives and without participating actively in their immediate social settings. What the Thurston students have, they keep and parlay for new achievements at a future time.

5. Students at Wayne are expected to be involved and committed toward making their world effective, whereas students at Thurston are concerned primarily with insuring that they maintain a current and valued position.

What are the potential strains for these different patterns of socialization? The students at Wayne are expected to be naive about realities of the social milieu that are different from their own. Consequently, their views of the world are expected to be cognitively more simple than the world view of Thurston students. In contrast, students at Thurston are expected to have a more realistic, if not cynical, view of how social institutions function and to have little emotional investment in actively participating to bring about change. On the basis of these ideas, boys with high preferences for exploration at Wayne would be expected to have more personally satisfying and adaptive high school careers than Thurston boys with high preferences for exploration. Furthermore, the high-explorer students at Thurston would be expected to feel more psychic strain as they attempt to engage and participate in a vague and unresponsive environment.

The ecological thesis is that competences will vary as a consequence of participating in different environments. A longitudinal study, hopefully, can clarify how natural features of different social environments affect their members. On the basis of the work presented in this volume, it is possible to offer some initial statements of principles. These five statements relate to the substantive findings as well as to the ecological perspective.

1. Tenth-grade boys in the two high schools vary substantially in their development.

The research reported by Edwards (Chapters 5 and 6), Gilmore (Chapter 7), Barbara Newman (Chapter 8), and Jones (Chapter 9) illustrates the wide ranges of response to life events, to the school regime, to such activities as going steady, and to beliefs such as trust of authority and commitment to maintain themselves in school. This variability, which reflects rich individual differences in development, forces the developmental researcher to suspend judgment on what is acceptable or normal behavior. It also prompts the formulation of a system of governance for secondary education in which small groups of students are encouraged to educate themselves at their own pace.

Increasingly, secondary schools are moving to decentralized modular scheduling. A developmental conception of adolescence as a period of variability and searching was popular several decades ago, and such a view may come back again. The contributions of Piaget, Erikson, and their followers receive support from the preliminary findings, which clearly articulate the transitional and variable nature of the developmental process.

2. Tenth-grade boys place strong emphasis upon personal athletic competences and bravado.

The repetitive theme running through the protocols, interviews, and responses to research instruments was the focus on — almost preoccupation with — self-expression via body movements. It was apparent that the young person who has excelled in athletics has it made. If the 10th-grade boy has tried nothing else, he will be tested by athletics; and only a few will be lucky enough to be encouraged to develop other skills and competences. This finding, which was discussed by Edwards (Chapter 5), Gilmore (Chapter 7), and Barbara Newman (Chapter 8), has important implications for planning educational programs, as well as for a continued appraisal of this age period. If the performance of physical and athletic activities is germane upon entry at high school, then a variety of intramural and extramural sports, graded by difficulty level and readiness for performance, can become a dominant part of high school life for the 10th-grade boy.

Psychologists, both for research and action purposes, can increase their authenticity as observers of the high school period by understanding how sports and athletic competence are related to the identity, self-esteem, and self-regard of the 10th-grade boy. The prominence of energy and physical activity, along with the benefits of knowing how to use the body, are topics that are rich for extending the theoretical foundations for adolescent psychology. It would seem that the future coping potential of 10th-grade boys can be positively affected by the extent to which they understand and use the body in athletic competition and sports programs. Leisure activities and diverse sports programs can serve a preventive role for youth as they express their personal competences, first through athletic activities and then in other social and interpersonal activities.

3. Social exploration is an emerging behavior that is worthy of study in the 10th grade and beyond.

When the research began, emphasis was given to measuring social exploration as an individual difference variable that would illustrate how boys develop preferences for engaging social structures. Considering the difficult measurement and research tasks, definite progress has been made in developing a research assessment procedure that reflects preferences for social engagement from the eighth to the 10th grade. As an individual difference variable, the predictive validity of the exploration construct is encouraging. Boys who initially had high preferences retained them, and boys with low preferences did so.

Social exploration concepts, as operationally developed by the assessment techniques of Edwards (Chapter 5), reliably assess an aspect of adolescent behavior that is divergent from other personality measures. Although further research will be required to determine how valid the scale is for diverse populations, the interview data (Gilmore), the observations of groups (Barbara Newman), and the experimental intervention (Jones) described in this volume affirm that the concept of exploration is alive and worthy of attention. It is a personality concept that is free of references to pathology and that refers to self-actualization preferences for active participation in the social structure of the school. Boys can vary in level of exploration and not be "sick." What is more important for boys who are high in this preference for exploration is the possibility of assessing the effects of their environments upon the expression of future exploration.

Will the boy with high exploratory preferences find new channels within the high school social structure, or will he be a "victim" of the socialization processes of nonsupportive environments? The questionnaire measure of exploratory preferences developed by Edwards seems quite appropriate to assess the differential effects of participation in contrasting environments. This measure can also help to focus on the developmental correlates of a behavioral disposition that seems likely to have an adaptive function for adulthood.

4. Multiple methods are preferred for research on adolescent development.

Given both the variability and surging growth of the adolescent, it is limiting to assess this particular period of life without using several different methods. The portraits of "Dave" and "Harold," revealed in the questionnaire data reported by Edwards (Chapter 5), the interviews reported by Gilmore (Chapter 7), and in Barbara Newman's observations (Chapter 8), provide a generally consistent picture. Yet each of these methods also brings out and highlights facts that were not reflected in the other methods.

The reports from questionnaire, interview, and group observation data all conveyed "Harold's" lack of intensive involvement in the activities of the school. Each method also illuminated a possible source of this behavior. Though all three methods reported the intensive involvement of "Dave" in multiple settings and activities at Wayne, the three investigators all spoke of their concerns that "Dave" was moving too fast to be settled; and there seemed to be a feature of "flight" in "Dave's" adaptation to his environment. The three vignettes about these two students present a comprehensive view of the boys' general orientation to their social and academic world.

The combined effect of the independent reports of the behavior of these boys raises additional questions about the benefits and the limiting qualities of these boys being nonvisible participants in their high schools. "Harold" was involved only with the academic regime at Thurston; he returned to his junior high school associates or to friends elsewhere for his social contacts. Apparently "Harold" was not involved in school, and the Thurston environment was not actively engaging him. Is it possible for Thurston High School to involve an able and relatively engaging student? A question for the Thurston faculty is whether the school seeks out talent.

"Dave," on the other hand, is a very active and spirited person who is very much involved in the multiple opportunities at Wayne High School. All three reports of "Dave's" behavior, however, inquired if he was not unhappy and ill at ease in spite of this spirited activity. It is hypothesized that a "test" for students at Wayne is whether outgoing, energetic participation can be a "false-positive" sign of environmental mastery. An important task in differentiating the socialization process at Wayne lies in distinguishing between the realities of adaptive mastery and the signs of pseudomastery.

5. Social environments can be assessed in terms of their psychological effects upon individuals.

Multiple methods sharpen the analysis of the socialization process in different social environments. The development of the Environmental Assessment Inventory by Philip Newman (Chapter 11) provides tangible data that the faculty and students at *each* high school agreed with each other in the perceptions of the quality of life in their schools. These reports also indicated that the settings for socialization and social interaction can be identified. The compelling and striking differences in the number and quality of social interactions at the two high schools — e.g., the number of settings for interaction among faculty and students and between students — provide a frame of reference for assessing the effects of participation in these demographically similar yet psychologically distinctive environments. If Wayne students do in fact have more occasions for social engagement and informal chitchat than the students at Thurston, will the Wayne students take with them more confidence and more ease in social interactions after graduation from high school? Will the high-explorer boys at Wayne emerge as more outgoing and competent because their surrounding environment was more congruent with their personal style?

The development of a multimethod study of both persons and settings is a comprehensive undertaking. The five topics noted above suggest different qualities about the two high schools that were evaluated and reflect some of the unique psychological properties of these varied social environments. It seems apparent that no single method, whether interview, survey, or field observations, can provide comprehensive answers to questions about person—environment fit. Each method can illuminate different facets of the student's expressive behavior that describe something unique about the individual, as well as reflecting the social structure of the environment. Each method, attending to varied levels and facets of person—environment interaction, adds clarity or suggests new dimensions, both of which are needed in ecological inquiry.

The research reported in this volume on the interaction of settings and persons was conducted within the context of a commitment to improvisation. Within this context, the authors have designed specific studies in accordance with our general research goals. We hope that we have given the reader a coherent orientation to our expedition.

REFERENCES

Biber, B., & Minuchin, P. *The role of the school in the socialization of competence.* Working paper presented at the Social Science Research Council's Conference on Socialization for Competence. Puerto Rico, April 1965.

Brim, O. G., Jr., & Wheeler, S. *Socialization after childhood: Two essays.* New York: John Wiley & Sons, 1966.

Clausen, J. A. Perspectives on childhood socialization. In John A. Clausen (Ed.), *Socialization and society.* Boston: Little, Brown & Co., 1968.

Inkeles, A. Society, social structure, and child socialization. In John A. Clausen (Ed.), *Socialization and society.* Boston: Little, Brown & Co., 1968.

Smith, M. B. Competence and socialization. In John A. Clausen (Ed.), *Socialization and society.* Boston: Little, Brown & Co., 1968.

Author Index

Subject Index